MW01287361

THE DONOR BILLIONAIRE

A FAKE RELATIONSHIP ROMANCE

THE FRAZER FAMILY

ZOE DOD

Edited by
V. STRAW

MILKY DOWN PUBLISHING

Copyright © 2024 by Zoe Dod

All rights reserved.

No part of this book may be reproduced in any form or by any electronic or mechanical means, including information storage and retrieval systems, without written permission from the author, except for the use of brief quotations in a book review.

This is a work of fiction. Names, characters, places, incidents and dialogues are products of the author's imagination or are used fictitiously. Any resemblance to actual people, living or dead, or events is entirely coincidental.

The Donor Billionaire is written in British English.

ISBN: 978-1-917413-01-5

Editor: Victoria Straw

Cover Design by ChristineCoverDesigns

For my Family and Readers,
You continue to support me in my dream.
I couldn't do this without you.

xxx

CHAPTER 1

LEAH

he buzzer sounds.

I run a hand over my face and into my hair, grimacing at the knotted mess I find. I glance down at the crumpled loungewear and realise I'm still in my PJs.

A hammering starts next as someone thumps the door with their fist. The buzzer goes again, although this time, it's as if someone is leaning on it.

"Okay, okay," I huff, pushing my laptop to one side and making my way to the door.

"We know you're in there," comes a familiar voice. "We come bearing gifts."

I look through the peephole to see a bag with the name of my favourite Chinese restaurant plastered on the side. A grin spreads across my face.

I throw open the front door and am confronted by two smiling faces.

"About time. We wondered whether you'd died," Stella says as she pushes past me and into the apartment, holding up the bag of delicious-smelling food.

"Not forgetting the important stuff," Nat adds, following

1

closely behind, waving a couple of bottles of wine in my face as she passes.

"Come in," I say to my two best friends retreating backs.

"Come on," Stella shouts from the main living area. "We're here to cheer you up. Get you out of your funk."

I close the door, adding the chain, before trailing after my two besties.

My feeble excuse for staying in this evening has clearly fallen on deaf ears.

I pause at the entrance to the main living area. Both are busy at the far end of the room, making themselves at home in my open-plan kitchen. Stella is unloading boxes of mouth-watering food onto the kitchen island. While Nat is rummaging through a kitchen drawer on the back wall, searching for the ever-elusive corkscrew.

"Found it."

Nat holds up the offending item, receiving a cheer from Stella.

I grab some plates from another cupboard and head towards them.

Stella's eyes are locked on something behind me. "I'll never get tired of this view," she sighs.

I turn and follow her gaze, watching as the lights of the city blink on as the sun sets.

"It really is quite something," I say, my throat thickening. I've spent many hours imagining holding Vince and my child, pointing out the people and sights below. I give myself a mental shake. "We need to enjoy it while we can," I add, offering my friends a weak smile before handing each of them a plate.

"Sorry," Stella says, rubbing her hand up and down my arm.

"So, what happens to this place?" Nat asks, always the more practical one.

I sigh. "Vince brought an estate agent around. He's put it on the market."

"Oh," they say together, their eyes wide.

I let out a defeated sigh. "It's his name on the deeds. I suppose I should be grateful he hasn't kicked me out—yet."

Stella steps up and spins me towards her. Her hands grip my shoulders, shaking me.

"Grateful! He should be bloody grateful you didn't take a blunt knife to his balls after what he did! Especially after he moved out and in with his little tart."

Stella hisses through gritted teeth.

I'm glad the food is on the side and not in her hands. I've just realised how hungry I am.

Nat steps up and pats Stella's hands before removing them from my shoulders. The action causes Stella to stop whatever else she's about to say. She's been very vocal about her feelings towards my ex-fiancé and his new lady-friend.

I pat her arm and smile at her outburst. "Too messy," I state, wrinkling my nose, before turning to Nat.

"Vince has put the apartment on the market."

I stop, accepting the generous glass of wine Nat places in my hand before taking a large sip. "There are quite a few viewings booked for this week. It's a prime location. The estate agents don't think it'll be long before he has a buyer."

It's amazing how those words sting. I'd always seen this as *our* place. We'd moved in together. Chosen all the furniture *together*, of which I'd paid for a large portion. Plus, I was the one who'd taken a holiday and decorated every room. But the fact of the matter is. He owns it. I'm just a lodger.

"Bastard!" Stella hisses. "What are you going to do?" she asks, handing me a spoon so I can load some vegetable chow mein onto my plate. I love these girls and the fact they know my favourite comfort food.

My heart contracts. That *is* the million-pound question. If he gets a buyer, it won't be long before he kicks me out.

"I arranged to view some apartments this weekend. I'd be grateful for the company if either of you are free."

"Count us in. We can't leave you to make that kind of decision alone. You've been too closeted in all this luxury," Stella says, nudging my shoulder. My chest expands at my friend's words. I am lucky. This apartment, my home, is fabulous.

Nat lifts her wine glass and plate filled with her favourite chicken and cashew and motions towards the dining table. Stella follows, leaving me to trail behind. I look at the dishes lined up on the island and wonder why I didn't simply tell Stella to place the containers straight on the table. My brain is so foggy. I'm surprised I'm functioning.

After our second trip, we drop into our seats and tuck in. I moan in delight at the explosion of flavours on my tongue. They both look at me, their expressions smug.

"What?" I say, glancing at my best friends.

"Nothing. They say food is the best replacement for sex," Nat says.

"No!" Stella and I say together, laughing. Although my sex life is barren now, Vince is no longer in the picture. Not that it was much better when he was around. Was the writing on the wall, and I'd simply missed it?

"So, have you heard from the slimy rat?" Stella asks, shovelling a mouthful of food into her mouth.

The vice that seems a permanent fixture in my chest tightens another notch. "He called me yesterday at work. I think he hopes it's safer to contact me there, that I'm less likely to lose my temper."

"How you haven't lost your shit with him, I'll never know. No one would blame you," Stella puts in.

"No. But I'm tired, Stella. I've already expended too much

energy where he's concerned," I say. "He's given me six weeks to find somewhere else, but then I need to be out." My stomach recoils, and I put my fork on the table. "He says he'll reimburse me for all the furniture I've bought. That he can use it in their new apartment. To be honest, it's a blessing. I can use that money as a down payment for somewhere else."

Stella growls but holds her tongue.

"I still can't believe him," Nat says again.

She's disappointed in Vincent. She thought he was a *good* guy. But then, so had I. Maybe he's right. Maybe I have become obsessed with moving our relationship forward, but after ten years together, was that so wrong? I'm thirty-four. Is it so wrong to want a family?

"Have you told your parents?"

I shake my head. "No. They're only four months into their trip around Australia. I know Mum. She'll only worry and want to come home."

"But, Leah-" Nat says, her brows wrinkling.

"It's not an option, and there's nothing they can do. They've rented their house out for the year. If they come home now, they'll be in the same position as me—homeless. They've been looking forward to this trip for years. My love life, or lack of it, will not ruin that for them."

Nat and Stella share a look but stay quiet. They know I'm right. Mum and Dad would be on the next flight home.

"Are you getting tested?" Stella asks, the ever-practical friend.

"I went to a walk-in clinic a couple of days ago. Tonight's a celebration. He hasn't given me anything nasty."

Nat's eyes shoot to mine, her skin taking a greenish tone, her horror transparent. "Oh my, you thought he'd given you something?"

I give her a gentle smile. She's always been the gentler, more innocent one of the three of us. She feels things more deeply. I try to smile, although I think it's probably more of a scowl. Her eyes widen. It's Stella who comes to my rescue.

"No, Nat. But Leah needs to be sensible. If Vince has been having sex with another woman, Leah needs to know he hasn't given her anything. It's for peace of mind."

Stella knows how it feels. Her last partner had been messing around behind her back. She wasn't as lucky, but a course of antibiotics had fixed her up, and made her more cautious.

I nod in agreement, and Nat's shoulders drop as she exhales loudly. I'm so lucky to have these two wonderful women in my life.

"To hell with him," Stella says. "We'll find you somewhere to live, and you can give him the middle finger. Close the door on this chapter." She grabs my hand over the table and squeezes. "There's someone better for you out there. Someone who will adore you, not make excuses. Vince may be wealthy, but he's a dick. He's always been punching above his weight. He never appreciated what he had, and I hope he comes to rue the day."

I know what she's trying to do, but the stabbing pain in my stomach increases. It's not only the end of an engagement. It's the end of my dreams. Dreams of finally starting a family, having a child of my own. Children. I'm not getting any younger, and now I'm on my own. I've given Vince the best years of my life, only to be pushed aside without a thought for my wants and needs.

"I know," I say, offering her a wan smile. "But it's scary. This has been my home. Vince has been in my life for ten years. I was twenty-four when we met. Twenty-six when I moved in with him. I don't even know where or how to start again."

Stella gets up and moves to my chair, pulling me up and into her arms. She rubs circles on my back before pushing me away, her hands gripping my upper arms. "You listen to me, Leah Walker. You deserve better than Vincent Lamont. Yes, he might be some big-shot investment banker with more money than taste."

I stifle a giggle.

"Stella's right," Nat says, shaking her head. "Vince definitely missed the fashion memo. A designer label does not automatically mean stylish."

"Perfectly put, Nat," Stella says. "Do you remember that florescent green patterned shirt? I can't remember which designer it was, but it looked like someone had puked up radioactive avocado all over him."

I bite my lip, and a snort escapes. My hand flies to my mouth, and it's not long before we're all doubled over, tears rolling down our cheeks.

"He never understood the importance of matching against your skin tone."

I gasp, trying hard to catch my breath.

"Hopefully, the next man you meet will have taste." Nat chortles.

"Some taste would be an improvement," Stella says, moving to the wall and pointing to a picture of Vince and me that highlights her point perfectly, setting us off in another round of giggles.

"You can and will move on. You're a strong, intelligent and independent woman. And don't you forget it," Stella says, sitting down again. "Now, my wine glass is empty."

Before Nat can open her second bottle, I get up and move to Vince's prize wine rack. I grab a bottle. "He may not have any taste in clothes, but his wine? Well, that's another matter."

Stella and Nat look at me and grin. Stella waves me over, opening her hand before taking the bottle I'm holding. She reads the label and snorts.

"Really? Pretentious prick," she mutters, making both Nat and I laugh. "But I don't mind if I do," she adds, grabbing the corkscrew and making quick work of the offending cork.

It may be a school night, but I need to let my hair down. I hold out my glass, which Stella fills. Together we swill, sniff, savour, and swallow.

"No point in wasting it," Nat says, giggling.

"That's it," Stella shrieks, making Nat and I jump. "Friday night... a girls' night." Stella raises her glass, motioning for us to follow. "We're going out. Starting your new life... or is that restarting?" Stella gives me the once over. "No more loungewear or bird's nests."

We clink glasses.

"Why not!"

Maybe this is just what I need. "To new beginnings," I say, holding up my refilled glass.

"To new beginnings," my friends chorus.

"And just make sure you wear that sexy little number you bought and your killer heels," Stella adds, winking at me over the top of her glass. "You too, Nat."

"I'm in a relationship," Nat says.

"It's called moral support, and I'm sure Rory will appreciate you making an effort when you get home," Stella adds, making Nat blush to the roots of her hair while Stella and I laugh.

"In for a penny," I say.

My friends are correct. It's time for my life to begin again.

CHAPTER 2

GABRIEL

*A*s always, I hear him before I see him and prepare myself for the coming onslaught.

"Morning," a cheerful voice says, breaking my concentration.

I look up and stare at the mirror image of myself standing in the doorway. At six foot two, we are both imposing figures. Caleb's olive skin is slightly darker than mine as he spends more time outside. However, we have the same dark eyes and prominent cheekbones, a throwback from our Italian heritage. The main difference, however, is Caleb plays on our good looks, while I'd rather sink into the background.

"How's my alter-ego this morning?" He grins, pushing off the doorframe and entering my office uninvited. He's always so damn cheerful.

"Working. Something you seem to be averse to," I say, knowing that statement is an out-and-out lie. Caleb runs his successful property development firm. That's redeveloping half of the city. He may not be as wealthy as me, but he's doing his best to catch up.

"Glad to see you got out of bed on the usual side this

9

morning. I'll probably die of shock if I ever walk in here to a warm, fuzzy welcome," he says, ignoring me as he drops himself into the chair opposite.

I roll my eyes and grunt before leaning back in my chair. I cross my arms over my chest, staring at my brother. "So, what do I owe this early morning pleasure?"

Caleb's smile never falters. "I wanted to let you know. I've booked us a night out. It's in your diary. Amanda has just added it."

I lean forward and pull up the recent addition to my calendar.

Night out with twin...no you can't cancel it.
Place: Tristan's Wine Bar.

"Why on earth would I want to go to a wine bar?" I stare across the desk. "Dinner, maybe, but—"

"Before you go into a full-blown rant, hear me out." Caleb holds up his hand. "Tristan's opening a new wine bar around the corner, and he's invited *us* to the opening night. As an old friend, he's asked us to join him and celebrate. We will be supporting him. It's just a few of us, having a drink, in a bar. A relaxing night out."

"Tristan's your friend," I grumble. "I don't need to attend."

Caleb leans back. "Our friend," Caleb repeats. "When was the last time you went out?"

I drop my gaze. I'm not playing this game with him. "You know I hate socialising," I say, wiping a speck of something off my desk.

"I heard Rachel got engaged," Caleb says, my eyes locking with his before I can stop them. I know I'm scowling, but that was low, even for Caleb.

I shrug, fighting against the growing pressure in my chest. "It doesn't surprise me. She's met someone who can give her what she wants," I say, trying to ignore the painful tightness in my chest.

Caleb tilts his head as if trying to analyse me. I hate it when he does that, so I school my features.

"You need to get out and live a little. Get away from your computer and boring spreadsheets!" Caleb jiggles in his chair. "Let your hair down."

I raise an eyebrow and stare across the desk at my brother. "Why is everyone in our family obsessed with my social life? Let my hair down... really?"

"It's not that." Caleb sighs and runs a hand through his hair. "Rachel left you after five years. You were about to propose. Since she left, you never go out. You go from the office to your apartment and back again. All work and no play. You're twenty-nine, not sixty-nine. You should be out, getting laid."

"Accept I didn't go out before she left. So, there's no change there. It's actually *why* she left." I lower my hands and sit upright, leaning forward. "Red carpet, charity events... not my thing. Crowded pubs and wine bars are definitely *not* my thing." I let a visible shudder wrack my body to get my point across. "You, Mother, and whoever else need to stop worrying about me. I'm happy. I'm not interested in having someone invade my life or my privacy. I have friends and date when I need to," I add.

The women I date are happy with our arrangement. They get a night out and a very satisfying end to the evening. For both parties.

"I'm just saying, would it kill you to come out and have fun with me, your brother, for one night? Apparently, Tristan's got some new wines coming in he wants us to try," Caleb cajoles.

I grunt and roll my eyes. "You're going with that, are

you?" Tristan supplies all my wines. I must admit, the man has great taste.

Caleb grins and spreads his arms. "Whatever works," he says. "I promise if you hate it, you can leave. I won't force you to stay. Well, not for more than an hour." He winks before adding. "What harm will a night out with your charming older brother do? You might even have fun. Come on, *Mr Pipe and Carpet Slippers,* one drink. Tristan will be really pleased to see you. And if it's truly awful, then I'll let you leave. Then it's all the more for me." His expression turns serious. "You're never going to meet anyone if you don't at least try."

I drop my chin to my chest and shake my head. He's right. It can't hurt, and it has been a while since I last saw Tristan. If I agree now, I can guarantee another six months' grace.

"Okay. But if it's awful, then I'm out of there."

I send him a look that lets him know I'm serious, and his grin gets wider. "Don't worry. It will be a life-changing evening," Caleb chuckles, getting up.

"Really?" I say sarcastically, knowing my brother has something up his sleeve.

"Look at it this way. You've got six months until Mum's birthday and The Frazer Foundation weekend," Caleb adds. "If you don't have a date by then, it will be open season on your ass. All Mother's friends with their single daughters." Caleb lets out an exaggerated shudder, clearly for my benefit. "Just think about it. You're wealthy, share my stunningly good looks, and I hate to say it, brother, but you're a *catch.* Even if you don't want to be."

I glare at him over my desk, but I know he's right. My brother is a *babe* magnet. They flock to him, often multiples at a time, like moths to a flame. It's never been any different. The social climbers, however, know he's a lothario, while I'm the quieter, more sensible twin. Obtainable, perfect marriage material, I think one mother described me as. It's why I avoid these things like the plague. Only Mother's birthday weekend is non-negotiable.

A knock sounds at my office door, making us both look up.

Caleb looks down at his watch before meeting my gaze and grinning. "Right on time... Come in, Leah," he calls out.

The door opens, and Leah, my communications officer and right hand, enters. She is the consummate professional in her tailored suits and never a hair out of place.

"Hi, Gabriel, I just wanted to remind you. You have a ten-thirty meeting," Leah says, looking over at me.

"Hi, Leah," Caleb says, giving her his most dazzling smile, which she returns with one of her own.

"Hi, Caleb."

I watch their exchange, my stomach hardening. No, and double no. Leah is off limits, especially to my brother. Before I know it, I'm on my feet.

"It's okay, I'm just leaving," Caleb says, returning his attention to me, his eyes sparkling with mischief. "I've got my own meeting to attend. Some of us do *actual* work for a living."

Leah's eyes flit to my brother before coming to rest on me. "Are you ready for our meeting?" she asks politely. "I can come back later."

"No, I'm leaving." Caleb walks towards the door before turning at the last minute. "Remember Friday, Gabriel. No excuses, even if I have to drag your sorry ass kicking and screaming. You *are* coming."

Leah waits silently in the doorway as he approaches. "Such impeccable timing, as always, Leah," he says, shooting her a wink before turning around to face me. "Do you know Gabe? Leah is one of the few people who can tell us apart. It's a shame she has a fiancé."

A rosy tint appears high on Leah's cheeks, and she drops her gaze.

Strange.

Caleb stops next to her. "Leah, if you ever get bored with working for my grumpy *little* brother, you can come and work for me," he says, drawing her attention to his face.

I pick up my stress ball and throw it at my brother's head. He ducks, leaving the ball to fly out the door and into the main office. Hitting a nearby cubicle wall with a thump. Caleb stares at me wide-eyed before doubling over and laughing.

"I think that's my cue to leave," Caleb says, dashing out the door, leaving Leah staring at me, open-mouthed.

"Less of the *little brother.* You're only ten minutes older than me," I say loudly at his retreating back, only to hear his laughter. "And stop trying to poach my staff. Find your own."

Leah peers around the doorway, watching Caleb leave. "See you Friday. Bye, Leah," he shouts, causing everyone on the office floor to raise their heads and stare at him.

"Always has to be the centre of attention," I mutter, sitting back down.

"Did you say something?" Leah asks, a frown appearing between her brows.

"It's nothing," I say, waving my hand in the air. "Although, care to explain what Caleb meant?" I ask.

Leah looks at the ground, her hand going to her wrist where she usually wears her bangle. I notice it's something she does when she's thinking or feels unsure. Instead, she pinches the skin before letting it go. She clearly forgot to put it on this morning.

"Er..." A flush creeps up her cheeks as her eyes return to mine.

I let out a loud sigh, her eyes flying to mine. "What did he do?"

Leah shrugs. Her mask of professionalism back in place. "He came into my office and pretended to be you."

"What?"

Anger bubbles in my chest. What had my brother been thinking? How dare he come into my place of work and mess with my staff?

"It's fine. He did nothing improper. He tried to pretend to be you. I think he wanted to see if I really could tell the difference between you."

Most people can't, even with our very different personalities. Even our family has difficulty if we want them to. Can Leah really tell us apart?

Interesting.

"Yes. You're very different. I don't know how or why. But I don't see identical twins when I look at you. I've always seen a difference. It came as a shock to me that people struggle to tell you apart."

My breath catches. Shit, does Leah fancy Caleb? I need to nip this in the bud. I'm not losing my communications officer because my brother can't keep it in his pants. Although I'm sure Leah has better taste than liking Caleb. It's not like she doesn't know what a man-whore he is.

As Leah reaches the door to leave, she turns back and grins, "I think Caleb's onto our fake meeting."

I can't prevent the smirk that tips my lips, especially when Leah's eyes widen in surprise.

"He is, but he loves turning up unannounced and disrupting my day. Our meeting keeps him honest and gets him out of my hair. If anything, he probably relies on it to ensure he's not late for his own meeting."

I'm not being entirely honest. We both know what we're doing with this dance of pretence. He stops by when he wants to check up on me as he knows I can't hide from him in the office. I'm thankful Caleb knows my limits and doesn't stay long on his impromptu visits. I appreciate him taking time out of his busy schedule to ensure I commune with the real world, and don't get lost in my spreadsheets. Our little scheme to get rid of him is brotherly banter, him being the sociable brother, me the anti-social. He's just never let Leah know before.

"Is there anything else you need before I get back to work?" Leah asks, pulling me back into the present.

I shake my head and watch as she approaches the door.

"How's the Callahan presentation going?"

Leah stops and turns, stepping further into the room. "The presentation is complete. I'm about to send it across for your final approval. Jim and Stephan have already checked it. The client pack is almost complete. I was uploading the latest performance reports. I should have it done by the end of the day."

As efficient as always. I know the presentation and pack will be perfect.

"Callahan will be a huge win for us," I say unnecessarily. Leah has been with me from the beginning. She knows the importance of clients like Callahan. She has a way of dealing with even the most powerful and irate clients. She has a look, and then they are *Leah'd.* She calms situations down and takes control.

"On it," she says, turning away.

"Leah, is everything alright?" The words are out of my mouth before I can stop them. Something about her seems – off.

She freezes. "Everything's fine. I'll get the presentation sent across as soon as possible."

I watch her leave. I really will have words with my brother about him poaching Leah.

CHAPTER 3

LEAH

"*L*eah." Gabriel's voice sounds from my office doorway.

I stop what I'm doing and look up.

"Gabriel?" I ask.

He fills the doorway. His dark hair and olive complexion are witness to his Mediterranean bloodline. Dark eyes lock on mine, framed by thick dark eyelashes most women would die for.

"Do you need me to go over those press releases again?"

I watch as a tick starts along his strong jawline.

"No, everything is under control," I reply, giving him a quizzical look.

His shoulders sag at my words. The movement is only visible because, having worked closely with this man for over eight years, I know his tells inside out.

"Is everything all right?" I ask.

He shoots me a look of surprise before running a hand through his hair.

"Everything's fine," he replies, the harshness of *fine* making me want to laugh.

"Have a great night with Caleb," I say, biting the inside of my lip to stop them from forming a smile.

The humph that comes from the door has me coughing as I choke on the air I'm holding in.

"Sorry," I say, holding up my hand as Gabriel steps closer, passing me the glass of water on my desk.

"Here," he says, his fingers cupping mine until he knows I've grasped it.

"Thanks," I croak, surprised at their warmth.

"Are you really sure there's nothing I can do?" He places his hands behind his back, pulling his shirt tight across his already broad chest. My eyes are drawn to the movement.

"No," I say firmly. "You need to go out and have fun with your brother."

"Don't you start," he says, his eyes once again locking on mine. "You're supposed to be on my side."

"I am," I say. "If an emergency arises, you'll be the first to know. However, the market is fine, and it's time you clocked off. Celebrate! The Callahan presentation is done. There is nothing more you can do until our meeting. Go! Enjoy yourself."

"When did you get so bossy?" Gabriel asks, raising an eyebrow.

I grin. "Two hours ago, when your brother rang to forewarn me you'd be trying to get out of tonight."

His forehead wrinkles, and his lips twist.

"He's got no right," Gabriel mutters.

"Caleb knows you too well." I drop back in my chair. "If you don't go tonight, you're only postponing the inevitable. He's not going to let you off the hook."

This time, I don't hide my smile as he huffs.

"Go," I say, waving him out of the door. "I have work to finish before my friends arrive. You're not the only one with plans."

Gabriel scowls at me before he turns and leaves.

"Have fun!" I shout after him.

A hand in the air, appearing over his shoulder. The only acknowledgement I get that he heard me. By his reaction, anyone would think his brother was asking him to donate a kidney or right arm, not socialise with friends.

I shake my head and smile. The man has no idea how devastatingly handsome he is. He just needs to loosen up and let someone in. Maybe tonight is the night.

I finish the last couple of emails I need to send, the whoosh of the last leaving my outbox has me dropping back in my chair and closing my eyes. Should I have shown Gabriel more sympathy? It's not like I haven't been restless all day with the prospect of going out tonight. Our drunken girls' night turned into *Project Leah's Reintroduction to Society*. I take a deep breath before opening them and power down my laptop.

My phone pings on the desk next to me.

STELLA:

We'll be with you in 20.

ME:

See you soon.

I look up at one of the many clocks on my wall.

How the hell did that happen?

It's been over an hour since Gabriel left my office.

I grab my bag from under my desk and head to the ladies' room.

I lean against the sink unit, my eyes locked on my reflection. Dark circles have appeared around my eyes, and my skin is becoming pinched. Butterflies dance in my stomach, and the temptation to call off this evening's shenanigans is almost too strong to ignore.

19

I puff out a breath and bend down, unzipping my holdall and pulling out my makeup.

"In for a penny, in for a pound," I say to my reflection as I repair the day's wear and tear, adding a little more eyeshadow and blush than usual. Tonight is, after all, a girls' night out, and I am single.

I unzip my clothes bag and pull out the little black dress Stella convinced me to wear. I purchased this for one of Vince's work events until management had decided not to include partners anymore, or so I believed. More fool me. Anyway, tonight, it will get its first airing. I step out of my trouser suit and blouse before shimmying into my dress. Folding the other items into my bag. I stand back and observe the finished effect in the mirror, smoothing the material over my hips and stomach.

My hands go to my chignon, pulling out my clips. I let my hair cascade down my back before pushing my fingers into the roots and shaking it, bringing body and volume back.

I turn left, then right, checking my appearance. The dress hugs my figure in all the right places. But then again, it should. I spent enough on it. Hair, makeup, clothes.

The door crashes open, making me jump.

"Oh, sorry, Leah," Amanda says, coming into the room. "Wow, you look amazing." Her grin helps to calm the desire to flee the building in my chest. "Going anywhere nice?"

"Thank you. Just out with some friends," I reply. "You're welcome to join us."

Amanda gives me one of her motherly smiles. "I'd love to." She winks. "But I have a husband and two *hangry* teenagers at home waiting for me."

I return her smile, knowing Amanda's husband and children are her life outside the office. Something I envy. At fifty-five, she's worked for Gabriel almost as long as I have, initially being employed by his father. When Frazer Investments took off, Amanda made the move and took over my role as PA, which allowed me to focus on the communications role I'd trained for.

"Another time," I add.

She smiles. "Most definitely."

I grab my things as she makes her way into one of the stalls. "Have a lovely evening, Leah."

"Thank you. I'll try," I say, as the empty feeling in the pit of my stomach returns.

I make my way back to my office to dump my bag. No point taking it with me. We're only going around the corner. I can collect it before I head home tonight or over the weekend. I'll be around tomorrow when I start apartment-hunting.

I pick up my phone and find several messages from Stella and Nat.

STELLA:

Makeup, dress, HEELS!

NAT:

She's made me wear heels, so you definitely are!

STELLA:

Five minutes out.

I look at the message stamp and realise it was ten minutes ago. As if on cue, my phone rings. Stella's name flashes up.

"Where are you? We're in reception," she says.

"Just about to head down. Perfection takes time," I say dryly.

Stella laughs. "See you in a minute. And Leah... remember your heels!"

I look at my bare feet before digging into my bag and pulling out the shoes Stella chose earlier in the week. I slide them onto my feet, rebalancing myself. I reserve wearing heels for specific occasions, such as client meetings or parties, where limited alternatives are available.

Grabbing my clutch bag from the desk, I head to the door, switching off the light before closing it behind me. The office floor is relatively empty, and only a few people remain at their desks. I wave goodnight and walk to the elevator, my muscles twitching the closer I get.

Waiting in reception, the girls are sat on one of the many leather sofas littered about.

"Wow," Stella says, pulling me in for a hug. "I knew that was the dress. You look..." She places her fingers on her lips and kisses them, throwing the kiss into the air. Her exaggerated movements make me laugh.

Stella and Nat have also dressed up. Nat is in her preferred navy trouser suit, with flared legs, while Stella has opted for a red, fitted dress, showcasing her natural curves, topped off with killer heels.

"Girls on the town," Stella says, linking arms with both of us and pulling us to the door.

Nat gives me a sympathetic look over Stella's head. Oh heck, what have I let myself in for?

"Change of venue," Stella adds. "Mr Dyer was giving away invitations to a trendy new wine bar that's opening tonight. I snagged three tickets. Wine tasting, with cheese and charcuterie, and hopefully plenty of young, sexy men for us to choose from."

The butterflies in my stomach settle. How raucous can a wine tasting bar opening get?

CHAPTER 4

GABRIEL

*T*ristan's latest wine bar is not what I expected. It's in an old, converted brick building that he has repurposed with a modern twist. The once boarded-up arch entrance has received a modern makeover. The old wooden doors have been replaced by a vast expanse of glass, housing a double glass doorway. I step inside, past the doorman, flashing the ticket Caleb sent me. The murmur of voices and laughter makes its way down the wide wooden staircase. I breathe in, glancing at my watch, before going upstairs.

"You're late," Caleb says, clapping me on the shoulder, grinning at my scowl. "Come on. Tristan can't wait to see you."

I follow Caleb over to the main bar area. The inside is even more impressive than the outside. The exposed brick and pipework give an industrial feel, but the expanse of glass and light brings the place into this century. Large tables grace the centre of the room, while smaller alcoves adorn the outside. Not that I can see much over the number of bodies present.

"Gabriel."

I hear my name shouted over the noise, and I turn to face the man of the hour.

"Tristan," I say. "Amazing place." And I realise I mean it. I may not like crowds, but I can appreciate the amount of thought and effort it has taken to create this atmosphere and setting.

"I'm so glad you could make it. It's been too long," he says, motioning to the bartender before placing a glass of red wine in my hand. "You're going to like this one."

I've been ordering wine from Tristan for years since he opened his first bar, although never in person. Until now.

"Thank you." I hold it up to the light and nod my appreciation, swirling the burgundy liquid around the glass. I breathe in the aroma. "That smells..."

Tristan grins at me, as I take a sip, letting the flavours explode on my tongue.

"Add twelve to my next order," I say, earning myself a clap on the back from our friend.

Caleb appears at my side. "Can I steal my brother away? There are a few people I want him to meet."

"I'll get those bottles ordered. Catch you later," Tristan says before disappearing into the crowd.

I follow Caleb, sidestepping the people jostling for space. "We're over here," Caleb says, moving me towards a large table surrounded by several people.

"Hi everyone, I'd like to introduce you to my brother, Gabriel,"

Everyone looks up, a number smiling and waving their greeting. I give a nod of acknowledgement.

"Oh Em Gee," a sultry voice appears to the side of us. "You really weren't joking when you said you're identical."

"Ruby," Caleb says, pulling the newcomer into his embrace before flinching as she makes a grab for me.

"As handsome as your twin," she purrs, running her hand

up and down my arm before leaning in and whispering, "I've never tried twins before."

"Enough, Ruby, or I'll get jealous," Caleb says, pulling her away from me and into his side before shooting me a look of apology.

"Oh, you're no fun." She pouts at Caleb, smacking his chest with her manicured hand, flexing her talons.

"Gabriel, over here. Come and sit with us."

I look down to see Xander and Quentin, another couple of Caleb's friends from school. Xander moves over, making space next to him. I want to decline, but when Ruby looks over, catching her lip between her teeth and twisting her dark locks around her finger. I drop onto the bench.

"Don't mind Ruby. She's harmless and infatuated with your brother," Xander laughs, slapping me on the back. "It's been too long, man. Where have you been hiding?"

Xander doesn't realise, being Caleb's mirror image, his statement offers little comfort. It wouldn't be the first time a woman has tried switching her luck when my elusive brother won't commit. I say nothing. I don't know the woman and wouldn't like to pass judgement.

Quentin leans forward and grins. "So Gabriel, when are you going to join us for poker night?"

It's not the first time they've invited me to join them. Boys' night is every fortnight at one of their houses.

"Don't push him." Quentin laughs. "Have you forgotten the guy's a genius with a photographic memory? He'll clean us out."

It's my turn to smile. Quentin has a long memory. They banned me from playing with them in college. "Maybe I will join you. Win some of the money my firm keeps making you," I say, earning myself a smile and another slap on the shoulder. All of them are Frazer Investment clients, and ridiculously wealthy. Also agreeing to a night in with my brother will keep him at bay.

"How's work?" I ask, letting Quentin and Xander do all the talking.

I forgot what great company they are. Before long I'm smiling at some of their and Caleb's antics. What is even better is that our seating arrangement has protected me from the growing number of people entering the bar. So much for Caleb's, *a few friends.*

As I reply to something Quentin says, I hear a loud shriek of laughter. Turning around, I catch a glimpse of a group of women entering the bar. My eyes do a double take. Is that Leah? No, it can't be. Before I can confirm, the woman is gone, absorbed into the crowd. I give myself a mental shake.

Leah's not about to turn up and rescue you, even if she knows how much you hate this kind of place.

She didn't even know where I was going. She's most likely out with her fiancée.

The crowd is growing.

How many people did Tristan invite?

Not that I can blame the guy. His business revolves around buying and selling wines and hospitality.

"Wow, did you see Leah?" Caleb appears at my shoulder. "She's very different out of her power suits," he adds, waggling his eyebrows at me.

I growl at him before I can stop myself. Does he remember who he's talking about?

"Don't scowl," Caleb says, a twinkle in his eyes, "You'll get wrinkles, and then you'll need Botox if you want to stay as handsome as me."

My scowl deepens, and his laugh echoes around us.

"Leah is off limits. Do not mess with my staff, Caleb," I say, standing up and facing my brother.

His hand clamps down on my shoulder, and he grins. "Don't worry, it's fun watching you protect her."

"All women need protecting from you."

I sigh.

"There are no complaints. I leave no one unsatisfied," he says. His eyes move to Ruby, who flashes him with her come-to-bed eyes. "And Leah is old enough."

I can't stop the hiss of air that escapes between my teeth. "She's engaged and works for me. Therefore, she is off limits."

I shake my head. There's no taming my brother.

To my surprise, he throws his head back and laughs. "Never fear. I like Leah, but not in that way. She's engaged. I do have some morals, even if you like to question them."

Although he's smiling, I can't miss the flash of hurt in his eyes.

I'm unsure how to reply, so stay quiet.

I glance down at my watch, and I'm shocked to see that it's been an hour and a half since I arrived.

"See, it's not been that bad," Caleb says, patting my shoulder.

I'm about to open my mouth to reply when shattering glass fills the air, followed by raised voices.

Caleb turns away from me and disappears into the crowd. I stand still as silence descends over the room, apart from the female voice echoing around the bar.

"You bitch. You just can't take it, he prefers me."

There's a loud sound of flesh hitting flesh, and I watch the crowd part as someone pushes their way through, and towards the exit.

"That's right, run away bitch," the voice yells after her.

The hum of voices picks up as the drama ends. Caleb makes his way towards me, his expression tight. "Gabriel, you need to go. Leah—" he says, his eyes wide, a muscle twitching at the corner.

I know I must look confused. "Gabriel," he says again, "That was Leah. She's just been slapped by some blond woman and run out." His next words knock the wind out of me. "Her fiancé is here with another woman."

I freeze, taking in Caleb's words. What? Leah's been with her fiancé for ten years. Has been planning their wedding.

"Has she said anything to you?" Caleb asks, his face a mask of concern.

I shake my head. "She's not said a word."

Shit, did she know?

"I'm going after her," I say, facing my brother.

Caleb nods before stepping aside and letting me pass. I know he wants to come. His protective streak runs deep for those he cares about.

"Go, Gabe, let me know how she is."

I don't reply, instead I push my way through the crowd only to find myself face-to-face with the man of the hour. Our eyes lock until a hand snakes around his arm, pulling him back. My eyes move to the blond. Her overly made-up face and fake tits are all I can see. She says something to him, her face screwed up, and he turns towards her. They look like they're arguing. If that's the woman he's traded Leah in for...

I turn around and head for the door.

CHAPTER 5

LEAH

Stumbling out the door, I make sure I'm away from the window and gawping crowd before gripping the wall and bending double. My free hand splayed across my chest as I frantically suck in air, trying to control the growing panic.

I hear Stella and Nat explode onto the street behind me, rushing to my side.

"That bitch," Stella hisses, her anger palpable. I tune out her rant.

I close my eyes as waves of dizziness wash over me. This is not how tonight was due to go. Vince never comes across to this side of town, but then again. He loves his expensive wines. Maybe I shouldn't be surprised.

Nat pulls me upright and into her arms, resting my forehead on her shoulder. "You'll be okay," she whispers in my ear.

I expel an audible breath, unable to think of the words that will calm my friends. Stella is still angrily monologuing.

Pulling back from Nat, I catch Stella's arm, hating the weakness I know will be present in my voice if I try to articulate anything. "It's okay," I rasp, giving her arm a reassuring squeeze.

"Nothing about this is okay," Stella argues, her eyes spitting fire.

"I'm sorry to have ruined our evening,"

Nat steps up behind me and wraps her arms around my waist.

"You didn't. Dickhead and his bimbo did that. Why couldn't he have simply left you alone?" Stella hisses. "He's the one who had to come over to you."

Stella's right. I spotted Vince as soon as we walked in. We joined some of Stella's work colleagues on the other side of the bar, keeping our distance. Vince approached me, tapping me on the shoulder and delivering his news.

Pain rips through me, almost pulling me to my knees as I choke down the wail that wants to escape. For once, I'm happy for my friend's support. I'd be a puddle on the street if it wasn't for the death hold keeping me on my feet.

"I need to go," I say, squeezing Nat's hand gently, letting her know she can release me.

"We all will," Stella says, her eyes roaming my face.

"It's okay. I've got to go back to the office and collect my things."

I give her upper arm a pat, trying to convey my need to be alone.

She nods, although I know from the tightness around her mouth, she wants to argue with me.

"Are you sure?" Nat says, her own eyes filled with concern.

I purse my lips. "I just need... time," I say.

They pull me in for a group hug. I blink rapidly, refusing to allow my tears to fall in public. I need to get out of here. Have my breakdown in private.

"I've got to go," I say, pulling out of their grip and starting off in the direction of the office. Pleased it's only a few streets away, especially as I'm in ridiculously high heels, cursing Stella for telling me to wear them.

The city streets are empty as I make my way back to my haven. I count my steps, not wanting the events of the evening to overwhelm me, but it comes back crystal clear.

"What the hell are you doing here?"

His voice appears behind me.

"Enjoying an evening out with my friends," I reply, turning to face him and holding up my wineglass. I then turn back to Stella and the people from her office.

"Don't ignore me, Leah," he says, stepping to my side and forcing me to acknowledge him. I shoot Stella a warning glance to stay out of it. We don't need a scene.

"I'm not ignoring you, Vince, I just have nothing to say to you."

"Have you found somewhere to live?" he asks, ignoring my statement.

Sighing, I turn to face him. "No, I'm apartment hunting tomorrow. I'll let you know as soon as I find somewhere." I take a sip of my wine, praying he gets the hint and leaves me alone. No such luck as a wave of blond hair appears at his side, gripping his arm, shooting daggers in my direction.

"Have you told her?"

I turn towards the new arrival and shoot her my most dazzling smile. "You must be Yasmin," I say, watching her eyes squint.

Ignoring me, she shifts her gaze to Vincent, whose eyes remain locked on me.

"Have you?" she asks again, her hand going to her stomach.

My mind freezes. "Told me what, Vince?"

Yasmin turns and gives me her brightest smile, although I notice it doesn't reach her eyes. "Vincent and I are having a baby. So, we're going to move into the apartment ourselves. My lease is up, and well, it seems silly to look for somewhere else when Vince already has such a beautiful apartment."

I watch her hand graze its way down Vince's chest, her eyes probing mine as she tosses her hair back and smirks.

Vince flinches, and I choke against the vice-like grip, squeezing my chest and heart.

"A baby... congratulations," I splutter out. My eyes go to Vince's. Guilt and something else flash across his features. "Are you sure it's yours?"

The words are out of my mouth before I can stop them.

The rest of the conversation is a blur. The sting on my cheek, the screaming. I grabbed my bag and left.

I look up and realise I've reached the office. A numbness has descended over my body. I push my way through the revolving door and into the main lobby. Its chandelier lighting glistens off the marble and tiles. I make my way to the security gate and flash my card. The security guard gives me a brief glance as the light turns green.

"Evening, Ms Walker," he says.

"Evening, James," I say, pushing through, not wanting to stop, needing to find a space to let go.

I push the call button on the elevator multiple times.

It finally arrives, and I fall into it, resting against the back wall.

"Shit, shit, shit!" I say, my voice hoarse.

My hand flies to my chest as a wave of pain envelops my heart.

My breath hisses out as I reach my destination, and the door opens.

The floor is dark.

I stagger out, the automated evening lighting coming on, dimmer than usual but enough to light the pathway to my office. My ankle twists, shooting me into the corner of one cubicle, pain lancing through my hip.

"Fuck!" I scream, glad no one is on the floor to witness my meltdown.

I rub the throbbing area hard with the heel of my palm. *That's going to bruise.*

I yank off my shoes, dangling them from my hand. I'm glad I haven't added a twisted ankle to the list of disasters racking up this evening.

I walk barefoot to my office, pushing open the door and flinging the offending footwear into the corner. They hit the wall with a satisfying bang. I sink onto the sofa in the corner of my office. I drop my head into my hands as the choking sobs I've been swallowing down finally make it free.

"Damn him."

My voice echoes around the empty office as I finally give way to the tears.

The elevator pings, letting me know I'm no longer alone.

CHAPTER 6

GABRIEL

I catch up with Leah at the end of the street but hold back. Hoping no one is watching and thinks I'm a stalker. Her body language clearly shows that whatever happened is taking its toll. She enters our office building, barely acknowledging the night security before making her way to the bank of elevators. I watch through the window as she frantically calls the lift, her shoulders sagging in relief as it arrives. When she disappears, I allow myself to enter.

"Evening, Mr Frazer." I jump as a voice breaks my focus.

"Evening, James," I say, acknowledging the man behind the desk. I keep moving, following Leah, not wanting to get caught up in pleasantries.

James takes the hint, instead hitting the button, allowing me through the security gate.

"Thanks," I call, pressing forward.

I arrive on the office floor. The overnight emergency lights are dim, the cleaners have left a while ago.

I notice Leah's office light on and make my way forward, unsure of what I'm going to find. I draw up short at the pain-filled sobs escaping the semi-opened door. Indecision wars in my gut, but Caleb's words echo in my mind.

Let me know how she is.

Leah's legs are visible, and I know she's sitting on the sofa in the corner of her office. Stepping up to the door, I rap my knuckles against the wood.

"Leah?"

"Gabriel."

A soft gasp comes from within, followed by rustling. I step around the door and into the room. Leah sits hunched over, black makeup runs, cutting tracks down her cheeks. Her hand comes up and swipes at the lines, smearing them sideways. I walk over to her desk and grab the box of tissues she always has there, handing them over.

"Thanks," she says, pulling one out. She wipes her face, making little difference to the disaster that is her makeup. I watch as she wrings the poor tissue in her hands, twisting and pulling.

"What are you doing back?" she asks, trying her best to put on her most professional tone, deliberately ignoring the elephant in the room.

"I was at Tristan's," I admit.

Leah's head drops, her face crumpling. She draws in a shuddering breath. "Oh."

An awkward silence descends.

After a moment, she looks up, offering me a wan smile. "That's embarrassing. But I'm fine, honestly."

I drop into the chair opposite Leah's desk, swivelling it to face her. "When my sisters say they're fine, it usually means they're anything but. After what I've just seen, I'd say you fall into that category."

Leah gives a little snort.

"And if I want to be alone?" Leah asks, raising her puffy, bloodshot eyes to mine.

"I'll grant your wish. But if you need to talk, I'm a surprisingly good listener." I stand up. "I'm going to make us both a drink. Tea or coffee?"

"Tea. If I drink *your* coffee at this time of night, I'll never sleep."

Leah's lips twitch. It's true, I do like my coffee strong.

"Tea it is," I say, leaving her alone.

I take my time making our drinks. By the time I return to Leah's office, she's washed her face and changed back into her work clothes. Her hair once again scraped up.

I place her drink on the table.

"Thanks," she says, picking it up and cradling it in her hands.

I return to my seat and wait.

Leah pauses.

"Vince and I broke up just over two months ago. As you can probably guess, he met someone else."

Her voice is monotone, and my stomach clenches. I think back over the past two months for any signs of this traumatic event. I knew something was wrong. But this—a broken engagement? How could I miss something this big in one of my employee's lives, especially Leah's? We work together side by side every day.

As if sensing my unspoken question. "Don't look so horrified. The fact you haven't picked up on it. I'm glad. This is my sanctuary. Work is work. My private life is for home."

I baulk at the words I've used many times over the years. The fact that I used the office to escape my heartbreak does not mean I expect everyone else to adhere to my screwed-up ways.

"You didn't have to."

"Yes, I did," she says, her smile hollow. "It meant I got through it."

I understand her logic.

"What happened tonight?"

Leah pauses, uncertainty clouding her features. Her shoulders drop. "Vince's new girlfriend announced they're moving into the apartment he and I lived in, and that..." Leah's face contorts as she wrestles with her emotions. "Announced that... announced that... they're pregnant."

The last words come out in a whoosh. Leah drags her trembling bottom lip between her teeth, her gaze returning to a spot on the floor.

We sit in silence as I let her words sink in.

"Where's he living now?"

Leah takes a deep breath and sits up tall, shaking herself off. "He's living with her, but apparently, her lease is up for renewal, and they want to move back into Vince's apartment. He's put it on the market... that's why there's been no rush for me to move out."

Leah must notice my confusion as she shrugs. "The apartment is Vince's. I'm his lodger." She's unable to hide the bitterness in her voice. "I'm lucky he let me stay while I find somewhere to live."

The words, *his* and *lodger*, make my blood boil. They were engaged, and not just for five minutes. Five years! Together ten! But somehow, nothing surprises me. I never liked Vincent Lamont. I've met him multiple times over the years. We may both be in financial markets, but he's brash and loud. A pretentious prick. The type of trader depicted in the movies. I've never understood what Leah saw in him, but then they say *opposites attract.* I only have to look at my family members and their partners to know how unlikely couples fall in and out of love.

Leah gets up, placing her cup on the table. Moving around the room, she gathers her belongings.

"Have you found somewhere?" I ask.

She stops what she's doing and gives me a tight-lipped

smile. "The girls and I are looking tomorrow. I've got about eight apartments lined up." Her chin falls to her chest, before her head comes up, her eyes locking with mine. "Then I can move out and put all this behind me."

"If you need any time off," I say.

She fiercely shakes her head. "Thank you, but No. What I need is for the office to be my sanctuary." Her eyes pleading as she looks at me. "Please."

"Okay, but if anything changes."

She nods, but her eyes don't meet mine.

I stand up and move to the door. "When you're ready to leave, give me a shout. I'll be getting my things together. I'll drop you home."

Leah freezes. "You don't have to do that," she says.

"I know, but you're on the way. Don't argue. Just accept it," I say, turning and leaving before she argues further.

CHAPTER 7

LEAH

I rest my hands on the edge of the desk and hang my head. Closing my eyes, I let out a shuddering sigh.

"Shit!"

Tonight was supposed to be a new start, a fun night out with the girls. A pounding starts behind my eyes, and I pinch the bridge of my nose. Damn Vince and his bombshell. Why tonight? Eight years of cultivating a professional persona in a male-dominated office, and *boom*. In a few hours, I become *that* whimpering, emotional woman. Not to mention the makeup disaster. I was shocked when I walked into the ladies' room, the streaks of black mascara and eyeliner coating my cheeks. I looked like something from a horror movie. Clearly, there should be a warning with make-up tutorials.

Sexy, smoky eyes-amazing. Avoid like the plague if likely to be caught in emotional dramas with your ex.

A shudder wracks my body. How did Gabriel keep a straight face? What the hell must he be thinking? I bite my lip to suppress a groan. He's still here... waiting for me. I can't even curl up in my heartbreak and wallow!

I disconnect my laptop and stuff it into my bag. I've already screwed up my dress and dumped it in my holdall. That can go to a charity shop on Monday, along with the heels. It will be too soon if I never see either of them again.

My phone flashes with several missed calls and messages. I stuff it in my bag. I'll deal with those at home. I need to get out of here before the thin thread I'm dangling from snaps and plummets me into a free fall.

Leaving my office, I make my way across the floor, past the team's desk cubicles.

Gabriel looks up from his desk as I knock on his open door.

"Ready?" he asks, his voice casual, offering no hint of the breakdown he just witnessed.

I move towards the window and stare out over the city. The lights give a surreal aura. "It's a beautiful view."

"During the long winter mornings, the lights reflect off the other buildings. In the summer, it's the sun," he says. I jump as Gabriel appears next to me. "Are you ready?" he asks.

When I nod, he turns away and grabs his laptop bag.

"I'm sorry," I say, breaking the silence as we walk to the elevator.

"What for?"

I want to laugh at the confused look on his face.

"Ruining your evening with your brother."

My stomach sinks when I realise it's not only Gabriel who witnessed my monumental downfall.

Gabriel huffs. "Saved me more like," he says, and I notice his lips twitch, but he holds back on a smile.

"Well, I'm sorry. What happened was totally unprofessional." I baulk at the last words out of my mouth, shocked when Gabriel turns to face me.

"Tonight, from what I understand, was not your fault. We can control our own actions, but not those of others." He pinches the bridge of his nose and closes his eyes for a second. "You have nothing to apologise for. I didn't hear you raise your voice, smash a glass or scream abuse. From what you've told me, it was not the *time* or *place* for that discussion. It should be Vince and his girlfriend offering an apology."

I hold my jaw in place. That's probably the longest sentence, not work-related, I've ever heard Gabriel give.

The ding of the elevator saves me. Gabriel stands back and lets me enter before following and pushing the button for the car park.

The doors open into the basement. The fluorescent lighting illuminates the parking bays and concrete blocks that support the twenty-five floors above us. This space is usually full of beautiful, expensive cars, but this evening, it's empty.

A movement at the far side of the car park reveals one of the building's many security guards. He waves over before continuing his sweep. I follow Gabriel over to his parking spot. My pulse speeds up, and I stop still, my eyes taking in the beautiful car in front of me. I've heard Caleb ribbing his brother about his car and seen a picture, but up close... It has a sporty, low-slung front, sleek headlights, and glistening ruby-red paintwork. It's a thing of immense beauty. If falling in love with an inanimate object was possible, the Alfa-Romeo 33 Stradale would be the one.

If Gabriel notices my drooling, he says nothing. Instead, he takes my holdall and clicks a button that opens the butterfly doors. I hold my breath as they rise like wings, exposing the stunning leather and aluminium interior.

"It's okay. I only had half a glass of wine. I'm safe to drive," Gabriel says suddenly.

In all honesty, it was not something I'd thought about. Instead of replying, I step forward, lowering myself into the passenger seat. Once I'm settled, Gabriel lowers the door, which closes with a gentle click. The faint aroma of leather invades my senses. I look in the mirror as the back raises like the doors. Gabriel drops our belongings inside. Once he's done, he makes his way to the driver's side, sliding into the bucket seat with ease and experience. His trousers draw tight across his thighs. The muscles flex as he positions himself to drive. His door closes, encasing us in luxury.

The fact he settled me into the car first shouldn't surprise me. He may be a billionaire, but his manners are impeccable.

Dragged up right, my mum would say.

I think it's more the case of *raised correctly*.

It's unlikely that there was much dragging up in the Frazer household.

I watch him out of the corner of my eye, his powerful hands confidently moving over the controls. It's clear he loves his car. The deep growl of the engine echoes around the car park, bringing a smile to my face. The movement catches Gabriel's attention because he turns to look at me.

"What? Can't a girl appreciate the start of a beautiful car?"

I shrug, grinning.

Gabriel returns my grin. The shock of it steals my breath. This is undoubtedly his favourite toy.

He nods and returns his attention to the car, putting it in gear and driving us towards the exit. The car's throaty roar bounces off the walls until we finally make it past the barrier and onto the street.

We travel in silence. I stare out the window before my eyes are drawn to the panoramic windows built into the roof. Their design showcases the buildings we're passing. I'm acutely aware of Gabriel as he manoeuvres this powerful machine through the city streets. My eyes lock on his hands as they grip the steering wheel. It's the first time in eight years, I've noticed how beautiful his hands are. His long, strong fingers and smooth skin, the way the muscles contract every time he moves. I turn once more to look out of the window before he catches my freakish behaviour.

What's wrong with me tonight?

I'm going to put it down to shock.

Gabriel pulls up outside my apartment building in record time. The lights from the reception area welcome me home. I can see Billy, our night security guard, at his desk. My heart constricts. I'll miss this luxury as a single woman living in the city, knowing someone is downstairs twenty-four hours a day, protecting me while I sleep. But then, I've grown accustomed to being spoiled. At the end of the day, it's Vince's salary that has allowed all this. Now, I need to find my own normal.

"Thank you for the lift," I say, but Gabriel is already out of the car. The door next to me lifts silently. Gabriel's hand appears in the gap. I make a move to exit the car. It doesn't take me long to realise there must be a technique for getting out. The bucket seat acting like a magnet for my ass. After failing three times, I accept the hand Gabriel offers. The strength in his fingers, as they clasp mine, sends shards of warmth and awareness down my arm.

"Thank you for the lift," I say, my voice sounding a little rough.

I look up to find Gabriel trying to hide his smirk.

"It takes practice," he adds, nodding towards the seat and door.

"Clearly," I mutter. "A pregnant woman would need a hoist."

A furrow appears between Gabriel's brows, and I realise what I said. Yasmin's announcement has had a profound effect on me. Gabriel says nothing. Instead, moving to retrieve my bags.

"Have a lovely weekend," I say as he moves to get back into the car.

"Good luck with the apartment hunting tomorrow," Gabriel replies, his brow still furrowed.

"Thank you," I say. "For everything."

"You've already said that," he points out. His expression is neutral, before he lets out a mini-huff and adds, "You're welcome."

I want to smile as his awkwardness returns. Instead, I say, "I'll see you on Monday."

He nods before effortlessly sliding into the driver's seat.

I walk to the entrance, and the automatic doors slide open. Billy looks up from his desk and smiles.

"Evening, Ms Walker. Welcome home," he says.

"Evening, Billy. Have a good evening."

I make my way to the elevator. My heart lurches as I step inside. Five weeks, and I'll be gone. A crushing pain grips my chest, stealing my breath as I think of Yasmin, Vince, and the child they're expecting. Yasmin will push a stroller into these lifts in the coming months. What was once our spare room, will become the nursery I always dreamed of.

My hands curl against the wall of the elevator as it ascends. I don't have to wait long before I'm deposited outside the apartment. I open the door and kick off my shoes, making my way inside. The beautiful view stretches out in front of me. The lights of the city reflect off the water. I sink down onto the couch and close my eyes, unable to look at my surroundings—the place I've called home for eight years. But it's not my home. It's Vince's, and now, it will be Yasmin and their baby's.

I bite my lip hard to stifle the sob that threatens to escape. I've cried enough tonight, and that just isn't me. It's time to face the truth. My life here is over. I'm about to begin a new chapter. What that will look like is anyone's guess. But crying over what *might have been*, helps no one.

I pick up my phone and see the dozens of messages from Stella, Nat, and Vince. I fire off a reply to Stella and Nat in our group chat.

ME:

I'm home safe, sorry to worry you.

STELLA:

Thank God. How are you doing?

NAT:

Hugs babes

ME:

I'm spent, both emotionally and physically.
Can I call you in the morning?

STELLA:

Of course. Try to sleep. We love you. xxx

NAT:

Love you xxx

ME:

Love you guys too xxx I'll call you tomorrow.

I swipe at my eyes as the screen blurs. No more tears, not tonight anyway. I can't think, let alone speak to anyone. I drag the faux fur throw off the back of the sofa, wrapping myself in its comforting weight.

My phone lights up with an incoming call. Vince's name appears. I send him straight to voicemail. It rings again, so I do the same. He's the last person I want to speak to this evening. A baby? Of all the things he could have done or said, nothing could cut me deeper. After six attempts, he finally gives up. I switch off my phone and drop my head back against the sofa cushion.

Tomorrow is a new day.

I have appointments to look at some apartments. I have my friends, my health, and my job. I'm not a trader, but Gabriel pays me well. I'm an independent woman. I've got this.

I close my eyes and try to ignore the painful tightness in my throat and vice-like grip around my lungs, unable to shake the feeling my world is caving in.

CHAPTER 8

GABRIEL

The burn starts as my arms cut through the water. I hit the end, twisting before pushing off to begin another lap. The water is tepid and refreshing. One other person joins me, but we ignore each other, lost in our own worlds. Few people are up and in the pool at five-thirty. The fifty-metre pool is one reason I chose this apartment building, that and my brother's company built it.

Last night has left me drained. For all my love for my brother, he's never understood the physical effect being around that number of people has on me. He thrives while I'm smothered.

My mind wanders back to Leah and the previous evening. I called Caleb as soon as I got in.

"All hell broke loose after you left," he says. *"Leah's two friends came back in and gave Vince and his girlfriend a piece of their mind."*

I can understand her friends. I wanted to give Vince a piece of my mind, too.

"What happened?" I ask.

Caleb gives me a rundown on how Leah's friends went nuclear on Vince's ass.

"Then Tristan's security threw them out."

"Who?" I ask.

"All of them," Caleb adds smugly. "But it's okay. I got the girls readmitted before I left. Vince and his girlfriend have a lifetime ban."

I grin. Karma can be a bitch, and my brother is a vindictive bastard when his friends are hurt.

I hit the side again, my fingers gripping the edge as I bring myself to a stop. My mind races over Leah's predicament. I drop my head back and stare at the ceiling, watching the ripples of light as they bounce off the hard surface. My ears encased, the whooshing of the water calms my frayed nerves.

My feet hit the bottom of the pool and I place my palms on the side, hauling myself out of the water and onto my feet. My arm and shoulder muscles protest at the seventy-seven lengths of free-style I forced on them. As my trainer taught me many moons ago, I stretch them out, not wanting to limit my movements for the rest of the day.

I grab my towel and head for the showers. My mind racing with possibilities. I'm a fixer, and I think I have the perfect fix.

CHAPTER 9

LEAH

*I*t's ten before I drag myself out of bed. I switch on my phone and make the mistake of listening to Vince's voicemails.

Leah, stop being so childish, answer your goddamn phone.

Leah, answer your phone, now.

Leah, I never realised you were this petty. I hope you're happy that you got me banned from Tristan's. Your bitch friends—

The voicemail cuts off before he can finish.

Leah, fine if you want to be like this... two weeks. Then I want you out of the apartment.

The voicemail cuts off again, my heart sinking this time. I shouldn't have turned my phone off. I've clearly poked the bear.

Leah... bloody hell, answer your fucking phone. I'm taking legal advice. Yasmin and I will move in in two weeks, so you need to leave.

The phone clicks this time, indicating he's finished the call. I run a hand over my face and rub the centre of my chest. He mentioned them moving in last night, that he decided against selling. But two weeks... I'll never find somewhere in time. Not anywhere I want to live. I've already received a message about three of the apartments I am scheduled to view. They're no longer available, having already been snapped up. I called the estate agent, only to be told, decent apartments are few and far between. "Anything decent goes on the day," she says. "There's no dallying, especially if you're on a tight budget."

Kind of her to tell me after the event. Especially as I am on a tight budget. Gabriel pays me well, but it still won't stretch very far with bills and taxes. Not on my own.

I sink onto the sofa and drop my head in my hands.

"No," I say out loud. "Get your act together, Leah. No more moping."

I straighten my back, pulling my hair into a topknot. Time to speak to the girls and get to these viewings—the ones left, anyway.

I pull up our group chat and dial. It takes seconds for Stella and Nat to connect.

"Hey, beautiful lady, how are you doing this morning?" Stella asks.

"I'm okay," I say, realising I mean it, even after Vincent's latest bombshell.

"Really?" Nat sounds incredulous.

"Honestly, Nat. I'm more embarrassed than anything."

"Why? What have you got to be embarrassed about?" Stella asks.

"I got back to the office, and Gabriel turned up... I wasn't a pretty picture." I sigh, thinking back to the black eyeliner and mascara streaks that made me look like a reject from an eighties heavy metal band. "Think disastrous makeup job, and you might be somewhere close."

"Oh." Stella coughs, well, it sounds more like she's choking.

"I take it something happened after I left," I fish. "Vince left me a few angry voice messages."

"Er..." It surprises me when Nat speaks up. "That was my fault. I heard what Yasmin said, and I kind of got into it with her."

My mouth drops open. Sweet little Nat *got into it*. My pacifist friend, who has never argued about anything with anyone.

"She smirked and I saw red," Nat continues.

I stare at the phone in my hand, not quite sure what to say. My friends are loyal to a fault. "Thank you, Nat, both of you. I'm not sure what I'd do if you weren't in my life."

"Vince is a lowlife. I can't believe he's knocked her up. Not after all his excuses," Stella says.

A pain lances through my chest. "I know, but it is what it is."

I tell them about Vince's voicemails and my two-week notice period.

"Can he do that?" Nat asks.

"It's his apartment. He can do what he wants," I say, knowing I need to be practical. Fighting him won't make a difference. It will only prolong the inevitable and cause me more distress in the long run.

"You know I'd have you stay here, but with my new flatmate, I'll be opening a can of worms," Stella says.

A new tenant moved into her spare room. She's been pushing the boundaries of their tenancy agreement, with Stella finding different men in the kitchen every morning. She's told her it must stop, or she'll go to the landlord. It's paused. A temporary truce. But I understand if I move in, it might upset the apple cart.

Nat stays quiet. She and her long-term boyfriend live in a House of Multiple Occupancy, so they have strict restrictions on guests. It's not surprising, given there are already seven of them and only two bathrooms. I'm not sure I could live like that, not after living here. It reminds me of my student days. But then, that's what they are. Nat has gone back to study law, and Rory has just qualified to be a nurse.

"Don't worry," I say. "I'll sort something out."

"*We* will," Stella says. "What time are your viewings?"

* * *

FIVE HOURS LATER, we sit in a coffee shop.

"Oh, my god. That last place." Stella groans. "I feel like I need to bathe in antiseptic. It looked like the furniture was trying to escape. When the agent said, they'd have the place deep cleaned, I'm not sure even she believed it was possible to make that place habitable. You'd require a hazmat suit."

I giggle. It's that or sob in despair.

"Or the apartment where that dodgy deal was taking place on the front lawn? They looked really shifty," Nat adds.

We all nod in agreement as the waiter delivers our coffee and a slice of *commiseration* cake.

"My absolute favourite was the shared bathroom," I add.

I laugh at Stella's look of absolute horror. "Can you imagine sharing a Jack and Jill bathroom with a man and his son? Having to remember to lock their door every time you wanted to pee."

Nat shudders. "Or the fact someone would always leave the toilet seat up!"

A constant complaint of hers from her own house-sharing experience.

"Or the pee on the seat and floor. I have yet to meet a *son* who can take aim," Stella adds, and we all groan in agreement.

"That certainly discounts that option," I say with a grimace.

At this rate, maybe I will need to ask Gabriel for some time off, especially now I only have two weeks.

"So, what's next?" Stella asks, taking a large forkful of the chocolate cake.

"I keep looking. Gabriel said he'd give me some time off if I need it," I say, digging my fork into the cake and stuffing it in my mouth. The chocolaty goodness explodes on my tongue and lifts my mood.

"Speaking of your boss," Stella adds. "His brother is H.O.T. and the way he stepped in." Stella fans herself dramatically. "You should seriously tap that now you're single."

I shake my head and laugh. "Never going to happen. Caleb is a friend and my boss's brother. He's also the biggest playboy in the city. No way, never going to happen."

Caleb is gorgeous to look at. Both brothers are. Their dark Italian heritage makes them more model than businessman. Something Caleb plays on. He hasn't made *Most Eligible Batchelor* two years in a row because he is mediocre. But it's not him I find myself wanting to talk to. It's my quiet, introverted boss, the man who sought me out, simply to check I was okay. As such, he most definitely *is* off-limits. He always has been and always will be. My job is too important to risk. Plus, he's never looked at me that way.

"Really?" She looks at me in utter amazement. "Well, if you don't want him...don't mind if I do." Stella laughs, and Nat rolls her eyes.

My phone rings, interrupting our conversation.

"If that's the jackass, ignore it," Stella says.

I check the caller ID, surprised to see Gabriel's name.

"Hold on, it's Gabriel, my boss," I say to the girls, shushing them as I accept his call.

Stella bites her lip, and Nat focuses on the cake. Cake that is almost all gone.

"Gabriel," I say. "What can I do for you?"

"Leah," his deep tone comes across the line, setting off little butterflies low in my stomach. "How's the apartment hunting going?"

Typical Gabriel, straight to the point.

I sigh. "It's been a bit of a disaster," I admit, unsure why I'm not just telling him everything is *fine.*

"I have a solution," he says. "I have an empty apartment."

I pause. Unsure what to say to his declaration. I know the properties Gabriel invests in. I couldn't possibly afford the rent on one of his.

"Leah, are you there?"

"Er, yes," I say, not sure what to say.

It's quite an embarrassing situation. He must understand that I live nearby solely because of Vince's salary. I can never afford somewhere like that in a million years on my own.

"What do you think?"

Maybe I'm mistaken. Maybe he has a tiny shoebox somewhere. One of his first properties.

My stomach tingles in anticipation. "Where is it?" I ask, holding my breath.

"It's in my building."

My heart sinks, and I bite the inside of my lip to smother my disappointment. "That's very kind, but there is no way I could afford the rent."

A lengthy pause leaves me questioning if we've lost connection.

"I can work something out. The apartment is currently empty and has been since I bought it. I use it as somewhere to house guests."

A multi-million pound plus apartment sitting empty, only for guests. Oh, how the other half live.

I smile, pleased he can't see my response.

"We can work out a rent that suits you. If I'm honest, you'd be doing me a favour. Only one person has ever stayed in it, and I haven't tested everything. The builder has sent a final warning on snagging lists."

His words warm my heart. I'm aware Caleb's company constructed the building, and thus, would readily address any issues.

"Have a think about it and let me know. If you want to have a look. I can show you around."

I cough to clear the lump that's clogging my throat.

"Thank you. Can I take a moment?"

"Take as long as you need. Call me when you've decided."

The phone goes dead, and I sit and stare at it.

When I glance up, Stella and Nat are staring at me wide-eyed.

"Did he just offer you an apartment in El Castillo?"

I look back down at my phone and nod, my head spinning.

"He did, but there's no way I can afford that."

I sigh.

"What did he say when you said that?" Nat asks.

"He said we could work something out. The apartment is empty, and I'd be doing him a favour."

Stella grips my hand over the table. "Is your boss a creep?"

"What? No... why?"

Stella laughs at my wide eyes.

"Well, if he's not a creep and 'work something out' is not code for you selling your body, why aren't you snapping his hand off?"

I slouch back in the chair, placing my phone face down on the table.

"Because..." Both of my friends give me expectant looks. "He's my boss."

"And?" It's Nat who raises the question.

I shrug. "It doesn't seem ethical." I huff out the words.

Knowing I sound stupid. "Gabriel's kind and thoughtful. I don't want him to feel I've taken advantage of him."

"Gabriel pays your wages?"

I give Stella my best, *really* look, and she laughs.

"Well, it's not like he doesn't know what you earn," she adds.

"I hate to agree with her," Nat says, smiling, as Stella shoves her shoulder. "But Stella is right. He knows what you earn. He knows what you can afford."

I shake my head, wrapping my arms around my churning stomach.

"Look," Stella says. "How about accepting it, in the short term? Move out of Vince's. Give yourself time to breathe, regroup." Stella leans over and grips my forearm, pulling it away from my body and clasping my hand in hers. "Let someone do something nice for you. Gabriel is trying to help. Is that so wrong?"

I huff out a breath before scooping up the last piece of chocolate cake and stuffing it in my mouth.

"Fine," I say when I finish my mouthful. "I'll take it, but only to get myself out of my current predicament. When I find somewhere else, I'll move out."

Stella and Nat clap hands. "Well, that's a relief. I'm not sure I could take any more viewings," Stella adds.

While Stella and Nat order more drinks, I drop Gabriel a message.

ME:

Are you sure?

GABRIEL:

Have you ever known me to do anything I've not thought through?

ME:

True

ME:

Okay.

I pause, not sure what to put next. Three dots appear to let me know Gabriel is typing.

GABRIEL:

You can view the apartment tomorrow. 2 pm?

ME:

I'll be there.

GABRIEL:

Get reception to call me.

ME:

See you then.

My heart is in my mouth as I type the last message. Am I truly doing this?

Nat and Stella return with a bottle of wine. Stella pours three glasses, raising hers in the air. "To Leah's new home."

CHAPTER 10

GABRIEL

*M*y phone buzzes, and the tension I've been holding since this morning dissipates.

I've spoken to Caleb about my plan, and he is fully on board. Especially if it means sticking one to Leah's ex-fiancé. The guy is a complete dick, while Leah is *family*. In Caleb's mind, he says I owe her. If for nothing else than her putting up with my *grumpy ass* for all these years.

ME:

She's going to take it.

CALEB:

Good. Don't scare her off!

ME:

Ha ha ha

It's not quite what she agreed, but I know she'll be willing once she's seen it.

I meet Leah in reception. Seeing her out of the office and in casual clothes is a shock. I did a double take when she first arrived, dressed in jeans and an off-the-shoulder jumper, her hair tied up in a messy bun. She looked so different from the woman who walks around the office, the epitome of professionalism. Only the dark circles under her eyes highlight the fact she's clearly not sleeping.

I open the door to the apartment and wait for Leah to enter ahead of me.

I'm happy she finally relented and agreed to view the apartment. It makes perfect sense for her to take it. If she feels uncomfortable staying here long term, it will give her the opportunity to find somewhere decent.

"Gabriel, this is stunning."

Leah turns to face me, her eyes bright with excitement.

I take a step in and make my way to the left. "This is the main bathroom," I say, holding the door open so she can enter. The room contains a large walk-in shower, sink and toilet. "Across from here is the second bedroom."

She follows close behind me. I can feel the excitement radiating off her. I don't think I've ever seen Leah like this. She's usually as reserved as I am.

"Wow," she says, walking into the room and around the large double bed in the middle. I added a comfy chair while the rest of the furniture in the room, including the television, is built in. Leah walks to the window and takes in the view. I hear her sigh, unsurprised, when she turns and faces me.

"Gabriel, this place is beautiful," she says.

"I know," I reply, unsure why she is making such an obvious statement.

"But that's the thing. I can't afford this. I wish I could. It's really stunning, but this is so far out of my price range."

"Ah." We're back to that. I thought I covered this, but then maybe I haven't. Caleb warned me to tread cautiously and avoid being too pushy, even if I can only see the benefits for Leah.

"Yes. Ah," she says, giving me her patient smile.

"The apartment is below mine. I keep it empty. It will remain empty if you don't take it. I currently use it for visitors, but only one person has stayed in it in five years. That was Mark and his wife." Leah goes to open her mouth, so I add. "They live in Australia. As you can see, the apartment is fully furnished. I hire a cleaner who comes in once a week to ensure it stays in good condition. I'm not renting it out to simply anyone. I never have, but it will solve your immediate problem."

The words tumble out of me. It's the truth, and I know Leah appreciates the truth.

"But there's still rent," Leah says, although she's no longer looking at me.

"What are you thinking?" I ask.

Leah looks up, her eyes bleak. "I currently pay..."

"What?" I interrupt. "You currently pay? But I thought Vincent owned the apartment you're living in."

She frowns at me. "He does. But I pay him rent."

I try to school my features. How can someone charge their fiancée rent? I cough, trying to smother my shock. "Sorry, I'm just surprised you pay your fiancé rent."

"It was like that from the beginning, and we never changed it. Initially, it was to protect him and the apartment, not that I want anything from him. I want a clean break."

I pull a piece of paper from my jacket pocket. "Here," I say, handing it over to her. "These are the management fees, which include the building's heating and my cleaner's costs. There are no separate bills." Leah takes the piece of paper from my hand and opens it, her eyes popping out of her head.

Damn, is it too much?

She shakes her head and hands the paper back to me.

"If it's a problem, you can remove the cleaning cost and

do the cleaning yourself. Anita can use the extra hours in my apartment."

Anita is one of the few people allowed in my space, and that's only when I'm not there.

"It's not that," Leah says. "That's not nearly enough for this place. This is less than I pay Vince for my portion of the bills."

Vincent is going down fast, in my estimation. Knowing what traders earn a year and the bank he works for, the fact that he's been charging his fiancée, the woman he professed to love and wanted to marry, turns my stomach. When Leah smiles at me, I hide the sigh of relief I want to exhale. I was concerned the number which Caleb and I arrived at was too high.

"Why then? This place is empty, plus you haven't even seen it all yet," I say, trying to entice her. "Let me show you the rest of the apartment, then you can make up your mind. The rest might disgust you, and I'll be begging you to take it."

When Leah quirks her brow, I find myself enjoying our banter. I also know I'll win in the end.

I always do.

I lead her back out into the main living area. A large open-plan kitchen sits against the back wall. The granite worktops reflect the sunlight streaming in through the floor-to-ceiling windows, giving the room an even brighter, airier feel. The kitchen overlooks the main living and dining area. A large, white, L-shaped sofa sits on a pale, long pile rug.

"The wooden floors all house the underfloor heating throughout the apartment and building," I say.

Leah nods, her eyes wide as she takes in the room. The room has been divided into zones. A seventy-inch flat-screen television is on the wall in front of the sofa. A glass dining table and chairs occupy the opposite wall. "The balcony sits below mine. It houses an outdoor seating area and heat lamp for nights when the temperature drops."

I move to the door, sliding it open and allowing her to step outside.

Leah walks forward, her hands gripping the edge of the balcony as she takes in the view. She sighs, closing her eyes for a second. When she reopens them, her eyes meet mine. I motion for her to follow me as I walk her back through the main living area and through another side door. It opens straight into a walk-in wardrobe, banked with a generous supply of enclosed hanging and shelving space.

"To the left is the master suite, and to the right is the ensuite," I say.

Stepping back I allow Leah to explore. The bathroom houses a claw foot bath, a large walk-in rainfall shower, a toilet and a sink unit. Caleb and I went all out when fitting the apartment out.

Leah squeaks, her hand flying to her mouth when she sees the bathroom, and I bite the inside of my lip to prevent myself from smiling. She then turns towards the bedroom itself. The bedroom holds a king-size bed, a television, and a small seating area. It's a tranquil area, just as mine is. She remains silent, taking in her surroundings before dropping herself onto the bed. She bounces back up, shooting me an embarrassed glance.

"Well. What do you think?" I ask tightly, clearing my throat.

Leah looks at me, her eyes sparkling. "Just until I find somewhere else," she states.

"I'm happy for you to stay, but if those are your terms," I say. "It's yours for as long as you want it."

"Let me at least pay you what I pay Vince," she says. "This is too little."

She waves the piece of paper I gave her.

I sigh. "I don't need your money, Leah. This place is empty. It's costing me money. If you cover the costs it incurs, then I'll be more than happy. Caleb wants to check that everything works, and I can only do that if someone lives in it. I want someone considerate living beneath me."

"What if I decide to have parties... loud parties?" she asks.

I scrunch up my eyes as I stare at her, unsure whether she's joking.

"Are you going to?" I ask warily.

"No," she says, grinning at me. "But it was worth seeing the look on your face. At least I've had none to date. But then, I haven't been single in a *really* long time."

I scowl at her now. "Then I don't understand. It's a moot point."

She looks at me, her head tilted to one side, as if she's weighing me up. "Why Gabriel? Why are you doing this? You don't owe me anything. I simply work for you."

"You've worked for me for eight years. Been loyal. Done everything I've asked, worked longer hours than most would have in your position. Helped me become what I am today. Take this as me paying back."

She gives a slight nod in acknowledgment of my words. Well, that was easy.

"If I take the apartment. Would you prefer I don't use the balcony?" she asks as we leave the bedroom.

The air around me becomes less suffocating.

I frown, confused by her question.

"You can use the balcony. This will be your home," I say. I trust her. This is Leah, after all. "There's also a gym, a fifty-metre swimming pool, steam and sauna rooms, a residents' lounge, a library, and you can hire out the cinema."

Leah's jaw drops before she clamps it shut, her lips pursing.

"What do you think? Do you want the apartment?"

She nods, her eyes twinkling, a wide smile splitting her face. "Yes... oh my goodness. Yes." She takes a step towards me but freezes, instead holding out her hand. "So, you're going to be my landlord. I promise to be the best tenant."

I take her hand in mine, surprised at how my large one engulfs hers. The awareness I thought I imagined the night I dropped her home reignites where our skin touches.

"I'll get the papers drawn up, and you can move in whenever you want. If you need help. Caleb has a company he uses."

"It's okay. Vince is purchasing all my furniture. He wants to keep the apartment as it is, for him and Yasmin." She sighs. "It will only be me and my suitcases. Maybe a few throws, pillows."

Jesus. What a fucking arsehole.

"Well, if you need a hand moving, we're happy to help," I say instead.

We stand in silence for a moment, before walking back towards the door. Leah touches my arm, sending more shivers of awareness down my spine.

"Thank you, Gabriel." She screws up her face. "That seems to be my favourite phrase around you. But I want you to know I truly mean it."

I look into her eyes, lost in the sincerity. "You're welcome. I'm glad I can help."

CHAPTER 11

LEAH

I call the girls as soon as I get home.

"Well, that's a relief," Nat says when I tell them I've accepted the apartment.

"I'm just glad you finally saw sense," Stella says. "Even if you don't stay and eventually look for somewhere else, it at least gets you away from Vince. But, just putting it out there, I think you'd be mad to move... just saying... but at least you can save some money with the low rent he's offering you."

I laugh. "I agree. Oh, my goodness, you should see the place. It's beautiful. I'm still pinching myself."

I doubted I could afford the rent at the start of Gabriel's guided tour. I wondered if he forgot how much he pays me. When he handed me the piece of paper, my heart almost burst its way out of my chest. I wanted to bite his hand off, but I've never been one to take anyone for granted. I happily paid my fiancé more than Gabriel was asking, and I lived with him. Although the look on Gabriel's face when I mentioned that. His eyes hardened, and his mouth pinched. He remained silent, but I could sense his disapproval.

The girls had been too. They'd not realised. When I told

them, they asked how Vince could do that when he professed to love me. To me, it hadn't been about that. I was happy to pay my way. But they couldn't understand, not when he was bringing in a seven-figure salary and happy to brag about it. I didn't tell them I also paid for all our food shopping.

My eyes are slowly opening where my ex-fiancé is concerned. Well, good luck to them both. I hope Yasmin enjoys picking up after him and having dinner ready on the table when he walks in. Then again, maybe she's wiser than me.

I finish my conversation with the girls and make some dinner. My phone rings and I answer it automatically.

"Oh, so you haven't lost your phone. I was wondering." Vince's sarcastic tone snaps me out of my good mood.

"No," I reply. "But I only answer it to people I want to speak to, and stupidly, I didn't check the caller ID before I accepted."

"Since I'm using Yas's phone, it wouldn't have mattered."

I smart at his smug tone.

"What do you want, Vince?" I say. Beginning to wonder what I ever saw in this guy.

"I want to check you got my messages?"

"Which one? You left me about twenty," I add, letting him know how excessive he's been.

"Well, if you'd just picked up your damn phone." I can tell from his voice he's getting snappy. And I don't feel like dealing with this side of him anymore.

"Vince, your little bombshell devastated me. You understand that, right? I would have assumed *you*, of all people, would know how that piece of news would affect me. I thought you would have more respect for me, than telling me in the middle of a crowded bar that your girlfriend is pregnant."

"Well, Yas is very upset. The fact you asked if the baby was mine."

My jaw drops. Has he not heard a word I've just said?

"She was upset? You know what, Vince, I'll not waste my breath."

I barely recognise the man I've been with for ten years. But then, did I ever know him?

He humphs down the phone. "Did you get the message about moving out in two weeks?"

"I did." A smile forms on my lips. Thanks to Gabriel, I'm no longer carrying that weight on my shoulders.

Silence descends.

"I can make it longer if you need me to," he says. "Maybe you can speak to Caleb Frazer and get his friend Tristan to turn a blind eye to Friday night's events. Your bitch friends really went to town on me."

Blood rushes to my cheeks, and a ringing starts in my ears. "If I get Caleb to talk to Tristan, then I can stay for another five weeks?" I question, wanting to confirm what he's saying.

"Yes. Yas is really upset. Tristan's bars are her favourite place. We've been given a lifetime ban from all of them."

I fist pump the air, a grin spreading over my face. I suspect Caleb had something to do with that. I make a mental note to thank him.

"Sorry, Vince. No can do. I've found somewhere to live. I'm moving out at the weekend. The apartment is all yours... and Yas's."

"What? How? Where?"

He chokes out the words, and I laugh. He thought he had me at a disadvantage. This is where I'd love to throw my arms around Gabriel.

"You heard me. I've found somewhere to live," I repeat more slowly this time, making sure he hears every word.

"Oh, and I'll email you the cost of the furniture that's mine. I expect full value otherwise, I'm coming back for it, with solicitors. I purchased it from my account, and like you, I have receipts.

"You don't have to be nasty," he says, his voice sulky.

"Oh, I'm not being nasty. I'm being practical. I just want what I'm owed."

"I don't recognise you," he says.

"No, I don't suppose you do, but when you mistreat a dog, you better watch out." I pause before adding. "I'll leave the key and pass with the concierge. Expect my email. Goodbye, Vince."

"Wait-what am I supposed to tell Yas?"

"I really don't care," I say, disconnecting before he can say anything else.

I drop onto the sofa, unable to keep the grin from my face. The doormat who has put up with so much for the past ten years has finally realised what a mug she's been. Friday night has helped to open my eyes. Yes, it hurts. I have amazing memories of our time together, memories I'm trying hard not to tarnish. But people change. I'm beginning to wonder if we've been drifting along in a bubble of convenience. As for *Yas* being upset. I can almost feel sorry for her, but then again, I don't. She slept with Vince, knowing he was engaged to someone else. If she had any morals, she'd have told him to leave me first. As for announcing she's pregnant in the bar...no. I have zero sympathy, she can suck it up.

* * *

I SPEND the next week packing my belongings and cataloguing the furniture. Over the years, I've been meticulous about keeping receipts and documents. Maybe subconsciously, I knew this day was coming. Should he dispute it, I send Vince the bill and photocopies of every receipt. Instead, he surprises me by paying me on the same day. Pocket change to him.

Saturday morning, Stella and Nat arrive early. I've packed up all my ornaments, photographs and soft furnishings. Choosing to ignore the fact my life at thirty-four fits neatly into eight boxes and two suitcases.

The apartment looks like a show home. The sides are empty. As things are packed away, I realise it is me who made this a home. All my trinkets and soft furnishings. It doesn't even look the same. Well, Yasmin has a blank canvas with which to work.

I wheel my two suitcases out of the bedroom.

"So, you ready?" Nat asks, coming to stand next to me.

"I am," I say, giving the apartment the once over.

Despite my better judgement, I'm leaving the place immaculate. I moved everything out and cleaned it meticulously. I don't want Yasmin to say I was slovenly to anyone. I've too much pride for that.

"Let's go," Stella says, taking one of my bags. "The taxis are downstairs in the car park. Security just called to say they've let them in. We should be able to load up quickly and get you moved."

I smile over at my friend and turn my back on the apartment. Time to move on. This is no longer my home. I don't even recognise it. However, that may have something to do with my rearranging all the furniture last night.

We move all the boxes out and down into the taxis. I climb into the first taxi, stacked with boxes. Stella and Nat are getting the second with my clothes. Before I can close the door, Stella clasps my hand.

"You've got this," she says, squeezing my fingers.

I pinch my lips together and incline my head before smiling. "I do."

One thing the past two months have shown me is that life without Vince is not what I thought it would be. The massive crater I feared when he first left doesn't exist. All I feel is a sense of relief.

"See you on the other side," she says, shutting the door and running back to the second taxi. The meters are ticking up, but I don't really care. I savour the moment. Realising I'm not the broken wallflower Vince wants me to be, that I'm stronger than that and always have been. Something I forgot every time I let him take charge. Well, that will not happen again.

I, Leah Walker, am in charge of my destiny from this moment on.

The taxi journey is short. El Castillo is only around the corner, so the two taxi fares end up being less than I feared. We unload the boxes into the underground garage. I see Gabriel's car parked to one side, along with many other beautiful cars. I really am moving into Millionaire Plaza.

"Wow, these are some serious motors," Stella whispers.

"I know," I say, hoisting the first box onto my hip and grabbing a case handle.

The security guard rushes over. "Ms Walker?" he asks.

"Er, yes," I say. "Is there a problem? I'm moving in today."

"I know Ms Walker," he says, smiling warmly. "Mr Frazer informed us. The concierge is sending someone down with a trolley. Are these your belongings?"

He motions to the boxes and cases.

"They are," I say, feeling a little embarrassed at my meagre possessions. No. I refuse to wallow. That time is past.

"Excellent," he says, his smile bright and welcoming.

We stop at the rattling sound getting closer. "If you'll let us, ma'am, we can bring everything up to your apartment."

"If you insist," Stella says, grinning as she links her arm

with mine. "Let's leave these lovely gentlemen to do the heavy lifting, and you can show us your new pad."

I look at the guy in uniform. "Are you sure?"

He looks confused for a moment before his gaze softens. "Absolutely. You head upstairs. We'll be right behind you."

With that, he and the other guys begin loading the boxes and my cases into the cages.

"I take it that's us done," I say as we make our way to the elevator.

Gabriel gave me a lift pass and apartment keys the day before. The tenancy agreement was on my desk the day after I agreed to move in, which hadn't surprised me. Gabriel is nothing if not organised. Both he and Caleb hold a vast property portfolio, so renting out one apartment is nothing new to him. He probably has each contract in duplicate.

I open the door and stand back as I let Stella and Nat enter before me.

"O.M.G," Nat says, her mouth open. "This is... I'm not sure how to describe it. You lucky..." Nat doesn't finish her words; instead, she throws her arms around me and buries her head in my shoulder. It's then I realise she's crying.

"Hey," I say, pushing her away and staring at her. "What are the tears for?"

She sobs even harder. Stella steps up and puts her arms around us, her own voice husky. "I think Nat's just saying, after all the crap you've been through lately, she's happy you've finally had a turnaround in fortune."

Nat nods and gives me a watery smile. I pull her in for one final hug, finding a lump forming in my throat. "I love you guys. Thank you for always being there for me."

Stella steps back, and we link hands in a circle. We started it in college when one of us required support. "Always," we say together, laughing.

"Now, where are those men? I've got some *bubbles* in a cool bag," Stella says, wiping her eyes.

As if on cue, there's a knock at the door. Opening it, the two guys from downstairs are standing with my belongings.

"Where would you like these, Ms Walker?" the first guy asks.

"If you just unload them here." I point to the corner. "We can manage from there."

They both unclip the cages and begin unpacking the boxes, stacking them where I'd indicated. When they're done, I grab my purse, open it, and grab some notes. They smile. "Oh no, Ma'am. Mr Frazer has handled all of that. Welcome to El Castillo."

With that, they leave.

Stella is busy opening a box with a large X on the side. I throw her a questioning glance.

"What? I needed to know which box contained the important stuff," she says, pulling out a bottle of champagne stored in an ice bag.

Nat is already in the kitchen, opening the cupboards. "Ah ha," she says, finding champagne glasses and putting three on the side.

"Isn't it a little early?" I say, looking at my phone. It's just gone ten in the morning.

"It's after five in Australia," Stella says, shrugging. "Besides, we're celebrating." She pours three glasses and holds hers up in a toast. "To new beginnings."

"To new beginnings." My chest tightens as we clink glasses. It signifies a fresh start. Frightening yet exhilarating. If anything, the past week has shown me that. I shake myself out of my thoughts when I notice the girls staring at me, concern in their eyes.

"I'm fine," I say.

"I hate those two words," Nat says. "Usually, when someone says *I'm fine*, they're anything but."

I think back to Gabriel, saying the same thing. Maybe I need to change my go-to phrase. Grabbing her hand, I give it a squeeze. "I promise you I will be fine. I may only be halfway there. But that's to be expected. I need to adapt. Ten years is a long time to be someone's *other* half. I need to learn how to operate as myself again."

Nat squeezes my hand in hers. "We need to arrange some more nights out. Rory's working night shifts at the hospital, so I'm free."

Stella grins at us both. "Get this girl back on the horse."

"I think I'll enjoy being single for a while," I say.

The last thing I want is another relationship, even if—

"Getting back on the horse doesn't mean a relationship. You need to get out and have some fun." Stella is much freer-spirited than either Nat or me. She was in a long-term relationship, but it turned nasty, and she's never been able to trust the same way since. I worry about my friend, but also don't want to find myself as cynical.

"Okay, okay." I laugh as there's another knock at the door. Did the guys forget something?

I open it, champagne glass in hand, before freezing.

Gabriel stands in the open doorway, dressed in faded jeans and a tight-fitting dark t-shirt. The material is stretched tight over his broad chest, revealing toned, muscled arms and abs. Wow. Who knew under his shirts, he was ripped.

Down girl. This is your boss you're gawping at.

My heart stutters.

"Hi," I say awkwardly as Gabriel looks over my shoulder, catching sight of Stella and Nat.

"Good morning," he replies. "I just wanted to check you managed to move in okay." His eyes move to the pile of boxes, and his lips twitch. "It looks like there have been no issues."

His head tilts at the glass in my hand.

"No...er, no issues. The guys were great. Thank you," I say before taking a breath. "Would you like to come in?"

"No, that's fine. You're busy. I just wanted to check that everything went smoothly."

"Thank you. And thank you for arranging for the guys to help move my stuff upstairs. It saved us a number of journeys."

"You're welcome."

"Come in." It's Stella who steps up, pulling me out of the way. "Hi, I'm Stella. One of Leah's best friends and chief mover." She holds out her hand to Gabriel, who stands for a moment, frozen. "This is a beautiful apartment," Stella continues, completely oblivious to Gabriel's awkwardness. I watch as he finally snaps himself out of it and takes her hand in his.

"Pleased to meet you, Stella."

Stella grins. "This is Nat," she says, motioning to Nat, who has remained quietly behind us. She gives a little wave as Gabriel nods his acknowledgment.

His phone rings, and he glances down at the screen. "I need to go," he says. "You ladies enjoy yourselves. I'll see you on Monday, Leah."

Gabriel swipes to answer the call.

Does the man ever stop?

"Frazer," he says before turning and heading back towards the elevator. "Can you hold for a moment?"

He stops and turns. "If you need anything, Leah, please call me. I'm only upstairs. Have a lovely day, Ladies."

Before I can say anything, he returns his attention back to his phone and the voice on the other end.

I shut the door, not wanting to eavesdrop on his call and turn into the room where Stella is busy fanning herself.

"That is one seriously *hot* man! Did you see that chest... those arms..." She grins like a Cheshire cat. "He's *the quiet, moody type.* I bet he's a tiger in bed." Stella lets out a growl, making me flinch and Nat giggle.

"Stop Stella. He's my boss and younger than me. No, simply no!" I say, shaking my head rapidly. However, since that night, I've seen a different side to Gabriel. He's not as distant and aloof as he likes people to think. He's a good listener, and he cares. This apartment is a prime example of that.

"Tell me you've not looked at him and wondered what he looks like without any clothes," Stella says, quirking an eyebrow in my direction, daring me.

"If it hasn't escaped your notice, I've been in a relationship for the past ten years. A serious one."

"Yes, but you haven't had your eyes gouged out. You're not blind! You're a red-blooded woman." Stella sighs, her expression dreamy. "I wish I worked with someone that hot. My days would fly by." Stella sighs again.

She works for a marketing company and is surrounded by *hot* men. The problem is her ex also worked there until he was fired.

"Okay, I admit, Gabriel is good-looking. I'm not blind. However, he's five years younger than me, he's also my boss. I love my job."

Stella and Nat exchange a glance.

"What?" I ask, starting to get a little annoyed with my friends.

"Nothing," they both say together.

It's my turn to huff. "Fine," I say. "Are you ladies drinking, or are you going to help me get these boxes unpacked?"

"Both," they say together, holding up their glasses for a refill.

Stella moves to place the rest of the champagne in the fridge.

"Did you get a food order in already?" Stella asks, turning towards me and holding open the fridge door.

The fridge is fit to burst with a variety of fresh fruit and food. I know there's only one person who would have done that.

"No, I was going to go later," I say, hiding my shock.

Stella quirks her eyebrow, "Only a communications officer... right... you keep telling yourself that."

THE BOXES ARE UNPACKED an hour later, and everything has a place. The empty boxes have been delivered to the recycle bins in the basement, and my clothes have taken up residence in a small portion of the enormous walk-in wardrobe. Photos and my collection of ornaments adorn the sides, while my throws and cushions add a splash of colour to the white sofa. When the girls leave mid-afternoon, I walk out onto the balcony, taking in the view.

When I turn back and stare through the window at my new home, a sense of calm descends.

CHAPTER 12

GABRIEL

$\mathcal{T}$he concierge called to inform me that Leah's things had been delivered, and she was now in the building. Before I could stop myself, I was outside her apartment. I had to divert my gaze when she opened the door, her hair in a messy ponytail, her hips hugged in tight faded jeans, the sloppy off-the-shoulder sweater showing glimpses of her ivory skin. Gone was some of the tension she's been holding all week. Instead, she looked stunning in her casual clothes.

My phone pings.

LEAH:

Thank you for all the food. You didn't need to do that.

ME:

No problem, I had an order myself.

I lie.

I keep in the basics but buy my dinner nightly from one of the local restaurants. But Leah mentioned earlier in the week that she would need to shop when she arrived. She didn't want to cart food with her, so I thought I'd save her the trouble. I've never been one for cooking myself.

LEAH:

Let me cook you dinner as a thank you.

ME:

You don't have to.

LEAH:

I'd like to. You've been so kind.

ME:

What time?

There's a pause. Oh shit, maybe she didn't mean tonight.

ME:

Don't worry if you didn't mean tonight.

LEAH:

It's fine. I'm cooking for myself. Say 19:30?

ME:

I'll be there.

LEAH:

See you then.

I spend the rest of the day in my home office, counting down the hours. A thought hits, will Leah's friends still be there? My stomach rolls at the prospect. They seemed nice, but...

I pick up my phone, ready to cancel, but put it down again.

Cancelling at the last minute is not cool. I jumped at the chance to see her, not even waiting for a formal invite, so it serves me right.

Grabbing two bottles of wine from my stash, I head to the elevator, taking the trip down one floor. Stepping out, an amazing smell assaults my senses. I follow my nose, and it leads me to Leah's door. I knock and wait.

The door swings open, and I take in the sight. Leah has changed into blue skinny jeans and a tight-fitting jumper. When she smiles, my mouth goes dry.

"Gabriel, come in," she says, stepping away from the door to allow me to enter. I step inside. The transformation in such a short time is unbelievable. This place has gone from a sterile apartment to a home in just a few hours. Photos, souvenirs, cushions, throws.

"Quite the transformation," I say, following Leah towards the kitchen and placing the bottles of wine on the unit. "I wasn't sure what we were having, so I brought one of each," I say, gesturing to the wine.

"That's kind, but you didn't need to. This is, after all, a *thank you* meal," she says, grabbing two glasses from the cupboard. "Would you like to do the honours? We're having a vegetable lasagne," she adds, colour rising in her cheeks. "I hope that's okay? I'm a pescatarian."

"It's fine," I reply, before realising *what* I've just said. I hold up a hand. "What I should have said is that no one other than my mother or Betsy, my mum's cook, has cooked for me in a long time. So, home-cooked food is well received."

A furrow appears between her brows, so I elaborate. "I don't cook. I get most of my food from the local restaurants." I list Monday, Tuesday, etc., and which restaurants supply which days.

Leah places her hands on her hips and gives me a stern look. "That's just sad and stopping now. If you enjoy tonight's meal, I'm happy to cook extra every night. I always cook for myself, and cooking for two is better than cooking for one. I can deliver it up, or you can join me. I'm easy either way."

I stare wide-eyed at the woman in front of me. I meant

what I said. No one ever has cooked for me, not nightly. Rachel and I didn't live together. One of her many bugbears. She also preferred eating out.

"I didn't mean. I don't expect," I say, suddenly wondering if Leah feels indebted, and this is her way of making it up to me.

"You might want to try my food first," she laughs. "Saying no won't offend me, but the offer is on the table."

She smiles, and I know I'll be taking her up on her offer.

"Can I do anything?" I ask.

"Pour us some drinks, and if you can grab the salad out of the fridge," she says, opening the oven to a whoosh of delicious-smelling air. My stomach grumbles, and I do as she asks.

I open the red and pour it into two glasses. It's the same red I tried at Tristan's. He delivered my latest wine order earlier in the week.

I move to the large American fridge freezer and open it. A salad bowl sits, pre-made, on the shelf. I pick it up and carry it over to the table, where Leah has set two places.

"Are your friends not eating with us?" I ask.

Leah smiles as she carries over a large oven dish bubbling with lasagna.

"No. They have prior engagements. It's also not much of a thank you if there are other people here too." She places the food on a mat and returns to the fridge, grabbing a small jug of something. She places it next to the salad as I return with our wine glasses.

When we finally sit, Leah dishes up.

"Help yourself to salad," she says. "The dressing is my mother's recipe."

"Thank you."

I help myself.

We sit in silence until Leah raises her glass.

"To new beginnings. Bon appetite," she adds, clinking her glass to mine.

"To new beginnings."

We eat and talk, and most surprisingly, I laugh. I'm shocked at how easily the conversation flows. I usually hate small talk, but Leah keeps a balance at work and at home. In the end, we've left the office behind and are sharing our likes and dislikes in movies, music and places to eat.

"So, what do you think?" Leah asks when we've finally finished. Not just the food but the bottle of wine.

"Delicious," I say honestly.

"Would you be interested in home cooked from now on? I cook for myself, so it's really no bother."

"Let me pay for the food," I say, only to receive a scowl.

"Hard no!" Leah says. "You can see this as another item on the list you gave me?"

"Only if I can supply the wine."

Leah picks up the bottle and studies it. "Deal. You have impeccable taste. Although I don't tend to drink during the week," she says, her lips tilting.

"I have the occasional glass, but it's not much fun drinking alone," I admit.

I have a feeling the comment about the wine holds more significance than I realise. But then her fiancé was at Tristan's. Maybe Leah is used to drinking good wine.

As if sensing my unasked question.

"Vince and his trader buddies drink expensive wine."

I notice she doesn't mention she does.

We leave the conversation, as I don't really want to talk about her ex and instead help Leah tidy up.

"Thank you," I say, making my way to the door.

"You're welcome," Leah says. "I'll draw up a menu, and you can let me know if there's anything you don't eat."

"I'm not fussy," I say. "Any home-cooked food will be a bonus."

I head back upstairs, not sure what to make of the evening, but knowing I'm already looking forward to our next meal.

* * *

OVER THE NEXT couple of weeks, Leah and I fall into an easy pattern. Some evenings, we eat together, but usually, if she knows I'm going to be working late, she plates me up a dinner and places it in my warming drawer. Those nights, I find myself missing her and her insights into business and life.

The Callahan presentation goes incredibly well, as I knew it would. Leah is present, along with the rest of the team.

"I'm impressed, Frazer," he says, shaking my hand after I walk him to the elevator.

"Thank you. I hope you will see it as a reason to move your business to Frazer Investments. As a boutique hedge fund, we offer a more personalised client service than some of our larger competitors." I use the words I've heard Leah sprout a hundred times over the years.

Callahan nods, his smile giving me positive vibes.

"I like you, and I like your team. A very professional outfit you have here."

It's at that moment Leah joins us.

"Here are the extra packs you wanted," she says, handing over the printed prospectus.

"Thank you, Leah," he says, motioning for his PA to take them. "I was just saying to Gabriel here what a professional outfit he has created. I like it. That and the longevity of the staff. You keep your staff happy, Gabriel. That's the sign of a good leader."

I freeze at his condescending tone. I may only be twenty-nine, young in terms of all I've achieved. But I know how to run a business. Callahan is in his sixties. Old school. One look from Leah, and I know not to take offence.

Leah nods and smiles at him. "I've been here since the beginning and wouldn't want to work anywhere else."

Callahan seems to like her reply. He shakes our hands and leaves. Leah follows me back to my office.

I motion for her to close the door.

"I think that went well," I say, only to have her squeal and throw her arms around my neck.

She steps back, her eyes wide.

"Sorry," she says awkwardly, smoothing down her dress. When she looks up, she gives me a shy smile. "I'd say it went better than okay. You were amazing. Looking at his response and everyone on his team. I'll be surprised if he doesn't come on board."

I stare at her, speechless. In eight years, I've never seen Leah so animated. She never really lets on how a meeting has gone. She'll congratulate me, celebrate with the team when we gain a new client. But she's always held herself apart, maintained her professional boundaries.

Now, there is this. Our growing friendship. We have spent quite a few evenings working on this presentation over dinner. Pride swells in my chest at her praise. Not that I need it. I'm good at what I do - better than good. But for some reason, her recognising it makes it feel—more.

"Tonight, I'll make us an extra special dinner to celebrate," she says, after we discuss a few additional points that came up in the meeting.

"I'll look forward to it," I say, watching her leave and finding myself meaning every word.

CHAPTER 13

*G*abriel's head appears around the door. His expression is pinched as he rubs frantically at his forehead.

"I'll send it straight over," I say, waving him in.

He enters, dropping himself into the chair opposite my desk. His whole body exudes tension, including the vein throbbing fiercely in his forehead.

I put the phone down and lean forward, resting my forearms on the desk.

"Callahan's PA," I say, grinning.

We are so close I can feel it.

"What can I do for you?" I ask, smiling at him, not wanting to jump to any conclusions.

"I've..." Gabriel stutters over his words before running a hand through his hair. "I've just received a call from the manager at El Castillo," he says. "There's been an incident."

It's almost home time. What can be so important that they're calling Gabriel at work, not waiting for him to get home? My mind goes into overdrive. What incident? An accident? A fire?

"The sprinkler system on the twenty-sixth floor has malfunctioned," Gabriel continues. His gaze locks on mine.

It takes my brain a moment to compute. Twenty-six... that's my floor... Twenty-six is my floor!

I stand up, knocking my chair back in a hurry.

"But..."

"You may as well sit. There is nothing we can do. Maintenance is in the apartments pumping out the water."

"Pumping out the water?" I squeak, sinking back down into my chair. "Exactly how much water are we talking about?"

"It looks like the system was on for quite a while. Most of the day. Apparently, one of your neighbours is away on holiday, and the others only returned from Singapore this afternoon. They raised the alarm." Gabriel drops his elbows onto his thighs and stares at me. "They're hoping you can get back in later this evening to retrieve any salvageable items."

"Salvageable," I hear myself mutter.

I run a hand down my face. And here I was, thinking life was finally looking up. I should have realised it was too good to be true.

"I'm sorry, Leah." Gabriel looks at me. "If there is anything I can do. Of course, insurance will cover any damages. We'll go later, together. You can stay —"

I shake my head, trying to absorb what he's saying, but my mind is whirling, his voice muffled. I know he's talking, so I offer him a weak smile and nod. *How bad can it be?*

* * *

How bad can it be? Ha! Water looks so innocuous, but there's a reason it's one of nature's most destructive forces. We are eventually allowed in later that evening, and Gabriel lets me sit in his apartment until then. I make dinner for us both, needing to keep myself busy, although I point out to him how he clearly lied when stocking up my fridge and cupboards. His are all but empty. He offers to shout us a takeaway, but I tell him I need to do something, and cooking is my go-to when I need to occupy my mind. He doesn't complain. Instead, he has the concierge send up a food parcel from one of the local stores.

When we finally gain access. I wish we hadn't. I might have only been here a couple of weeks, but the apartment felt like home. Now there's a strange smell in the air. One where things that shouldn't have got wet, have. Gabriel's beautiful furniture is ruined. My throws and pillowcases have left colour runs all over the white fabric. I gasp at the sight.

"Oh no," I say in horror.

Gabriel places a hand on my arm and squeezes. "It's all replaceable. Let's just see if anything is salvageable?"

I nod, not sure I trust my voice. I leave Gabriel and make my way to the bedroom. Sliding open the wardrobe doors. My suits hang in ruins, the water having seeped in through the gaps. They will most likely dry, but I'm uncertain if the *dry clean only* material will ever be the same again. The three evening dresses I have are in a similar, sorry state.

I sense Gabriel behind me. He has his phone and is making notes.

"Those look—"

"Don't say it... please," I say, trying to hold my voice steady. At least with the money Vince put in my bank account and Gabriel's low rent, I can afford to replace them. It will just be finding decent replacements. Most of these were custom fit. I take pride in my work appearance. After all, I represent the firm when I speak to our clients and potential clients.

"Is it the same with everything?" Gabriel asks instead.

I move to the enormous chest of drawers. Gabriel rushes

past me and hits the plug socket, switching off the television set at the mains. "Just in case," he says. The electricity should have been turned off in the apartment, but he's right.

I pull open the drawers, relieved to find that my jumpers and t-shirts have all been protected. I breathe a sigh of relief.

"Let's get these packed, and they can be moved upstairs," Gabriel says, pulling a suitcase out of the wardrobe. It's soaking, but the inside will be dry as it's a hard case.

"Upstairs?" I say.

"Yes, you'll move into one of my spare rooms until the renovations are complete," he says. He puts the case down on the mattress, and flinches as it squelches under the weight.

"Don't argue with me," he says. "Come on, let's get your things packed."

"But the concierge said they'll arrange for me to stay in a hotel until they finish cleaning the apartment," I say, not wanting to put him out. I know how important his privacy is. The man has an apartment purely for houseguests, for goodness sake, so they don't have to live in his space.

Gabriel looks around him. "This is going to take more than cleaning and a dehumidifier. The furniture is a write-off. I've told management you'll stay with me while it's fixed."

I open my mouth to argue, but Gabriel holds up a hand. I recognise that stubborn look and know I'm not going to win this argument. "My apartment is close to two and a half thousand square feet. I have a guest suite that I have never used. We already eat together. I'm kind of partial to vegetarian food now, and if you're in a hotel, you'll be eating takeaway or hotel meals for god knows how long."

When I go to open my mouth, he raises an eyebrow, so I shut it again.

I look at the case and head to the bathroom.

"I'll wipe it down," I say.

When I return, his eyes lock on the heavy towel dripping in my hand.

"I think that might be a lost cause," he says, moving to my bedside table.

"Don't," I say more forcefully than I intend, but I'm too late.

Gabriel turns to face me, the drawer open in his hand. I cover my face as he turns back and looks down.

He doesn't say a word. Simply shuts the drawer and turns away, a slight flush appearing on his high cheekbones. "I'll leave you to put your belongings in the case," he says, making a quick U-turn and leaving the bedroom.

I move to my bedside drawer and open it, grimacing at the tube of lubricant and the housewarming gift Stella and Nat purchased for me. The latest single-woman *must-have* accessory, according to Stella. Now my boss will think I'm a sex-starved desperado.

Ground swallow me up.

Can this day get any conceivably worse?

I pick the items out of my drawer and drop them in the case. I would have a bone to pick with Stella and Nat, but it's a pretty amazing present. Heat warms my cheeks, and spreads through my stomach. What if he thinks...

I get to work packing what's left of my dry clothes into the suitcase, burying my vibrator at the bottom.

I'm done within ten minutes, pulling the suitcase into the main area. Gabriel is busy documenting and ordering people around. Two men are busy boxing up any food that has not been destroyed. While another is moving plates and cups into plastic containers.

"Those can stay." He points to the kitchen goods. "Let's transport all food upstairs," he suggests.

He turns as I enter the room. "Do you have everything?" he asks.

"Everything that's dry. My suits..."

Gabriel waves a hand. "Leave those. I'll get Anita to collect, along with the pillows and throws. If we can save them, great. If not, the insurance will cover them. I asked maintenance to allow all your bits and pieces to dry before they pack them up. Some photos are damaged, but we may be able to get reprints. I'll speak to a friend of mine and see if they can get them digitally scanned."

I don't miss Gabriel's use of *we*, my eyes prickle, but I blink away the tears that have been threatening since he delivered the news. I look to the side, which holds a picture of my mum, dad and me. The water has seeped in at the edges, although the frame has kept much of the picture dry. As if wading through treacle, I make my way over and pick it up.

I sense Gabriel behind me. "Sorry," I say, wiping my eyes harshly.

"Don't be," he says, his voice gentler than I've ever heard him. "Your parents?" he asks, looking over my shoulder.

"My mum, dad and me," I mumble. "They're on a year-long tour of Australia. Dad's retirement present to them both."

"Is this the only photo you have?" he asks, his concern obvious.

"No, it's fine. I can replace it. They have the master copy. It's just... I miss them. With everything that's gone on..." I hold it to my chest before returning it to the side.

Gabriel leans past me and picks it up. "Then it's coming upstairs. We can try and dry it out. If not, there's the photo shop across from work."

"But it's wet," I say.

"Don't argue with me," he says. "Come on, let's get you back upstairs."

We leave the maintenance team on-site. Gabriel goes to

the elevator and calls it. He flashes a card, allowing the normal lift to go up to the penthouse.

"Do you have the card I gave you for my apartment?" he asks.

I nod, pointing to my purse.

"Great, you'll need that to get up and down. If you forget it for some reason, the concierge can help."

When we get to Gabriel's floor, the elevator opens, and the reality sets in. I stop in my tracks. "Gabriel," I say, and he pauses, turning slowly towards me. "You hate people in your space. You have an entire apartment designated to guests, specifically, so they don't have to live with you. Are you sure this is a good idea? I don't want to be in the way. I can still go to the hotel."

Gabriel's dark eyes lock on mine, and he shrugs. "I can always make an exception." He turns and lets himself into his penthouse, dragging my case behind him.

"Well, I promise to stay out of your way," I say, trailing after him.

He carries my case up the spiral staircase, depositing it in the most beautiful room I've ever seen. I thought the master suite in my apartment was special. The guest room is that and more. Even the ensuite and walk-in are enormous.

"Gabriel, this is—"

He holds up his hand.

"There are four guest rooms. This one has access to the balcony."

He doesn't get to finish, as a buzzer goes, making us both flinch.

"That will be the food and anything else dry enough for them to pack up. Why don't you get unpacked. I'll let them in."

With that, he leaves me standing in the doorway.

I don't argue. Instead, I set about doing what Gabriel

suggested. My eyes water as I undo my case, and I shake my head, staring up at the ceiling. There's no point crying over spilt milk... or a flooded apartment. Things could be worse. I could be unpacking in a hotel room rather than this luxury. I'm still not sure why Gabriel has opened his home to me. Dinner for a couple of hours differs from having someone in your space, morning, noon, and night. I make a vow to myself to stay out of his way as much as possible.

I turn around to the chest of drawers and realise Gabriel has placed the photograph of me and my parents on it beneath the television. I bite my lip at his thoughtfulness. Who would have thought the distant man I've worked for, for years, has a surprisingly caring side?

CHAPTER 14

GABRIEL

hit! What on earth possessed me?

From the moment I received the phone call, my entire focus has been on Leah and how I can fix this. This past *month,* she's become a huge part of my life. Not only feeding me, but I've also found myself enjoying our nightly chats. They've become the highlight of my day. She always has some random fact to share daily or an unfamiliar word, but most of all, she's up on world news and current events. We've had some interesting debates. I haven't truly had that since my best friend, Mark, departed for Australia. He's the only other person I've ever been able to share my space with.

I sit in the dark in my living area, nursing a whiskey, filling out the insurance claim, and approaching the interior designer we'd previously employed to furnish the apartment. I also booked an appointment with my personal shopper for Leah to replace her suits. I'm expecting her to complain, and the thought makes me smile. She hates it when I do nice things for her. Colour blossoms on her cheeks, and she can't quite meet my gaze. It makes me wonder if Vince ever did anything nice for her, at least in the last couple of years. I know the early years were different. She always had new jewellery or clothes. But then, that's what seems to happen in all relationships. The early years are full of romance, the latter years...

My brother Elijah and his wife. My older sister, Kat, and Zach. Only my parents seem to have been love-matched. Which is funny, seeing as their marriage was arranged. The coming together of two powerful families. My mum always laughs and says it was more the coming together of two souls. Before my father's untimely death five years ago, they were inseparable. As kids, we were raised in a sea of warmth and love. Strangely, not one of us has found that kind of happiness or connection.

I hear a noise. My breath hitches as Leah stumbles into the room. It's clear that she's been asleep, as her hair is mussed up. I watch in silence as she flicks on the under-cupboard lights before making her way to where I keep the glasses. She reaches up, and I bite the inside of my lip as her breasts press against the silky material of her nightdress, her puckered nipples clearly visible. I can't see her bottom half as the island is in the way, but my imagination has no issues filling in the gap.

She reaches for a glass before moving to the American fridge freezer, a replica of the one in her apartment. She fills her glass, taking large sips, her throat bobbing as she drinks the liquid. I can't take my eyes off her. As if sensing my gaze, she looks up.

"Sorry. I didn't see you there. I assumed you'd be in bed." Her cheeks darken, as if the thought of me *in bed*. No, that can't be right. That's my own mind...

"I was just filling out the insurance claim forms. The manager asked that they be done ASAP so the work could begin," I say, my voice husky. I take a swallow of whiskey, the burn helping to calm my libido.

"Oh," Leah says, sounding flustered.

She crosses her arms around her chest as if realising how much her night clothes reveal.

"I was just getting some water," she stutters. "I'll see you in the morning."

"Night, Leah,"

"Good night, Gabriel." I watch her leave. The nightgown skims the tops of her thighs. I take another swig of whiskey, the burn helping to temper the blood flow rushing south. Heaven help me. When did Leah become a temptation? She's my employee, not one of my friends with benefits. She's just got out of a long-term relationship.

I finish my whiskey before I get up and move to my office. I unlock the door and step inside, closing it behind me. The builders made the room soundproof at my request. I look at the clocks that line the wall, each showing a different time zone. It allows me to keep track of each market - when they come online and close for the day. Eleven hours time difference, so I dial his number.

"Wow, what did I do to deserve a call?" an amused voice answers. "Jen wants to know what the emergency is?" His voice then pauses, taking on a more serious tone. "There isn't an emergency, is there?"

I could be cruel, but... "No, no emergency."

"A social call then. That's unusual."

Mark has been my best friend since school. He, like me, was always on the outside, never really fitting in. He comes from old money. His parents were *older than most* when they had him. As a result, he was an only child and mature beyond his years, often finding the antics of the other boys our age tedious. A kindred spirit.

Unlike me, however, he wasn't top of the class, and was terrible at sports. A misfit. The perfect friendship formed. I helped him with his studies, and he kept me company. Since

Caleb was the school's main social butterfly and my twin, we were left alone to do our own thing. Mark was grateful. He listened and gave me advice on how to navigate the social niceties of the world when I struggled to see the point in them. He understood me and was a great people reader, which made us the perfect pair.

"Leah's moved in," I say as if that explains everything.

"I'm good, Gabriel." Mark laughs, then pauses. "Who is Leah, and what do you mean she's moved in?"

I huff, realising it's been quite a while since we last spoke, but Mark waits patiently.

"Leah is my communications officer," I say. "You met her when you came over."

"Oh, the dark, haired, beaut... ow!"

I hear the smack at the other end of the phone. "No harm in appreciating beauty. You know you're the only woman for me."

I hear Jen in the background and smile. She's the only one who can keep my friend in line, and he adores her and their son.

"Yes, that's Leah," I say, not wanting to add any more.

"Are you dating?"

"No," I reply quickly.

"Then, my friend, I think you need to start at the beginning."

I can imagine Mark making himself comfortable as he waits for me to begin.

"I'm confused," Mark says when I finally bring him up to date. "What's the problem?"

"I can't stand people in my space. They drive me mad."

Mark is aware of how hard I find sharing. He's the only person I could share with. It's why I never invited Rachel to move in.

"Okay, that's nothing new. I'm struggling? What's

happened? Has she done something, and now you don't know how to deal with it?"

I growl, making Mark laugh.

"No, Leah hasn't done anything," I say, letting out an exasperated huff.

"What *is* the problem, exactly?" Mark asks.

"What if I screw up? What if I get snarky because she's in my space, and I mess up? She's the best damn communications officer. Oh hell, how did I let this happen?"

I run my fingers through my hair before tugging it at the roots in frustration.

I can tell from his tone that he's deliberating on the words about to come out of his mouth. "Let me get this straight, Leah hasn't done anything to annoy you so far?"

"No, of course not, but then she hasn't been living with me. She only moved in tonight."

"Maybe not, but it certainly sounds like you've been spending a lot of time together."

"We have, but then I come home, and I have my space."

"How did it feel tonight when Leah was there?"

"I don't know. She disappeared into her room, and I didn't see her until about half an hour ago when she came to get some water."

My body stirs at the memory of her nipples pressed against the material of her nightgown.

"So, she stayed out of your way?"

"I just said that," I reply. Where the hell is this conversation going?

"Does she have any awful habits? Suck her teeth? Eat with her mouth open? Pick her nose or toenails."

"Now you're just being ridiculous!" I say, my tone sharp.

Mark laughs. My heckles rise. "Are you listening to a word I say?" I ask.

"Every word, but Gabriel, you need to chill out. Leah

living with you is not forever. You do nothing on the spur of the moment. You're the least impulsive person I know. As a result, your body has already accepted Leah in your space. Your brain just needs to catch up. Stop worrying. Enjoy her company. It might surprise you."

"What's that supposed to mean?"

"You may find I'm not the only person you can live with."

"Leah works for me."

Mark chuckles. "That she does," he adds cryptically.

"You were supposed to help," I huff.

I drop back in my chair and stare at my phone. Why did I ring him? He knows me too well, cuts through my BS like a razor-sharp knife.

I decide to change the subject. "How's Josh?"

I spend the next ten minutes listening to Mark tell me all about Jen, Josh and parenthood. Every time I listen, a twinge hits my chest. It's one thing I envy about my friend. I might have a few more billion than him, but he has a family. When I held Josh in my arms not long after he was born, my heart melted. I swore I'd be the best godfather, knowing it is unlikely I'll ever have a little Josh of my own. I hate the fact my friend lives so far away with his family.

"Send me some videos," I say when Mark ends his latest update.

"On their way."

My phone pings with a tirade of incoming messages. "And Gabriel, don't overthink it. I know it goes against your nature, but not everything in life is clear-cut and predictable."

I know he's right. It just isn't the answer I want to hear.

We say goodbye, and I tell him to give his wife and son a hug from me. When the phone disconnects, I stare at my desk. I need to get some sleep, especially if I want to make the pool by five.

CHAPTER 15

LEAH

I arrange to meet the girls at our favourite coffee shop for lunch the next day.

"Hey, where's the fire?" Stella asks, standing up and giving me a hug when I move to the table.

"Not a fire," I say, pulling out my chair and dropping into it. "More of a flood."

They both fix their eyes on me.

"The apartment flooded last night," I say.

"Oh, Leah," Nat says, gripping my hand over the table.

"How?" Stella asks.

"The sprinkler system malfunctioned," I say. "The entire apartment was underwater. Everything is ruined."

They both stare at me open-mouthed.

"Where are you staying?" Stella asks.

"That's the thing. Gabriel invited me to move in with him."

"He what?" Stella shrieks, bringing stares from the nearby tables.

"Sorry," she says, her voice more restrained. "What do you

mean, you've moved in with Gabriel? We want details and fast."

I update them on the flood, and how Gabriel came with me to survey the damage.

"Maintenance was going to put me up in a hotel. Gabriel wouldn't hear of it. He insisted I move into one of his spare rooms."

"I'm sure he did," Stella says, waggling her eyebrows.

"It's not like that. Gabriel knows I like to cook. He knows if I stay in a hotel, I'll be forced to eat takeaways. His apartment is triple the size I was renting from him and is spread over two floors. The bedroom he's put me up in is more like a hotel suite. I will hardly have to see him."

My friends stare at me wide-eyed. I haven't told them about Gabriel and my dinner arrangement, mainly for this reason. I don't want them to jump to any conclusions. It's already a strange set-up. I don't need them adding to it.

"So, you're telling us you're now living under the same roof as your boss?" Stella says.

"Technically, they were already living under the same roof," Nat interjects, making me chuckle.

"True —but she's now sharing living space with her sexy boss."

"Boss, being the operative word," I say firmly. "Before you get any romantic ideas about Gabriel and me. We don't see each other that way. He's my boss, and he's five years younger than me."

"Ooh, toy boy." Stella chuckles. "Think of the stamina."

Nat swats Stella on the arm, making her yelp playfully.

"Come on, you'd have to be blind or a nun not to notice how *hot* he is. Not to mention, he's the identical and very single twin of the man voted The City's Most Eligible Bachelor. Voted and agreed by the majority of women in our fine city."

I groan, sounding like Gabriel when Caleb was voted the city's most eligible bachelor for the second year running.

"Stella's right. He is gorgeous, and you are now single," Nat says.

"Don't you start," I say, turning to Nat. "You're supposed to be the sensible one. It's not happening, ladies. He's my boss. I'm sorry to disappoint you both, but we're friends and colleagues."

Stella and Nat share a look, making me sigh. "Whatever I say, you're not going to believe me, are you?"

"It's not that." It's Nat who speaks, surprising me. "It's just... he's a friend who left his night out to track you down when he knew you were upset. He offered you his empty apartment at a ridiculously low rent when you had nowhere else to go. Now he has you move in with him when your apartment floods. Are you sure he sees *you* as *just* a friend?"

"Stop," I say. The words come out harsher than I expect. "I know you mean well, but you need to stop reading into this. That's just who Gabriel is. He's loyal to his friends," I tell them, knowing it sounds strange, but it's the truth. They haven't been privy to this side of him. It's only recently I've come to witness it.

"You have to admit, he is gorgeous. Can you blame us, now you're single? You'd make a beautiful couple, just imagine the babies you'd make," Nat continues, before her hand flies to her mouth. "Oh, Leah, I'm so sorry, that was completely thoughtless of me. I wasn't thinking." Nat's eyes fill with tears, and it's my turn to grip her hand.

"Hey, don't worry. Since when do we tread on eggshells around one another?" I ask.

At that moment, our food arrives, acting as the perfect distraction for everyone.

"Gabriel got an eyeful of my housewarming present," I tell them.

There is a clatter of knives and forks as they hit their plates. Stella starts choking, making Nat slap her hard on the back.

"What?" She chokes, still gasping for air, and her face flushes.

"He was helping me move and opened my bedside drawer."

My memory returns to Gabriel's flushed cheeks and his inability to look me in the eye as he left the room.

"Maybe he'll volunteer, save on batteries," Stella says, when she's finally caught her breath.

"Boss," I say again for the umpteenth time.

"Yes, but you can't tell me he won't be lying in bed thinking about you using it," Stella says, waggling her eyebrows at me.

I groan, wondering what possessed me to tell them, so I try another distraction.

"This afternoon, Gabriel has arranged for me to see his personal shopper. My suits were ruined in the flood."

Once again, my friends share that look, but this time, I'm thankful they hold their tongues.

"How the other half live," Stella sighs. "I'd love a personal shopper."

Unlike Nat and me, Stella hates shopping, so I can understand the draw.

"I'll let you know whether it lives up to the hype," I tell them.

We spend the rest of our lunch break talking about our next girls get together. It was supposed to be at mine, but Stella agrees to host, although I tell her I'll provide the food and drinks.

We finish lunch, and I head off to meet up with Gabriel's personal shopper. I'm greeted by Mario, who leads me to a private room equipped with the comfiest-looking sofas, racks of clothing items, and a changing area. Natural daylight floods the room from the high, discrete windows. Once he gets me settled, he introduces me to Chloe, who will be my stylist for the afternoon.

"Mr Frazer mentioned that you require work suits. That yours were unfortunately damaged in a flood?" she asks, sounding confused.

"Malfunctioning sprinkler system," I say, taking a sip of the wine Chloe has just presented me with.

"Wow, okay. Not a problem," she says, smiling warmly. "Mr Frazer has told me to put everything on his account."

"Er...no...that's okay. I can pay for my own clothes," I say.

Gabriel definitely won't be paying for my wardrobe expenses.

"Apparently, he is, and I don't argue with him. He also instructed me to tell you, you aren't allowed to argue either."

I raise my eyebrows at her, and she laughs.

"I know, but who am I to argue? I work on commission and do as I'm told," she says with a wink, and I realise I'm going to be in for a fun afternoon.

"I'll take the argument home with me," I say.

"Let's get started," Chloe says, wheeling out a clothes rack full of the most beautiful business suits I've ever seen.

"I..." I go to say. There's no way I can afford one of these, let alone the five I need to replace.

"Oh, I should mention, Mr Frazer had me remove all the price tags. You are to have what you need."

When I go to open my mouth, she holds up her hand. "I've been styling Mr Frazer for five years. I do as he asks," Chloe says.

"Well, I've worked for him for eight." I grin back at her. "And you have impeccable taste." My final statement earns me another grin. "Let's do this. I'm too tired to argue."

The next couple of hours fly by, and I realise I like Chloe

a lot. She's funny and smart. She has a first-class honours degree in fashion. She designs and sells her own brand online, which I promise to look up later. One day she hopes to set up her own clothing line.

"You're all done," she says, marking up the last of the suits, blouses, and shoes. "I'll have the altered suits delivered to Mr Frazer's apartment by lunchtime tomorrow."

"Thank you, Chloe. This afternoon has been an experience."

Chloe grins. "I hope to see you again soon."

I nod as we shake hands, but I know there's no way in hell I can afford this luxury. But today was something every woman should have the chance to experience at least once in their life. Who am I kidding? This is a taste of how the other half live. Even Vince doesn't use a personal shopper... or maybe he does.

I'm not sure whether to be disappointed or relieved when I arrive back at Gabriel's apartment to find it empty. I move to the kitchen area and notice a note left on the side.

Leah
I've gone to meet with Caleb. I won't need dinner.
Hope your shopping trip went well.
Gabriel

WITH GABRIEL OUT, I sit in the main living area. The view over the water is spectacular, highlighting the vibrancy of our city.

I grab my laptop and look up Chloe's clothing line. I scroll through the pages of clothes.

Wow, she is truly talented.

I click on a couple of summer dresses and a top, placing an order. I smile before flashing the URL to both Stella and Nat. A small boutique, what's not to love?

My email pings.

It's my weekly update from my parents detailing the friends and ex-colleagues they've met up with.

I click on the photographs, taking in their healthy glow and relaxed postures. I miss them, especially now, but there's no way I will have them mar their brows with worry as they think of me at home.

The last picture is of my mum holding a baby. She's added a caption. *Can't wait for grandbabies of my own.* Pain lances through my chest. Damn Vince. It's not only my dreams, but he's also shattered theirs.

I stare at the picture of my mum holding their friend's grandchild, my dad looking down at them both, his finger being gripped in a tiny hand. I bite down on my hand to stifle the sob that threatens. My mum had a rough pregnancy with me. As a result, the doctors advised them not to try for any more children. My mum, blessed to have me, followed the doctor's advice. Both my parents smothered me with love. Love and laughter always filled our house, but it hasn't stopped me from dreaming of a large family. Vince always knew this. I thought we were on the same page.

My mind wanders back to my lunch date with the girls. The thought of dating again leaves me cold and detached. The effort it will take to get to know someone, to be able to trust them. I'm not sure I want that, at least not yet. But then, do I have time to waste? If I want to see my dreams of a family fulfilled. I'm not getting any younger. From next year, any pregnancy means I fall under geriatric, meaning the risks go up for both me and the baby. That's not including if I have any issues getting pregnant.

When I look back on my relationship with Vince, I can see how naïve I was. There was always an excuse to take the next step to start a family. A friend's wedding, another fancy holiday, a promotion at work. That's why I was surprised when Yasmin announced she was expecting. Vince has always been super cautious, taking charge of birth control even when I was on the pill. We never had unprotected sex in the whole ten years we were together.

"Can't be too careful," he used to say. "There's plenty of time for that."

Well, my time with Vince has passed. Do I hope Mr Right appears? Of course. But what then? A year, maybe two, as we get to know each other. I'll be thirty-six, maybe thirty-seven, and that's if I meet someone immediately. Not if I end up dating a few idiots along the way.

I rub my eyes. My hopes and dreams for the future are slowly dying.

I flip back to the internet and pause... typing and hitting return before I can change my mind.

Pregnancy options for single women

The search engine spits out its results.

Wow, who knew there'd be so many options.

I click on one website.

IVF: the option to freeze my eggs for later use or to have them fertilised by donor sperm.

IUI: or intrauterine insemination using a donor at a fertility clinic.

Artificial Insemination comes up next. The DIY of pregnancy. I smile as I read more information on the subject. I'm astonished by the vast amount of information that is accessible. YouTube videos on how to use the kits, where to go and what to look out for. I read several testimonials for one site and I decide to enter my details.

What have I got to lose?

I'm not signing my life away. Only looking for information.

I enter my personal details, only to have it ask me what I'm looking for in terms of a sperm donor. I enter my requirements and complete the procedure. The screen tells me someone from the company will be in touch in the next seven days.

I put my laptop to one side and bring my feet up. Clicking the remote for the enormous television Gabriel has attached to the wall. I flick through the apps and streaming services. Gabriel has a full house. Why does that not surprise me? Why do without when you don't have to? I find a rom-com I was hoping to see at the cinema a while back, but Vince blew me off for a work meeting, or so he said.

I push the thought aside and allow myself to sink into the story's romance. My eyes get heavier. I dream of romance, and babies, of love and family.

* * *

I WAKE WITH A START. The room is dark, except for one of the table lamps offering a subtle illumination. The television is off, and my laptop is closed on the coffee table. I stretch, only to find that one of the throws covers me.

Oh, help! Gabriel must have come home and found me sprawled out on his sofa.

I throw back the blanket and stand up. After folding it carefully, I make my way up the stairs. The last thing I want or need is for Gabriel to come back downstairs and find me still asleep in his living room. Way to irritate the person who's opened their door to you. A thought hits me - What if he brought a woman home? How awkward would that have been? Oh, I'm so stupid. What was I thinking? Goodness, what happens if he *wants* to bring a woman home? My stomach cramps in protest. I need to raise it with him. Maybe we need to have a sign, then I can make sure I stay up in my room, out of the way.

I creep upstairs and into my bedroom, collapsing on my bed.

I need to find a way to apologise.

CHAPTER 16

GABRIEL

"*H*ow's Leah doing? Has she settled in, okay?" Caleb asks.

I freeze at my brother's question. It's been a week since Leah moved upstairs, or in, or whatever I want to call it. My conversation with Mark was unhelpful, to say the least. I know I could live with him because I did. That wasn't my point. But then again, I'm not sure what my point is any more. I'm used to being in control of my thoughts, feelings, and actions. A certain communications officer has uprooted my life on a monster scale. And now Caleb is asking after her.

What's with all his interest in Leah?

I want to ignore him, but I don't.

"She's settled in fine. I don't see her, apart from at the office," I lie, squeezing my eyes shut in case he calls me out on it. I still haven't told him about the flood or about our dinner arrangements. I don't want or need him ribbing me or reading things into it.

I know Caleb. He will probably try to snag himself an invitation and the thought of that. Not happening.

"Not surprising," he says, shrugging. "It's a big place."

He should know. He's the person whose company designed and built it.

My mind wanders back to last week.

When I finally made it down to the pool for my early morning swim. I found Leah swimming laps in an otherwise empty pool. I stood for a moment before I eased myself into the water, submerging myself before swimming the entire length underwater, popping up next to her and grabbing her waist. Leah shrieked before turning in my arms and splashing me, her laughter filling the air. Suddenly aware of her close proximity, I let go, pushing backwards.

Shit, what was I thinking.

"God, you scared me," she says, splashing another round of water in my face. I'm relieved to see her smile.

I return it with a grin of my own, the tension leaving my shoulders. I wipe the droplets away. We're still the only two people in the pool, which is not surprising as it's just gone five am.

"You're up early," I say. "I'm usually the only one here."

Leah grins. "I needed a wake-up. I used to go to the gym all the time before work when—" She stops herself. "Anyway, I saw the pool last night and decided it looked too tempting to pass up."

I can't fault her there. Caleb's architect did an amazing job designing the pool area. It's unusual to have a pool this size in an apartment block. But El Castillo is not just any block.

"I agree. I swim in the mornings and hit the gym on weekends."

I'm unsure why I'm telling her my schedule.

"Speaking of swimming. I want to get in a few more lengths," Leah says, grinning before pushing herself away from the side.

I watch her for a second as her body cuts through the water. Her form is impeccable, a clear sign she was a swimmer in her younger years. I set off after her, my larger frame and strength meaning I do about two lengths to her one. We continue. I'm impressed with her stamina.

"I'm done."

Leah's voice echoes over the water, so the next time I touch the side, I bring myself to a stop. I shake my head to clear my eyes.

I notice Leah haul herself out of the water, her arms take her weight as she lifts herself. Her toned arm muscles ripple, her waist bending as she pulls her feet under her and stands. My eyes travel up her smooth calves, toned thighs, and stop at the swell of her ass, suddenly remembering how it felt to have my hands on her waist. I drop my head forward so as not to be caught gawping. Leah's black swimsuit leaves little to the imagination.

"Are you coming?" she says. She grabs her towel from one of the loungers around the pool and wrings out her hair.

"No. I'll just do a couple more lengths."

She gives me a strange look, her eyes flick to the enormous clock on the wall. "No worries, I'll see you at the office."

I'm going to be late, but leaving the pool in her presence is out of the question. The hard-on I'm sporting, despite the cool temperature of the water, is not something I can hide.

"See you at work," I say, pushing off.

I pound the water as I try to get my mind and body under control. It's clear I've been too long between dates. Something I need to rectify before my sudden infatuation with Leah becomes too much.

"Gabriel. Have you heard a word I've said?" Caleb asks, as he pulls me back into the present.

"No, sorry, I was miles away." Realising my mistake too late.

"You appear distracted, brother," Caleb mutters.

I humph at him.

"Don't humph. What were you thinking about that had you so engrossed?" he asks.

"Swimming," I blurt.

"What?" Caleb sounds truly confused, although I'm not sure why. Swimming was a common activity for all of us during our early years and teens. Elijah even earned a spot at the Olympics.

"I remembered I need to pick up some new swim shorts."

"Whatever," Caleb says. "I swear, brother, you're becoming stranger and stranger with every passing year."

"And from you, I shall take that as a compliment," I say. "And now I really have to get back to work."

* * *

WHEN HE LEAVES, I slump back in my chair. That was last week, before she was living with me. Before I came home to find her sound asleep on the sofa, her hand tucked under her cheek, her thick eyelashes framed against her pale skin. She looked so comfortable curled up in a ball. Instead of waking her, I grabbed one of the replacement throws and covered her up with it. It was then I observed her laptop perched precariously by her feet, prompting me to move it.

"Hey buddy," Mark's voice comes across the line. "I don't hear from you in two months, and then two calls in two weeks. I'm honoured."

"What should I do?" I say, knowing my tone is frantic, but my lack of sleep is affecting me in more ways than one. "I need advice."

Mark's voice softens, but his amusement is clear. "Okay. I can try," he says, pausing. "But you may need to rewind a few steps and tell me what you need advice on."

"Artificial Insemination."

"Pardon? Hang on. What?"

"I said, artificial insemination."

"I heard you the first time." Mark pauses before adding. "My brain isn't on the same genius level as yours. I need you to back up and slow down."

I've tossed and turned with the knowledge I uncovered for several days. I've not wanted to broach it with Leah, but...

"Breathe, Gabriel," Mark's voice comes over the phone, his amusement clear.

"I'm not sure why I bother," I grouch.

"Me neither, but then again, here you are. Now start at the very beginning."

"Leah's looking into artificial insemination. I think she wants to have a baby," I say, almost relieved to be finally saying it out aloud.

Silence descends on the other end of the line.

"Did you hear me?" I ask.

"I heard you. What I want to know is, why are you so rattled?"

"If she has a baby, she'll leave," I say.

"But wasn't she engaged? That was always likely to be the case." I hate it when *practical-Mark* steps in.

"It was, but when her engagement ended."

"People's dreams don't die just because an engagement ends. Didn't you say Leah is thirty-four?"

"Yes."

"Maybe she feels her biological clock is ticking, and she doesn't want to wait around. Rely on the right man turning up," he says. "One of Jen's friends has just gone down this path. A similar situation to Leah, with a broken engagement."

I listen.

"She's going to co-parent. She's met a guy through an agency, and together they are about to become parents. They are not a couple, but they will share joint custody of their child."

"What?" I stare at my phone in shock. The thought of Leah having a baby with a complete stranger. No!

"I know. There are multiple agencies helping couples come together. Like dating sites, but different. There are as many men out there who want a child as women but, like their female counterparts, can't find *the right one*. This solves a problem."

"People do that?"

"Jen's friend has. Maybe you could mention it to Leah?"

"Over my dead body," I hiss. "I'm not encouraging Leah to have and raise a child with a stranger."

Mark laughs again. "But that's the beauty. They got to know one another over months. They became friends. Really good friends before they decided to try for a child."

"Sounds weird." A feeling of unease travels up my spine.

Could Leah go down this path?

"To you, maybe." Mark pauses again. "Am I missing something?" he says eventually. "You like Leah? You want her to be happy?" he asks, making my heckles rise.

"Of course I do. She deserves to be happy, especially after everything she's been through. It's just..."

I'm not sure how to word what I'm feeling. Is it wrong of me not to want Leah pregnant with some stranger's baby? Struggling as a single mum to raise a child alone. I think back to the picture she had of her mum, dad and her as a child. She grew up in a loving family environment.

"It's just what, Gabriel?" Mark pushes.

"I worry. Raising a child alone is difficult. She clearly wants a baby. She mentioned her ex kept putting it off. She was devastated when he told her his new girlfriend was pregnant."

It's then I realise I've missed a major sign.

"I can hear your brain ticking all the way down under," Mark says dryly.

"Sorry," I say, my brain running at a hundred miles an hour. "I just had a realisation."

"That's good. Care to share?" Mark adds.

"She wants a family," I state.

I hear a slap on the other end of the phone, followed by a groan. I stare at the phone in my hand and frown. What just happened?

"Sorry," Mark says. "So Leah wants a baby. You're worried about her doing this alone?"

"That's what I said."

"Do you like Leah, Gabe?" Mark presses. "Do you trust her? Think she'll be a great mum?"

"As close as anyone I know," I say.

Trust is not something I give easily, and Mark knows that.

"High accolade from you, my friend." Mark chuckles.

"I like her. She doesn't annoy me the way most people do. A female version of you."

I think about how we've been living together for the past two weeks and not once have I resented her presence. I have sat and chatted to her instead of disappearing into my office.

"I take it there have been no issues since she moved in?" Mark asks.

I know it's early days, but usually two days in and my grandmother always used to state, *"Visitors and fish stink after three days."*

For me, that is definitely true.

I hold the phone away from my ear. Leah walks past my office door and smiles. I left her a note this morning, needing time and space between us.

"I have to go," I say to him. "Leah's just come in."

"You know I'm here if you need me," Mark says quietly. "Can I just ask you to think, long and hard, before you make any decisions?"

I pause. My friend actually does know me better than I know myself. The crushing pain in my chest has eased.

"How?"

Mark chuckles. "Gabriel, I've been your friend for twelve

years. I am, apart from Caleb, probably one of the few people who truly knows you." He sighs. "It sounds like Leah may be on her way to joining us." He pauses before adding, "Leah may not be interested. If she says no, she's not rejecting you."

I freeze.

What? No?

"You've got the wrong end of the stick," I blurt out.

Leah and I -no. Hell no. But...

My brain whirls again. Mark is supposed to help, not make things worse.

Mark chuckles again, and I grit my teeth to stop myself from telling him to fuck off.

It won't be the first time, but then I think back. I may have uttered those words, but Mark is rarely wrong. No, this time he is.

"You're mistaken," I say.

"We'll see. Anyway, Josh wants me. Daddy duty calls. Call me anytime and let me know what you decide."

I humph at his words, which makes him outright laugh.

"Give my godson a cuddle," I say.

"I will do. Take care and don't be a stranger. Jen sends her love."

"Back at her," I say, hanging up the phone.

I lean back in my chair and stare at the ceiling. A knock on my door has me looking up.

CHAPTER 17

LEAH

*T*here's been no mention of *The Sofa Incident*, so I've just let it ride.

Tonight, I'm heading over to Stella's. I clutch a bag of our favourite Chinese, and a couple of bottles of wine. I know I'll need wine for the bombshell I'm about to drop.

"Come in," Stella says, throwing open the door to her compact apartment. "The witch is away, so we have the place to ourselves."

"The food is here," I say, holding up the bag and making my way to Stella's tiny kitchen.

"That smells amazing," Nat says from the sofa, before getting up to follow me.

"I'm starving."

We lay out the dishes, helping ourselves. The apartment is too small for a table, so we pick up books and use them as trays on our knees.

"Any news on when your apartment will be habitable?" Stella asks, pouring me a glass of rose.

"The apartment is still being dried out. They need to check the underfloor heating and electrics for damage. The furniture, however, is a right off. Gabriel has put in an insurance claim. He met with his interior designer earlier this week and ordered replacements."

"How's it going? Living with the illustrious Gabriel Frazer?" Stella asks.

"I've hardly seen him," I tell them. "I cook us dinner, and then he does his thing, and I do mine." I'm not being entirely honest, but Gabriel and my set up is complicated.

Stella's face drops, making me chuckle.

"Sorry," I tell her. "No salacious gossip. My life is boring."

I stop and take a deep swig of wine. "I *do* want to talk to you both about something."

"Fire away," Nat says, topping up my glass when I hold it out.

I inhale and exhale, trying to steady the butterflies that have taken flight in my stomach. "I want to have a baby."

Silence descends, as both of my friends stare at me.

"A baby?" Stella coughs out.

"As in a real baby?" Nat asks.

"Is there any other kind?" I laugh.

"You know what I mean," Nat says. "How? When? I suppose more importantly, who?"

I look at my friends and hope they're going to understand. "I've always wanted a large family. It's why I pushed Vince to bring our wedding forward."

"Forward! Leah you were engaged to the man for over five years!" Stella says, her exasperation clear.

"And I should have seen the writing on the wall," I admit. "His barrage of excuses is something I've thought long and hard about." I move my plate off my lap and put it on the tiny coffee table. "Our split hasn't lessened my desire to be a mother. If anything, his bombshell has strengthened it." I sigh. "I'm not getting any younger. Next year, I'll be thirty-five. Geriatric in terms of any pregnancy." I drop my head and clasp my hands in my lap. "I've never been pregnant. If I'll have any problems. I don't have time to sit around and hope Prince Charming shows up."

Silence descends, my friends taking in my latest declaration.

"You're considering becoming a single parent?" Nat asks, leaning forward and taking one of my hands in hers.

"I am," I tell her truthfully.

Stella leans forward and grasps my other hand. "Wow, it's a big step."

"It is." I give them a weak smile. "There are so many cons telling me I must be mad," I admit with a sigh. "I have no idea how I'll juggle full-time work with a baby. Where we'll live. Childcare."

"All those are doable. If you want them to be," Stella says, squeezing my fingers. "On a more serious note. You know you'll never be alone. You have us," she tells me, her gaze moving to Nat.

"We'll be the best surrogate mummies your little one could have," Nat adds. The look they share brings tears to my eyes.

"You are the best," I say, emotion clogging my throat.

"I love you guys," I say to my two best friends.

"The feeling is mutual," Stella replies, as they both squeeze my hands.

I'M NOT ENTIRELY honest when I tell the girls everything with Gabriel is fine. Ever since I fell asleep on the sofa, he's been acting strange. I initially thought he was annoyed with me for invading his space and taking liberties. But after today, I'm not so sure. The whole way through our afternoon meeting, he sat staring at me, like he wanted to ask me something but then changed his mind.

We should be celebrating. Callahan decided to give us his business, but instead, the atmosphere is thick and almost suffocating.

I'm relieved when it's finally time to leave the office. I need to speak to Gabriel and clear the air. Whatever it is, I can't ignore it any longer.

I grab a clean teaspoon and taste the chocolate chilli I've made for dinner. I need it to be perfect. Whatever is wrong, I need to fix it if I can. If I don't, the next couple of weeks will probably become more strained. Yes, I can stay in my room, but I don't want to damage our professional relationship.

I sag against the kitchen unit, exhausted. What with Vince's affair, the pregnancy bombshell, the flood, and now Gabriel, I'm not sure how much more emotional upheaval I can take. Hopefully, the offer of a hotel is still viable should I need to move out.

I hear the door go and freeze. As usual, Gabriel makes his way upstairs to get changed. I've tidied up the kitchen in case I need to make a sharp exit. The only things left are the pans containing tonight's dinner, and I must admit I've outdone myself. This recipe is delicious.

It's ten minutes before Gabriel reappears, his hair damp from his shower. He's changed out of his suit. Tonight, he's in a t-shirt and jogging bottoms. The casual look gives him a different air to the office version of Gabriel, but then the man would probably look amazing in a bin-liner.

"Something smells good," he says as he grabs two plates from the cupboard. This has become our nightly routine.

"Chilli Con Carne," I say, noticing how his eyes are looking anywhere but at me. I'm not mistaken. Something is undeniably up.

"Delicious. Can I do anything?" he asks.

"No, everything is ready. I'll bring this over."

He moves to the table while I carry the pans.

I take his plate and load it up, first with rice and then with the vegetarian chilli I've prepared.

I help myself before taking a seat at the table next to him.

An awkward silence descends. I look at Gabriel, his brows drawn, his face tight.

I place my knife and fork down. Resting my elbows on the table, I clasp my hands together over my plate.

There's a tightness around his mouth. As if sensing my gaze, he stops eating and looks up, his expression almost sombre.

I swallow past the lump that's formed in my throat.

"Have I done something wrong?" I ask. Gabriel flinches. Yep, something I've unquestionably done. "I can't fix it if you don't tell me what it is," I add.

He lifts his hand, running it through his nearly dry hair.

"It's not you," he says.

I raise an eyebrow. Is he really going with the it's-not-you-it's-me pile of crock?

I wait, knowing the type of man Gabriel is. He's trying to find the correct words. Something I've learned about him over the past eight years.

"I saw your laptop," he says, his eyes meet mine.

It's my turn to look confused. He saw my laptop?

"I saw what was *on* your laptop when you fell asleep on the sofa," he expands when he clearly sees a lack of understanding in my expression.

What was on my laptop?

The world closes in. Memories of the last thing I looked at before I put the movie on, flood my mind. *Oh shit!* Did I not close my browser? What the hell was Gabriel doing looking at my laptop?

"It was an accident. It was by your foot, and I was worried

you'd kick it off. When I picked it up to close it, the screen opened."

"Thank you for moving it," I say, unsure what else to say.

This is not a conversation I want to have with my boss. What I do in my private life is none of his business, but then again, I rent his apartment. Maybe there's a rule against children, or perhaps he doesn't like children.

I pick up my plate and move towards the kitchen area, my appetite suddenly gone.

I sense Gabriel following.

"Leah," he says. His tone causes me to stop.

"I'm not sure what you want me to say, Gabriel?"

I turn my face to his, my back against the kitchen unit. "What you saw was private." I sigh. "I'm not sure what it has to do with you?"

He puts his plate down and runs a hand down his face, stopping at his mouth.

"I don't either." He sighs before adding. "I've been trying to work out what to say all week."

He stands next to me, his back resting against the unit. We stay there in silence, staring out of the window. The silence is comforting as my brain tries to decide what to say next. I could walk away and tell him to mind his own business, but that's not who I am.

"I'm thirty-four, and I've wanted a baby for years," I stare at the floor in front of me. "But it was never the right time. A friend's wedding, a fancy holiday, the apartment. There was always a reason to put it off." I pause as my voice catches. "Now I'm single. It might be years before I meet someone who I feel comfortable bringing a child into the world with." I shoot a glance at Gabriel, but he is staring straight ahead, listening. "The other night, my mum and dad sent me some pictures of them holding a friend's grandchild. They looked so happy." I pinch the bridge of my nose, hoping it will alleviate the pressure building behind my eyes. "I realised the end of my relationship with Vince also ended my dream of becoming a mum, and I can't stop the pang of longing."

Gabriel turns his head to look at me. I meet his gaze, unsure what I'm going to see there. I'm surprised when I see understanding. "It started me thinking, there are no guarantees." I shrug. "No guarantees, I'm going to meet someone. That they will want a child. That I can even get pregnant."

He nods before diverting his gaze.

"You're going to try for a baby by yourself?" Gabriel asks.

"It's one option. I'm worried if I wait for Prince Charming—"

Gabriel scoffs at my words, and I shoulder bump him, making him chuckle, which surprises me.

He sinks his hands deep into his pockets.

"Look, I won't be offended if you tell me it's a problem. That you want me to find somewhere else to live if I go down this path," I say quietly, not able to meet his gaze.

I watch Gabriel's brows furrow as he removes his hands and crosses them over his chest.

"What about me?" he says, his eyes still not meeting mine.

"I don't—"

He turns to face me, his hip resting on the counter. His eyes once more on my face.

"What about using me as your sperm donor?"

My jaw drops as my muscles go weak. I can't have heard him correctly. I cough and raise a trembling hand to my mouth.

"What?" I squeak.

He takes a deep breath as if giving me a chance to catch up on his announcement.

"What if I act as your sperm donor?"

"Gabriel... I..."

I stumble over my thoughts. This is not what I expected.

My eyes lock on his face. His expression tells me he's been thinking long and hard about this.

Gabriel takes my hand and leads me over to the sofa. I follow in a trance. "Sit. I'm serious," he says, taking a seat opposite me. "I want you to hear me out."

I nod, too shocked to say or do anything else.

"I think we can help each other." He looks at his hands, his forearms resting on his thighs. "I don't ever see myself in a long-term relationship. I'm grumpy, self-absorbed and a workaholic. Not good husband material. Therefore, the prospect of me having a child or children of my own... let's say they're minimal." He runs a hand through his hair, leaving it mussed. "I don't want a marriage of convenience, or to marry someone only to have my children caught in the middle of a messy divorce, or being used as pawns."

I bite my lip when he returns his gaze to me. It's then I realise he's deadly serious. Gabriel continues.

"I need an heir. Want an heir." He tilts his head and gives a small smile. "I could leave everything to my godson or my nieces and nephews, but they already have enough. I've been thinking recently that I like the idea of my own child."

Oh shit, my billionaire boss is asking if I can make both our dreams come true.

He wants to be my baby's daddy!

Adrenalin floods my system, and my heart rate kicks up several notches. My mouth falls open, and I know my eyes must be bulging. This is not what I was expecting.

"That's er...wow."

I stutter, realising that all my years as someone who values their ability to communicate clearly have abandoned me in my moment of need. I close my mouth and swallow, taking a moment to let my thoughts percolate.

"I don't want to be a surrogate." The words leave my

mouth in a rush. "I want to raise my child," I say, unsure if he understands that.

Gabriel smiles. "That works perfectly," he says. "As I mentioned before, I'm a workaholic. A surrogate wouldn't work. Any child I have that way would require nannies. That, to me, is a hard no. I was raised by my mother and father in a loving environment. I want that for my child."

It's my turn to look confused. "But we aren't in a loving relationship," I say, not quite sure what he's getting at. "We don't even officially live together."

Gabriel huffs as if I've missed the point. I shoot him my *seriously* stare, and he smiles.

"Maybe that came out wrong. I was loved by my mother and my father. I had the love of both parents. I would like that for my child."

My heart rate picks up, and heat rises in my body. He has clearly thought about this long and hard.

"I'm suggesting we co-parent," Gabriel continues. "Apparently, it's becoming the latest trend in thirty and forty-some-things. Two people decide to have a baby together and co-parent the child. Similar to a divorce, but without the animosity."

I stare at him. My mind flits back to an article I read. Agencies have been set up to help match potential parents. It's an option I discounted once I realised it meant sharing my child with a virtual stranger. Surely Gabriel can't mean this type of relationship?

I sink back into the sofa, my shoulders slump as my mind spins.

"Think about it," Gabriel continues. "You wouldn't have to raise a child alone or with a stranger. You'd have me to share in the parental duty. You know me, quirks and all." He smiles, and I return it with one of my own. "Any child or children we have will be financially looked after. I can see to that. Most of all, you'll have my support and that of my entire family, as well as your own."

I draw in a shaky breath, spots appearing at the edge of my vision. This is most definitely *not* where I saw tonight's conversation going. "You've really thought about this," I say.

Gabriel leans forward and grabs my hand, squeezing it. "I can have my lawyer draw up an agreement that works for us. When I say *together*, I mean together."

The feel of his hand in mine sends tingles up my arm. Am I dreaming, or is this really happening?

I look Gabriel in the eye. "You're saying you want to have a baby with me?"

He nods.

"You've decided all this after looking at my laptop?"

He frowns. "Yes," he says.

"Maybe we both need to take five," I say, wanting to kick myself but knowing this is important. "This is a lot to take in."

Having a baby with someone, especially if that someone is also my boss—younger, incredibly wealthy boss, is not something I want to jump into lightly, even if my ovaries and brain are doing a happy dance. Nat's comment about us making beautiful babies comes back to me.

Gabriel's hand squeezes mine. "I won't change my mind, but I understand you need to process it."

I chuckle. That is such a Gabriel thing to say.

"I do," I say, extracting my hand from his and placing it into my lap. The warmth and closeness do strange things to my insides. "You've taken me by surprise. This is not what I expected this evening." Gabriel shrugs, and another thought enters my head. "Did you say, children?"

Gabriel smiles. "Well, if we have one, and it works, there's always the potential to introduce a brother or sister at a later date. If you're on board."

I know I'm staring. He really has thought about this.

"What about if one of us meets someone? You're younger than me. Not even thirty."

I'm not sure I can start this process and then have Gabriel change his mind because another woman has come on the scene. I know he doesn't date per se. He has ladies he takes to social events he can't get out of, but that could change.

His expression is similar to someone sucking a lemon. "We will co-parent. Believe me when I say I have no desire or intention of meeting anyone, let alone dating them."

I stare at him. "How can you be so sure?" I whisper. "You're not celibate." Or at least I don't think he is. My stomach contracts at the thought.

In my heart, I know Gabriel will be a good father, even if he does meet someone. The past eight years have shown he has a strong moral compass. Co-parenting is no different to a divorce, simply less messy. Gabriel doesn't give me the impression he'll shirk his responsibilities.

"I won't be," he says. "Although I will while we are undergoing treatment. I always have safe sex, and I will be discrete."

I feel my cheeks flood with colour. I can't believe I'm having this conversation with Gabriel. This is a different side to the man I've worked alongside for the past eight years.

"What if I meet someone?" I blurt out, not wanting to put him off but knowing I have to be honest. Gabriel's eyes lock on mine. "I don't want to be on my own for the rest of my life. I want the chance to have what my parents have," I admit. "The only reason I'm contemplating this route is because time is running out. I could freeze my eggs and hope... but ..."

Gabriel sighs. "I understand if you want a relationship. Remaining single won't be a condition of our co-parenting agreement. I know there are a lot of things we're going to need to iron out. This isn't a straight road. We can discuss any issues we foresee arising and include them in any legal agreement we have drawn up. I'm happy to support you and any child or children we have, but I won't support another male. And Leah, if we are trying to have a child, you will need to remain faithful while you conceive. I don't want to find I'm raising someone else's child further down the line."

It's my turn to touch his arm. "That would never happen," I tell him. "If, and I mean, *if*, we do this, I would be fully invested. You do not need to fear that. I'm not asking for financial support. I was...am prepared to do this alone. There are several reasons for me not rushing headlong into this process. The financial implications are but one of them. Childcare is another. A stable home. What you saw the other night was me checking out my options. A want doesn't mean I'm going to do it." I inhale before exhaling slowly. "Having a baby is a pipe dream."

"Why?" Gabriel asks.

"Why, what?"

"Why does it have to be a pipe dream?" Gabriel sits up in the chair, his elbows resting on his knee, his body leaning towards mine. "I'm offering you a solution, so it doesn't have to be a pipe dream. I have more than enough money to support you and a child. As for accommodation, there's an empty apartment below here that is being renovated as we speak. We are both single, so we won't be hurting anyone."

I know I'm staring at him open-mouthed, but I can't stop.

"What would we tell people? Our colleagues? Family?"

Gabriel shrugs, and I glare at him.

"Gabriel, I'm being serious," I say.

He looks at me, his expression becoming serious. "Fine. What were you going to tell people?"

"I hadn't thought that far ahead," I tell him honestly. "Pipe dream, remember?"

"What would you have told people?" he asks, pushing me.

"I'd have told them the truth. That I used a sperm donor. Gabriel, that's not going to work if you step up and admit to becoming my child's father. Can you imagine the rumour mill?" I cover my face with my hands and groan.

"What if we pretend we're in a relationship?"

I drop my hand and stare at the man sitting in front of me. "Excuse me?"

"We pretend to be in a relationship. As far as the office goes, that's up to you. If you want to keep it a secret until you're pregnant, that's fine. We can then announce we are having a baby together. You'd then go on maternity leave, and by the time you come back, everyone will be used to the idea. Problem solved. As far as my family are concerned. This is perfect. They'll be so taken by the fact I have a girlfriend that they won't be able to contain themselves. You'll keep the social climbers and my matchmaking mother at bay and get a baby. It's a win/win."

How have we gone from work colleagues to co-parenting to being in a fake relationship?

Gabriel grabs my hand again, and clasps it in his. "We're both single. We pretend to be a couple to the outside world. Keep the gossips at bay. You've worked for me for eight years, and we already have a professional relationship. When people realise you and your fiancé split up, it might not be such a leap as you think."

His logic isn't as far off as I thought. I've read enough romance books to know this is how it works. Only mine won't have the *Happily Ever After*, although I will have a child to call my own. Is it really beyond the realm of possibility? Even Stella and Nat have suggested I hook up with him. It's then I realise Gabriel is still talking.

"Caleb already knows you are renting the apartment downstairs. It won't be hard for him to believe things between us developed. Which is not a lie. When the baby arrives, we can drift amicably apart and continue as we've agreed. As co-parents."

My heart rate speeds up. His enthusiasm is contagious, but I need to take control. "But what about our living arrangements? Won't they think it's strange I'm living downstairs and not with you?"

"If you haven't noticed, you're already living with me. It plays perfectly into the narrative. You moved in, and we couldn't keep our hands off one another."

I feel my cheeks flush at his words, thinking about some of the wayward thoughts that have been invading my brain recently. Gabriel doesn't seem to notice.

"In all honesty, my family rarely visits. If they do, I usually have notice. We let them see what they're expecting to see. To be honest. It's none of their business."

"What about our clients? Colleagues? Men like Callahan have chosen us because of our professionalism."

"Our professionalism will never be in doubt," Gabriel reassures me. "Our private life is ours."

I can't argue when it comes to the business. It is Gabriel's domain and I simply work for him.

"I can't lie to my parents or friends," I say

There is no way I can dupe my parents. I wouldn't want to.

Gabriel squeezes my hand.

"You're free to tell your parents and friends whatever you want. So, you're aware, I don't think I'll have to lie," Gabriel says cryptically. "When I drop into conversation with Caleb that you're living with me. They will draw their own conclusions."

I'm not sure whether I should be horrified or impressed. One thing is clear. He's deadly serious about the whole thing.

"Caleb will never believe us."

Gabriel retracts his hand and sits back, his expression hardens.

"Do you fancy my brother? Has something happened between you two I don't know about?"

I must look confused.

"I know he visits you in the office, Leah."

I laugh when I realise he's serious.

"No, I don't fancy Caleb. He only does that because he knows it winds you up," I say. I thought Gabriel had worked this out. "Half the time, he comes in, shuts the door, and leans back against it. He stays for five minutes and then comes to see you."

I watch a furrow appear between Gabriel's brows. "Well, I'm just warning you. If we do this, he will forever be off limits."

I tilt my head, a greater understanding of the brothers' dynamics coming to light.

I capture Gabriel's gaze with mine. "There is nothing between Caleb and me. There never has and never will be."

Gabriel's shoulders visibly relax, and he gives a curt nod. We sit in silence, the tension growing. This is not something I can decide now. My head starts to pound.

"I need time to think about it," I say, surprising myself. I should turn him down flat. This could compromise our working relationship and our newfound friendship. I love my job. If this goes wrong, my whole life will be ruined.

"Okay," he says. He gets up and moves away. So typical of the man I know. I'm unsure whether I've just offended him, or like any business discussion, he feels it's reached its natural conclusion.

I move to the kitchen and clear up the dinner plates. Gabriel disappears into his office. I lean over the sink and drop my head.

Have I entered the Twilight Zone?

I have a lot to think about. My stomach clenches as an unexpected warmth floods my body, making its way south. My breath hitches as my nerve endings stir to life. I bite my lip, as I lean forward. Flashes of me inserting Gabriel's sperm into my body rocks my thoughts.

The moment passes, and I draw in a shuddering breath. I make my way to my bedroom and close the door. I move to my bedside table, and pull out my housewarming present from the girls.

CHAPTER 18

LEAH

I meet the girls at our favourite coffee shop over lunch, having spent the entire night tossing and turning.

"So, how's it going with your new roomie?" Stella asks, dropping herself into the chair opposite me.

I arrived early, unable to concentrate at my desk.

"Er... good," I say, not quite able to meet her eyes.

"O.M.G." she shrieks before tamping down her voice when people look over, instead switching to a loud stage whisper. "You've slept with him. I knew it. All that hotness. I just knew you were going to crack!"

I flinch, my eyes dart to the tables surrounding us. One of the older women gives me a scowl, and I give her an apologetic smile.

"Stella," Nat hisses, taking a seat, having just arrived.

"Sorry," Stella says. "But our best friend here has slept with her boss."

"Stop," I say, shooting Nat a look before she can start screaming too. "I have *not* slept with my boss... with Gabriel."

Stella sinks back in her chair, disappointed. "Oh, you're

no fun. There I was, thinking you'd been spontaneous and spent the night having orgasms."

I had, but not at Gabriel's hand. My *gift* however had a full-blown workout.

The woman on the table next to us shoots us another glance before getting up and moving. Luckily, the cafe is still relatively empty.

"Fine, but you clearly haven't slept, so it's time to spill the beans," Stella says.

"Here you go, ladies," Daphne, our waitress, says, delivering the drinks and food I ordered.

"Leah?" Stella's voice takes on a desperate tone.

I take a deep breath. "Last night, Gabriel offered to be my sperm donor."

Stella showers the table with the mouthful of coffee she was swallowing. Nat smacks her on the back as she gasps for breath.

"What the?" she says finally, although her voice is gravelly.

"You heard me," I say, not wanting to repeat it in case someone overhears.

Stella takes a long gulp of water from the glass Daphne appears with. "Thanks," she says as Daphne leaves again.

"I think you need to start at the beginning," Stella croaks.

I tell them about Gabriel finding my search, how he has been acting strangely, and then last night's bombshell.

"What have you said to him?" Nat asks, her face giving nothing away.

"I told him I need to think about it," I tell them honestly.

Stella sits back and stares at me, her forehead creasing.

"Responsibility or no responsibility?" she asks.

"Responsibility," I reply.

Stella pinches her lips between her fingers. "As in co-parenting?"

I nod, surprised she's heard of it. "You'll need a legal agreement," Nat adds.

"Agreed and discussed. It was the first thing Gabriel said."

"Other than offering to donate his sperm, you mean." Stella smirks and I roll my eyes at her. "How is this going to work?"

I sigh. I can't lie to my friends. "He suggests we allow everyone to think we're in a relationship. Fewer questions or insinuations."

"He's gone up in my estimations already. Gorgeous looking and thoughtful. So why haven't you bitten his hand off?" Stella asks, folding her arms over her chest and raising an eyebrow.

"He's my boss. If it all goes wrong, I lose everything. My job and my home," I say, running a hand over my face.

"What is likely to go wrong?" Stella asks before her eyes widen. "Are you going to sleep with him?" she asks in a proper whisper this time.

"No," I say more loudly than expected, although Gabriel and I haven't discussed the method officially. He saw me looking at sperm donor sites and offered to be my sperm donor.

"Pity," Stella mumbles, making me laugh, and Nat pushes her sideways. "What?" She says, holding up her arms. "You have to admit, that guy is sex on legs and moody to boot. I bet he's an animal in bed."

I groan. The last thing I need is to think about Gabriel...in bed.

"That is not how this is going to work," I say. "If it happens at all."

It's Nat who surprises me with her next statement. "Why not? You want a baby. He wants a baby. Surely, it's got to be better for any child to know both its parents. And Gabriel has A-mazing genes. Just imagine the gorgeous babies you two will make together. The firm I'm working for has done a couple of legal agreements for co-parenting couples. If you want me to take a look, I'll be happy to."

We eat our food in silence, everyone caught up in their own thoughts.

"We're here for you, whatever you decide," Nat says once we've finished eating.

"Thank you. I love you guys," I say, meaning every word.

"The feeling's mutual," Stella adds, gripping and squeezing my shoulder as we prepare to go our separate ways.

I head back to the office, my mind semi made up. There are a few important topics that we must address, including the method of conceiving this baby. Since Gabriel mentioned his desire to become a parent, the possibilities have already begun to take root.

CHAPTER 19

GABRIEL

I enter the apartment to voices. Leah didn't tell me her girlfriends were coming around this evening.

"There you are, darling," a voice says before I'm enveloped in a floral hug.

"Mum." I pull back, my eyes meet Leah's over my mother's shoulder.

Leah holds her hands up and shrugs, her shoulders close to her ears. This is not what I expected when I walked through the door. I revert my attention back to my mother, holding her gently away from me by her upper arms.

"This is a surprise," I say. "What are you doing here?"

"Surprising you," she says, patting my arm. "Isn't a mother allowed to come and visit her son?" she says, turning away from me to smile at Leah. "Aren't you a sly one, keeping all this quiet. It's a good thing I have called in."

From my mother's tone, I know there is going to be a long phone conversation, in my future. She's not going to let this rest.

My gaze locks on Leah, who is smiling back at my mother. What the hell? We haven't even finished our conversation about family from a couple of nights ago. I've done as she asked and left her to think about it. Now this? Mum clearly thinks she's my girlfriend. Is this Leah's way of telling me she's on board?

"I can't believe you've been working together for eight years now!" Mum says, moving back towards Leah and linking an arm through hers, patting her forearm. "How time flies. You really should let me into the office more, Gabriel."

"The office is where I work. It's not a place for family gatherings," I say.

God help me, it's bad enough Caleb feels the need to drop in all the time, let alone if my mother starts.

"Caleb visits you all the time," Mum adds, as if prompted, and I see Leah's lips twitch.

"Not by choice," I grumble.

"So, Leah, you know Caleb?"

I suppress a groan.

"I do," Leah says, biting her lip to stop herself laughing.

A trait I notice more and more now she's living with me. Leah extracts herself from my mother, her attention fixed on the pot of food bubbling on the stove. Is she enjoying this?

"Leah is one of the few people who can tell us apart," I say.

"Really?"

Leah's eyes fly to mine as her cheeks flood with colour.

"To me, they are very different," she says, shooting me a look that promises retribution.

"That's interesting," Mum adds, her expression thoughtful. *Oh shit,* I recognise that look. *What have I started?*

"Not really," I say, deciding to change the subject.

"Can I get you a refill, Mum?" I move to the cupboard and grab myself a wineglass.

"That would be lovely, darling."

I refill Mum's wine before walking up behind Leah. I rest my hands on her waist as I stare over her shoulder.

"Sorry," I whisper in her ear. "I had no idea."

I'm not sure what I'm doing, but before I can stop myself, I lean forward and drop a kiss on her cheek.

"This smells delicious," I say against her ear, surprised as goosebumps rise along her forearms.

She turns her head sharply, our lips millimetres apart. I can feel her breath on my skin. Leah's eyes drop to my lips, my heart rate picks up, and my muscles tense. She turns away before I can respond and directs her attention to another pan.

I look up, my mind racing, only to find my mother watching us. A slow grin spreads across her face. If we want my family to believe we're a couple, we've scored the first goal of the game. Leah in my apartment, cooking dinner for us both, working for me. This could not be more perfect, if I planned it.

A pressure builds in my chest and my stomach clenches as I think of Leah agreeing to carry my child. Of her stomach growing swollen with our baby. My hands tighten on her waist, and she lets out a small gasp.

"Would you like to stay for dinner, Francesca?" Leah asks.

I freeze as Leah pats, then squeezes the hand still wrapped around her waist. I retract it, the sense of loss immediate. Having Leah in my space is playing havoc with my senses.

"Oh, I don't want to intrude," Mum says, although her eyes tell a different story. If I know my mother, she wants all the gossip. This is her dream come true. Finding her youngest, socially awkward son, me, with a woman in his house, cooking him dinner.

"It's no trouble. There's plenty," Leah says, turning off the stove.

She turns towards me and raises an eyebrow, her eyes full of mischief. She's telling me two can play at this game.

"Gabriel, lay a place for your mum."

Mum looks over, her grin reminiscent of the Cheshire Cat in the Alice in Wonderland book she read to us when we were little. I do as I'm told and lay an extra place.

"Oh, Leah, this is delicious," Mum says on her second helping. "It's amazing you come home after working such long hours and cook for my son."

I roll my eyes. Mum never approved of my restaurant-supplied diet. She's probably fallen in love with Leah purely because she knows how to cook.

"It's no trouble. I enjoy cooking, and I'd rather know what I'm eating," Leah says. "I grew up cooking alongside my mum. She taught me everything I know."

"How lovely," Mum says. "It's a skill so many of the younger generation are losing."

"To mum and I, it was a bonding session. We still cook together when I visit."

Mum clasps her hands in delight, holding them to her chest. "That's lovely. Do you see them often?"

"Usually once a month. They're currently travelling around Australia. I miss them," Leah says.

"Then Gabriel, you need to bring Leah home one week-end. She can have some family time at our house," Mum says shooting me a look that garners no argument.

"Of course," I say. I need to change the subject before she's locked us in. "Did you have a pleasant lunch with your friends?" I ask Leah, garnering a shocked look.

"Er, I did," she says, inclining her head, questioning how the hell I knew she went to lunch with her friends. I smile and raise an eyebrow.

"Oh, that's wonderful," Mum says. "It's so important to maintain your friendships when you're in a relationship. I kept all my friends from before your father and I married. They've kept me going... after I lost him." My mother's voice drops. She and Dad were inseparable, but she always maintained her own friendships and hobbies.

Leah squeezes my mum's shoulder as she collects her plate, and I'm shocked when Mum pats her hand in acknowledgement. Who is this woman bewitching my mother?

Mum helps clear up. I can tell that Leah is shocked. Mum might be worth billions. Dad took the family business and grew it during their marriage. But there was one thing Mum ensured. We were never too big for our boots or too wealthy to muck in.

I watch as my mother and Leah fall into an easy conversation. I might as well have not been there. Having taken their drinks to the sofa, they have barely come up for air.

It's only when my mum's phone beeps she looks up in shock.

"Oh gosh, is that the time? I'm sorry I've monopolised your evening. That's Freddy, my driver. I'll leave you two lovebirds alone," Mum says, carrying her glass to the kitchen and rinsing it under the tap.

"Well, it was lovely to meet you, Mrs Frazer... sorry, Francesca," Leah says, following behind her.

"You too, Leah. I'm so happy he's found you." Mum pulls Leah in for an impromptu hug, which Leah accepts. Her arms wrap around my mother.

Together, we walk her to the elevator.

"I'll take Mum down to the car," I say, stepping in beside my mother.

"See you soon," Leah adds.

"Oh, Leah, will you come to the Frazer Fundraising Weekend this year? We have a family get-together to celebrate my birthday, and the next day, it's all about raising as much money as we can for the causes we support."

"Er," Leah says, as her eyes shoot to mine.

"Of course, Leah will be there," I say.

If I've got to go, there's no way in hell I'm going to expose myself to the society mothers and their daughters, who flock to our country estate every year without Leah by my side, especially if the world thinks we are a couple.

Leah shoots me a look that tells me we will discuss this later, but steps back to allow the doors of the elevator to close.

"Oh, Gabriel, she's lovely," Mum says as soon as the doors shut, and we begin our descent. "I should have seen it. I'm surprised I didn't. No wonder you've not been interested in any of the women I've introduced to you. Not when you were waiting for Leah."

Her face brightens, and I feel a flash of guilt. This is what she wants for me. Tonight has made her happy. My mind wanders to Leah and what I will face when I return upstairs. It's her fault. She's done an amazing job of making my mother fall in love with her. Now she'll have to deal with the fallout.

"She is," I reply, unsure what else to say.

"I remember meeting her briefly years ago. I can't believe she still works for you?" Mum fishes.

"She does. She's my communications officer. My right-hand woman."

Facts... only facts, a safe subject.

"It makes sense," she says.

"What makes sense?" I ask, confused.

"Leah working for you. She's perfect. I know you over-think things, but, really, Gabriel. Eight years?"

My heckles rise at her words. "Excuse me, Leah was engaged until recently. She wasn't available."

"Oh." Her face drops. "This isn't a rebound thing, is it?" Her concern for me is evident. Maybe my mother hasn't taken Leah's side over mine. Yet.

"No, Mother, we've very much entered this relationship with our eyes wide open."

Not lying.

"I trust you. More than any of your siblings. You're the sensible one."

Her words leave me speechless.

"Pardon?" I say.

I listen to her chuckle. "You're my thinker. You weigh up every option and nuance. I trust in you, Gabriel. You need to trust in yourself. Don't overthink it." She pauses. "I like Leah. She's open and honest. It's obvious she gets you." Mum pats my cheeks. "And she's normal, not like some of those other social climbers."

I wonder if she means Rachel. She never really liked her.

Her eyes twinkle when I look down at her, surprised.

"Let it follow its own path."

The doors open, and Mum's driver is waiting in the basement. He holds open the car door. She turns to me and pulls me down for a hug and to rain kisses on my cheek.

"I love you, Gabriel. Now get back upstairs to Leah."

I smile, certain that I have a cheek covered in fuchsia pink lipstick.

When she's seated in the car, I step back into the elevator and make my way back to the apartment.

I find Leah waiting near the kitchen unit.

She turns to me in a flash. "I tried to set her straight, but she appeared to have made up her own mind the instant she saw me," she says, her voice panicked.

"I believe you," I say, grabbing another glass of wine. "I did warn you. This situation, you being here. My mum is a romantic, and you are everything she wants for me. She just told me as much."

Leah blanches. "But—"

I step towards her but refrain from touching her again. "I

told you we wouldn't need to lie. My family will jump to their own conclusions because of what they see."

I make a sweeping gesture.

Leah rubs a hand down her face.

"Have you thought any more about what I said?" I ask. "I take it you spoke to the girls about it?"

Leah sinks onto one of the stools positioned along the kitchen island.

"I did. I hope you don't mind." She looks at me cautiously.

I shake my head. "I take it they're watertight. That if we do this, they won't run off and sell our story to the press?"

Leah looks at me in horror. "No. They've been my friends since secondary school. We're more like sisters."

I nod, letting her know I trust her judgement.

"What did they think?"

I'm surprised at how much this has interrupted my thoughts. Waiting.

Leah's shoulders sag. "I don't know. They were surprisingly positive. It's just—"

"Just what?" I push.

"It's just... I work for you. You're now my landlord. If something goes wrong, I lose my job. Something I love, and my home."

I pull out one of the stools and sit down next to her.

"We will have a legal contract. We can include helping you find another job if something goes wrong. As you've probably guessed, Caleb would employ you in a heartbeat, or Elijah, Kat. Any of my siblings."

"You can't guarantee that."

"I can and I will. I promise if we do this and something goes wrong, and you feel you can no longer work for me—which I don't foresee happening by the way—Then I'll ensure there is no comeback on you," I say, knowing I mean every word. I won't let Leah suffer.

"What else is bothering you?"

I sense she has another question but is holding back.

I watch in fascination as colour creeps up Leah's neck and spreads across her cheeks.

"We never, er, discussed..." Leah stumbles over her words. For the second time in as many days. My communications officer, the most adept communicator I know, is lost for words. I clamp down on the smile that threatens.

"Leah, whatever it is, spit it out."

"How do you see me getting pregnant?" The words rush out in a flurry, and I have to take a moment to comprehend what she's asking. "I can't sleep with you... sorry, have sex with you. That would be totally unprofessional."

I bite the inside of my lip to stop myself from laughing.

I take a deep breath before carefully choosing my next words.

"I thought you were thinking of artificial insemination."

Leah visibly releases the breath she's been holding.

"That's what I was thinking," she says, giving me a small smile.

"I can arrange for us to be seen at a clinic," I say next, surprising myself.

Leah looks at the ground, her colour rising again. "I was wondering if we can try here...at least at first. A clinic sounds so impersonal. If I have problems conceiving, then maybe."

"Not a problem. It may be better, as my brother and I share the same face. It could set tongues wagging if I'm seen at a fertility clinic," I say almost too quickly. The thought of having to perform while Leah waits anxiously in the other room. Maybe I should have thought this through a bit more.

Leah hops down from the stool and turns to face me. "Are you sure?" she asks, the uncertainty in her voice makes my heart clench.

"When have you ever known me to suggest anything I'm not one hundred per cent behind?"

Leah lets out a shuddering breath. "Okay," she whispers.

"Okay, what?" I ask, needing clarification.

"If we can come to a legal agreement on how this is going to work." Her gaze locks with mine. "I don't want either of us to go into this unprepared. Once that's done, I'll come off the pill and order the kits."

The shy smile she gives me stops my heart, and I swallow past the tightness in my throat.

Leah holds out her hand, and I envelop it in mine. "But we are both within our rights to back out if something changes. Promise me," she says, her voice pleading, but it appears more for me. She's trying to give me a get-out-of-jail-free card. Warmth spreads where our skin touches.

"I'll speak to my solicitor tomorrow and get the ball rolling."

Leah says nothing. She silently nods, her eyes focused on our hands. I let go but find myself immediately missing the connection.

Leah looks up at me. "Thank you, Gabriel," she says.

"Thank you? This is mutual, Leah. Let me know what you need."

She nods in affirmation. "I'll see you in the morning. I'm going to bed."

When she turns and walks away, I miss her presence. Leah, in the three weeks we've been living together, has turned my ordered life upside down, and now I'm about to add to that with a child.

CHAPTER 20

LEAH

*A*s promised, Gabriel appears at my desk with an envelope in hand. He spent the morning out of the office with his solicitor.

"Leah?" he says, standing in the doorway.

"Gabriel, do you need something?" I ask, beckoning him in and offering him the seat opposite my desk.

He looks around and enters, shutting the door behind him. He's carrying a large brown envelope.

I wait for him to get himself comfortable.

"I have the initial draft of our contract for you to look over," he states, leaning forward and placing the envelope on the desk. "My solicitor has said if you have any questions, he is happy to go over anything with you. If not, you can take it to your own solicitor."

His face is the mask of professionalism. It's hard to imagine the contract he is talking about is the one where we bring another human being into the world.

A custody agreement without the hostility of a divorce.

I place a hand on the envelope. "Thank you. My friend Nat, is training to be a solicitor. One of the partners in her

146

firm has agreed to look over it for me. They have apparently been involved in a number of co-parenting agreements."

Gabriel doesn't say anything, he just stands and makes his way to the door. He pauses, his hand rests on the handle, as he turns back to face me.

"Let me know if there are any issues. I'm happy to discuss anything you feel uncomfortable with. I'm serious when I say I want this to work."

The look reflecting out of his eyes tells me all I need to know. "Thank you, and I will." I hold his gaze. "I also want this to work."

He bows his head in acknowledgement before opening the door and leaving.

Gabriel in the office and Gabriel at home are two very different people. One thing I'm sure of having met his mother and his brother, he will, if this works out, make a wonderful father.

* * *

I CALL Nat and let her know I have the document, arranging to meet her at lunch to pass it over.

"Thank you for doing this," I say as I hand her the envelope. "I know I don't need to say it, but this must remain confidential."

Nat rolls her eyes.

"Give me five pounds," she says, smiling.

I reach into my purse and pull out the note. I tilt my head as she grins, accepting it.

"You've now hired my services. Neither I nor anyone who looks at this within the company I work for can divulge the details of this document to anyone. Client, attorney privilege."

"Thank you," I say, pulling her in for a hug. "I look forward to hearing from you."

I make my way back to the office, my mind racing. I haven't told Gabriel yet, but I've already come off the pill. The night I decided we were going to try, I put them at the bottom of my drawer. In for a penny, in for a pound, as they say. Excitement bubbles in my stomach every time I think about what I'm about to do. There is no way this can be wrong. I was prepared to do this alone. But this is so much better. My child...our child will have the love of both parents. A mother and a father. Gabriel and my relationship may be unconventional, but we will work to ensure that any children we have is unaffected. We can attend birthday parties together, school events, and even parents' evenings.

Who knew four months ago, when Vince walked out, my life was going to take this turn?

* * *

A WEEK LATER, Nat calls me at work.

"Hold on," I say, before I get up and close my office door. "It's okay, I can talk."

"Angela, the solicitor looking into your contract, would like to speak to you," Nat says.

"Oh shit," I say, surely this can't be good. I half expected her to come back via Nat. But then again, maybe she's not allowed.

"Don't worry," Nat laughs. "I'll put you through."

"Hi, is that Leah?" A new voice comes over the phone.

"Yes," I squeak. "Is this Angela?"

"It is," she says. "I want to speak to you about the contract you asked me to look over."

"Is there a problem?" I ask, crossing my fingers and hoping she's not going to find a major roadblock.

"Far from it," she says. "It looks like Mr Frazer has made this contract to be more favourable towards you, the mother of his child, than himself."

"Oh," I say, wondering what she must be thinking. Yet, not really wanting to know.

"I want to let you know that everything appears in order. You can come in and talk to me if you have any questions, but I can't see anything that raises any red flags. I will put together a breakdown of the terms and email them to you."

"Thank you. That would be amazing," I say. Lawyer speak is all well and good, but it's a headache to interpret.

"Oh, before I go. Are you aware Mr Frazer's solicitor contacted me? Added another clause," she says.

My heart sinks, although she has just said all is okay. What else has Gabriel added?

"Leah?"

"I'm here," I say.

"Mr Frazer has added a clause stating that if artificial insemination is unsuccessful, providing you are in agreement, he will fund as many rounds of IVF as required."

My hand shakes as it moves to my mouth, smothering the sob that is threatening to escape. "Gabriel really does want a child," I whisper.

"Are you okay?" Angela asks.

"Yes, of course. I'm just surprised. It's not something we've discussed," I admit.

"I'll leave you to think on it," she says. "I'll pass you back to Natalie."

Hold music plays down the phone until Nat's voice reappears.

"Everything okay?" she asks.

"Good... amazing," I tell her honestly.

After Gabriel left the contract, I briefly skimmed my eyes over it.

Gabriel added clauses that included time off work should our child get sick and need me at home. The ability to work from home should I need it. The apartment and a more than generous child allowance for both our child and me, to name a few points.

My mind snaps back to the present when I realise Nat is talking to me.

"He's also added a termination of your employment contract should you wish to invoke it, with a clause to ensure he assists you in finding another job of equal standing," Nat says. "You need to bite his hand off. This man is desperate to have a baby with you. Hell, it might be a little unconventional, but Leah, this is your dream."

"I know. I'm in shock right now. But thank you, Nat. For everything."

"Leah, I'm not saying a word to Stella. When I said this was confidential. I meant every word."

"Thanks, Nat. I love you. I'll speak to Stella."

"Love you too. Now go and sign that contract!"

CHAPTER 21

GABRIEL

I look up and follow Leah's path as she walks into my office and closes the door. My heart rate accelerates.

"I've heard back from my solicitor," she tells me. "Everything appears to be in order."

Leah drops into the chair opposite me. I can tell from her expression she wants to say more. A pressure builds in my chest. Is she having second thoughts?

"Do you have a question?" I ask, as I decide to bite the bullet.

I would rather not discuss this in the office, but we've both been avoiding each other since my mother's visit.

Leah plays with her wrist, which is still bracelet-free. She pinches and twists the skin, making me flinch.

"Leah?" I ask, making her look at me.

"I don't understand?" she says. "You've put everything in my favour. Why?"

I lean back in my chair and steeple my fingers. I wondered if her solicitor would notice. Mine nearly burst a blood vessel when I told him what I wanted to do. He advised me against most of it.

"It only seems fair. I'm in a position of power as your boss. I don't want you or anyone else to think I've taken advantage of you. Especially when I asked to join your party, not the other way around. I want to even the stakes, at least where our child is concerned."

"But the IVF?" She looks at me, her large eyes staring almost in shock.

I smile and shrug, deciding that honesty is the best policy.

"The more we've discussed this, and I've thought about it. I can't imagine having a child with anyone else. I'm fully committed to seeing this through."

Leah raises her eyebrows and inhales deeply. "Okay. I'm not going to say no. And just so you know. I feel the same way. I can't imagine starting this journey with anyone else."

I let the tension seep out of my body.

"Good. Are you happy to sign?"

"I am," she says, giving me a genuine smile, that makes my heart stop in my chest.

"I'll arrange for us to call in to my solicitors this evening," I say. "Get the ball rolling."

Leah stands up and moves towards the door, pausing just before she reaches it.

"Just so you're aware. I stopped taking the pill the night we discussed this."

My jaw opens, but Leah doesn't wait, leaving me sitting open-mouthed at my desk.

We're really doing this. Warmth spreads through my body.

I look at the clock and pick up the phone.

"Mark," I say when my friend answers.

CHAPTER 22

LEAH

*T*hree weeks have passed since Gabriel's mother's impromptu visit and we signed the co-parenting contract Gabriel had drawn up. Life has pretty much returned to normal. Gabriel is all business. The man is undeniably a workaholic, his phone or laptop always close at hand. He comes home, has dinner and then disappears into his *man cave* for hours. When I'm in the apartment, I spend most of my time in my room, reading or watching television. If not, then I'm making the most of the well-equipped gym or fifty-metre swimming pool. When Gabriel pointed out that I wouldn't be in his way, he wasn't joking.

The flood damage to the apartment has been fixed, but we're now waiting for the new furniture to be delivered. It's being shipped in from Italy and various other places in Europe. Not sure why a rental needs a twenty-thousand-pound sofa, but it's his place, so who am I to argue. It's not like I'm slumming it in the penthouse of the El Castillo. The only issue is I wish he'd kept it quiet. I'm going to be terrified to sit on it, or let Stella or Nat anywhere near it. I'm going to ban red wine permanently from the apartment.

My phone rings, and I look down at the caller ID. Mum?

"Hi, Mum," I answer. "I wasn't expecting to hear from you?"

We discussed when they left, that we would either video link or send emails. We have managed one link since they arrived, but with the time difference and their travel home's limited Wi-Fi, we've mainly stuck to emails.

"Hi darling," she says. "I've been trying to reach you. I finally got hold of Vince, and he said you and he... What's going on, Leah? Vince said that you've moved out."

Damn Vince, he could have given me the heads up. My heart sinks.

"Er, yes. We split up a while ago," I say.

"And you didn't tell us?"

The hurt in my mum's voice makes my heart clench.

"I didn't want you and Dad to worry. And, honestly, it's for the best," I add, needing her to believe it.

"But Leah." Her tone changes to my super-efficient mum. "Where are you living? Have you found somewhere safe to stay? I know some places in the city. They're a nightmare."

"I'm fine. I'm staying in El Castillo," I say, holding my breath, waiting for the fallout.

"El Castillo? As in *the* El Castillo, on the waterfront? How? What's going on?"

Of course, Mum would remember the El Castillo. It was being built when she and Dad came to visit Vince and me. Even in the early stages, the building was impressive, making its mark. It was also one of the first buildings to embrace smart, sustainable architecture. It had been big news when Jaxson Lockwood and Caleb Frazer joined forces to transform the city.

I take a deep breath and begin to fill her in on what's been happening. From Vince and I breaking up, to Gabriel offering me his apartment to live in. I miss out the part about

Vince getting someone else pregnant. She doesn't need to know that when she's halfway around the world. Instead, I tell her we fell out of love. A conclusion I've come to over the past couple of months. I don't miss him and realise we were already living separate lives. Yasmin had merely been a catalyst for us to do something.

"Leah Walker. Are you in a relationship with your boss?"

Wow. How did she jump to that conclusion?

"Er..." the door to the apartment opens, and Gabriel walks in.

"Why would you say that?" I ask my mother, my heartbeat speeding up to painful levels. Gabriel looks over and raises an eyebrow.

"Your boss offers you a multi-million-pound apartment. No one does that out of the goodness of their heart unless they're after something."

I flinch, knowing Gabriel can hear her words. The fact he offered me the apartment out of the goodness of his heart rankles.

Gabriel shrugs and walks towards the door. Why the next words escape my mouth, I'll never know.

"You're right. I just didn't want you to worry. It's such early days. We're trying to keep it low-key."

Gabriel pauses and turns to face me, his expression questioning. I told him I wasn't prepared to lie to my parents, and now I find myself doing exactly that.

The phone falls silent for a moment. "Is it wise? You know the saying about never messing around on your doorstep?"

"I do, but I promise this is different."

I sigh, needing to put her mind at rest. I know my mother, she'll be cutting her trip short and flying home if she thinks there is something wrong. "It's not like I haven't known

Gabriel for years. When Vince and I ended, things changed between us."

"But you and Vince had so many plans."

I know she's talking about our wedding and grand-children.

"We did, but there was always an excuse. Vince and I should have ended about five years ago," I tell her truthfully. That's when I wanted to begin a family and Vince began his barrage of excuses. He pacified me by placing an engagement ring on my finger but looking back.

I let the past unravel in a way I've been too blinkered to see until now. Talking things through with my mum is opening my eyes.

"I just worry about you. It's a mother's prerogative," she says.

"And a father's," my dad chips in from the background.

"I know," I sigh. "It's one reason I haven't said anything." The guilt of that decision weighs heavy, now she's finally on the phone.

"We may be over fifteen thousand kilometres away, but we're still your parents. You don't need to hide things from us. We just want you to be happy. If Gabriel makes you happy, then we look forward to meeting him. We love you, Leah."

"I know. I love you both, too, so much. I have everything under control." For the first time in months, I feel that is true.

"I'm glad. So when do we get to meet this *new* man of yours?" Mum asks, the tone of her voice becoming mischievous.

I cover my eyes, not wanting to look at Gabriel.

Gabriel's hand encloses mine as he extracts the phone from my hand.

"Mrs Walker," he says, my eyes lock on his. His lips tilt, and he moves the phone out of my reach.

"Of course, Louise."

I sit in silence as Gabriel schmoozes my parents. First my mum and then my dad. I'm not sure what I'm more surprised about. The ease with which he talks to them, my awkward boss, or that he's talking to them at all.

Eventually, he hands me back the phone.

"Mum?" I say.

"Oh Leah, he's lovely, what a beautiful deep voice. I can't wait to meet him. Maybe we can talk face-to-face next time we arrange a video call."

"Er, I'm sure you can—" Gabriel took my phone off speaker while he spoke to them, so I'd only been able to hear one side of their conversation.

I shoot him a quick glance, but he goes into the kitchen area and concentrates on pouring us both a glass of wine.

I'll need one after this conversation.

"Perfect," she says, sounding much more vibrant than at the start of the call. I have Gabriel to thank for that.

"Okay, well, I better go. Keep sending me pictures and let me know when you want to video call," I say.

"We will. We love you, Leah. Say goodbye to Gabriel from us."

"I love you too," I say, my throat tight. "I will. Bye."

I disconnect the call and take the glass of wine Gabriel is holding.

"Thank you."

"You're welcome. It's the same wine we had the other night," he replies, misunderstanding.

"No, I mean, thank you for helping to put my parents' mind at rest."

Gabriel sits down on the sofa opposite.

"They're halfway across the world. I get you not wanting

to worry them. I'd be the same with my mum." He surprises me by saying.

"Well, thank you anyway."

He nods before placing his glass down and getting up. He leaves the room, returning with a large brown box.

"This was downstairs waiting for you," he says, handing it over.

I stare at the box, before realisation dawns on its contents. I ordered artificial insemination kits online. They promised discrete delivery, and they haven't failed.

"It's the insemination kits," I say, heat emanating from my cheeks.

"Great," Gabriel says. "Let me know when you need me."

I take a large swallow of wine, praying not to choke and spit it all over the white rug and sofa. My lower body contracts at the thought of what *needing me* means.

I drop my gaze, unable to look at Gabriel, instead letting out what sounds little more than a squeak.

"Is there a timeline?" Gabriel asks, his voice calm.

"Timeline?" I say, my voice still higher than it should be.

"When you'll need my sperm?" Gabriel says as if we're talking about the weather. "It's just that I read I'd be better off abstaining for several days before giving a sample."

Ground swallow me up.

We're discussing him relieving himself. My clothes instantly feel hot and uncomfortable. The thought of Gabriel in the shower or in his bed, dick in hand. What does he think about? Oh hell, my mind needs to stop.

I cough, trying to clear my throat and adopt the same matter-of-fact tone. "I've stopped taking the pill. My period is due in a couple of days. I'm tracking my temperature and using an ovulation app and kits."

We are doing this together, after all.

"Let me know, and I'll do what is needed."

Unsure what else to say, I get up, carrying my wine towards the kitchen area, needing to put some space between us. If we do this, I'll be giving up my evening glass of wine. That thought does strange things to my insides.

"Are you ready for dinner?" I ask.

* * *

I STARE AT THE THERMOMETER. It's happening. My temperature has increased. The ovulation kit is saying *it's time*. My heart is pounding in my chest, and my insides feel like they're vibrating. I stare at the bathroom door. What am I going to do if he changes his mind?

"Grow up, Leah!" I say, giving myself a harsh talking to. Gabriel is not going to change his mind. The man took you out to dinner after we signed the contract. We both knew this day was coming. I'd had my period, so everything has been leading up to this. I already opened one kit and read the instructions. Everything was straightforward and clear. I just need Gabriel to provide his sperm, and then I can do the rest... and pray for nature's kindness.

I'm thankful it's Saturday morning as I head downstairs in search of Gabriel, unsure if he's around. He usually swims early, so he may be in his home office.

I knock on the door and wait. There's no reply.

I leave and walk back into the living room to make breakfast.

An hour later, I hear the door click, and Gabriel walks in.

He throws his bag onto the unit. "Morning," he says.

"Morning," I reply, unsure how I raise this. It's not like we're in a relationship.

He stops and looks at me. "Is everything okay?" he asks.

I bite my lip, drawing his eyes to my mouth.

"Leah?" he says again, stepping closer.

"It's time," I say, watching his brows furrow before the realisation hits. I watch as colour floods his cheeks. Oh no, is this where he tells me he's changed his mind?

He coughs and nods, his face growing serious... an expression I'm used to seeing in the office, less so at home.

He inhales. "What do I need to do?" he asks, coming to stand in front of me. My body responds to the heat radiating from his. I tell myself it's my hormones, my body wanting to create a baby.

I pick up the container that arrived with the kit and hold it out to him.

I feel my colour rise as our fingers graze.

"If you can..."

He nods, taking it from me and turning away.

"I'll be in my room when you're ready," I say, as he heads for the stairs.

A flush of warmth hits me as I watch him leave. A tingling ache floods my body as my mind wanders to what he's about to go upstairs and do. Will he be watching porn? Read some girlie magazines? Daydream about the weather girl he likes? Think about me?

Shit. I'm being ridiculous. My skin tightens, and a flush of warmth spreads through the lower half of my body. I bite down hard on my lip, squeezing my thighs together. I shouldn't be horny. I need to get ready.

I make my way upstairs and pull back the covers. I grab the hip-raising pillow I purchased. It's a sex pillow designed to help your partner hit your G-spot, but I hope the angle will help the sperm find its way home.

I sit on the edge of the bed and wait. Gabriel's been gone a while. Is there a problem? I make my way to the door as a knock sounds.

He holds out the container. "Here you are," he says.

I reach out and take it. Our fingers graze, my awareness

skyrockets. "Thank you," I say breathlessly, hoping I don't look like a beetroot. I need to be professional and not think about what he's just handed me.

"All yours," Gabriel says, before he turns away, walking back towards his own room.

I exhale the breath I didn't realise I was holding, and make my way to the bed and the syringe I have waiting for me.

CHAPTER 23

GABRIEL

I leave the apartment and try not to think about what is going on in Leah's bedroom. How she'll insert my cum into her body. The thought alone had me erupting into the sterile container, my teeth clenched tight to stifle any cries. Who knew abstaining for a week and a half would have this kind of effect?

Instead, I go to see Caleb.

"Is it true?" he asks as soon as he opens the door.

"Depends on what? There are many things that are true. There are an equal number of false."

"Don't be smart with me," he grumbles. He steps back and lets me enter his apartment. Jet lag visibly taking its toll. He's been in America for the past month, working with an old friend of Elijah's. An architect renowned for his work in sustainable, eco-friendly buildings.

"If you're talking about Leah, I take it our mother has been gossiping?" I say, as I follow him into his kitchen.

Caleb moves to his wine cooler and grabs a bottle of beer for us both.

"It *is* true then?" Caleb stares at me as if trying to read my soul. "I always wondered," he adds cryptically.

Directing us back into his main living space.

"Wondered what?"

"About your feelings for her."

I drop onto his sofa, drawing down a large swallow of beer.

Feelings? I catch the word before I say it out loud. Caleb is too perceptive, not only as a person but also as my twin.

"What changed? I've only been gone a month," he asks.

I sit back and stare at the bottle of beer in my hand. "That night, after Tristan's," I say, realising it isn't a lie. That night changed everything between Leah and me, or at least started us on our current path. I saw Leah as more than someone who works for me. I saw her as a person. It also made me realise how distant I am from those working for me. Something I need to rectify.

Caleb stares, and I lock my muscles to prevent myself from fidgeting under the scrutiny of his gaze. He takes a swig of his beer before leaning forward, his elbows resting on his knees.

"I'm going to say this, and I know you will not like it."

I lock gazes with my brother. I know what's coming. He's always been protective, even when I've not wanted him to be.

"I like Leah. You know I do, but are you sure this isn't too soon? She and Vince were together a long time."

It's my turn to lean forward. "Most people will think it *is* too soon." I think back to Leah's conversation with her mother. "We've discussed it. Leah's relationship with Vince was over a long time ago."

Caleb looks sceptical, and I can't blame him. "She was pretty upset the night of Tristan's opening for someone whose relationship was over."

"She was, but then Vince's girlfriend announced she was pregnant."

Caleb's eyes widen, and his head draws back. "I was not expecting that."

"No, nor was Leah," I say drily. "Vince had been putting off starting a family for years. That's why Leah was so upset. It was the ultimate betrayal," I add, hoping Leah forgives me for sharing this information with Caleb.

"I don't get it. I don't get Vince," Caleb says, shaking his head, making me wonder whether my brother has, in fact, developed feelings for Leah over the years.

"After Leah moved into the apartment, we started spending time together, and our relationship changed," I explain.

"I'm not surprised," my brother says, smiling over at me. "It was always going to take someone like Leah to break down your walls. You were always going to need to get to know someone without any stigma or pressure."

I stare open-mouthed at my brother.

"You forget how well I know you, Gabe," he says.

Something I can't deny, even if I want to. Caleb has always had an innate way of knowing what I need or how I'm feeling.

I close my mouth, pursing my lips. "Leah wants to keep it out of the office, at least for the moment," I tell him.

"I'm not surprised. She's never been big on gossip." Caleb leans forward and taps the top of his bottle to mine. "I really am happy for you both." I take that as his agreement not to come in, shouting his mouth off the next time he *pops* in.

It shouldn't, but it always surprises me when the romantic side of my brother rears its head. For the ultimate playboy, he certainly has a romantic heart.

"Enough about me. How was America? How's Jaxson?"

"America was good. We made a lot of progress on the plans for the new development," Caleb says.

We move on to talk about the plans for his new project. By the time I leave him, I've pushed aside all thoughts of Leah and what she is doing with my cum. I message her, telling her I won't need dinner. Instead, I head into the office. I spend the rest of the day reviewing the latest market news, drawing up potential lists of new investments before finally tiptoeing back into the apartment.

* * *

TWO AND A HALF WEEKS LATER, Leah walks into my office, her brows drawn and her face pale.

I stand and walk towards her.

"I'm not feeling great," she says, her eyes not quite meeting mine. "Is it okay if I work from home this afternoon?"

"Of course," I say.

I frown at her. Something is off, but she doesn't want to tell me. It's not appropriate for me to pry, even if I want to.

"Do you want Amanda to order you a taxi?" I ask.

"No, it's fine. I think some fresh air will do me good, plus the tube will be empty at this time of day." I'm annoyed when she gives me a weak smile. What isn't she telling me? "I'll see you later," she says before she turns and heads for the door.

"Don't worry about cooking tonight. I'll get us a takeout from the Healthy Food Company."

Leah pauses but doesn't turn around. She nods once before leaving.

* * *

I LEAVE THE OFFICE EARLY. The need to get home and check on Leah increases throughout the day. Something is wrong.

Maybe she's picked up a bug.

I enter the silent apartment. The main living area is empty. No sign of Leah anywhere. I head upstairs and listen. I hear the television coming from her bedroom.

I knock. "Leah?" I call through the door.

"Come in, Gabriel," she says.

I enter, walking through her closet area and into the main bedroom. Leah is sat up in bed, her nose and eyes red. A wad of tissue screwed up in her hand.

"Can I get you anything?" I ask. She looks ill. "Is everything all right?"

She gives me a watery smile, and I watch as a tear trickles down her cheek. She shakes her head. "I'm fine. It's just my period has come. I forgot how painful they were before I went on the pill."

She flinches as she moves.

Having grown up with two sisters, periods are nothing out of the ordinary. It takes my brain a moment to catch up... period also equals no baby.

Before I can think, I step forward and sit down on the bed. I pull her into my arms.

"I'm sorry," she mumbles into my chest.

My brow wrinkles, and an icy chill settles over me. "Sorry for what?" I ask.

"I failed."

She sniffles, my shirt getting damp under her cheek.

"You have nothing to be sorry for. So it didn't work this time. You've just come off the pill. That can have an enormous effect on a woman's fertility. Do you think we're going to give up after one attempt?"

"I should have known you'd have read up on everything

possible," she says, trying to make light of the situation, although her voice catches.

I take her head in my hands and make her look at me.

"Talk to me?"

She swipes at her eyes. "Probably not a good idea. I'm a hormonal and emotional wreck. Sorry." She gives me a watery smile. "My period is the only time I get like this... well, that and around unfaithful fiancés." Her breath hitches, but I think it's supposed to be a laugh. She covers one of my hands with hers. "You're a wonderful man, Gabriel Frazer. How did I get so lucky to have you want to father my child?"

The look in her eyes floors me. So much so I want to do a double-take.

"Remember, we're in this together now. You're stuck with me. Come on. Get showered and come downstairs. I brought dinner with me," I say.

I stand up. Leah nods and climbs out of the bed.

"I'll be down in a moment," she says, not looking at me.

I catch her hand as she makes her way past me. "I meant what I said."

She nods. Her gaze is on the floor.

"I know. I don't know what I was hoping." Her eyes finally rise to mine. "That it would just magically happen. I know that's highly unlikely, but you just hope. My biggest fear is I've left it too long."

"Stop torturing yourself. You need to relax. If you want a bath, you're free to use mine," I add, surprising myself once more.

"No, it's fine, but I may take you up on that at another point in the future. If that's okay."

It's my turn to nod. At this moment, I would give her anything.

"I'll see you downstairs." I make my way to the door

before stopping and turning around. "If this doesn't work, there are many options we can try."

Leah's lip catches between her teeth, and I watch her throat bob. I leave her with my words, knowing I will do everything in my power to give Leah the child she wants.

I lay out our dinner. The Healthy Food Company is a take-away service Leah introduced me to. Unlike restaurants, it provides home-cooked meals minus the salt and cream. The healthy option. I feared it would not be as tasty as the meals I got from the restaurant around the corner, but it pleasantly surprised me.

"I'm here," Leah says, looking washed and refreshed. Her eyes are still a little bloodshot, but she has more colour in her cheeks.

I move to the microwave and remove the beanie bag I've heated for her. "Something my sisters always swear by when it's their time of the month," I say.

Leah takes it, the look of shock on her face, a picture.

"I ordered your usual," I say, pointing to the food I've laid out. Not that we have ordered many times, but there have been a few occasions when we've worked late and not taken anything out of the freezer.

Leah takes a seat, resting the bag against her stomach.

I realise I meant every word I said. I want her to grow big with my child.

"Gabriel?"

Leah's voice pulls me back into the present.

"Sorry, I was miles away," I say.

"Are you okay? You look a little flushed. You're not coming down with something?"

I cough. "No, I'm fine," I lie, trying hard not to fidget in my seat. My semi-hard dick becoming a pain. "What were you saying?"

Leah chuckles. "You were miles away. I wondered if you

were going into your *man cave* this evening, or if you wanted to do something?" She pauses, her bottom lip disappearing between her teeth again. "Sorry, that's not any of my business. I shouldn't have asked. Forget I said anything."

"Leah, we need to set some ground rules. Tiptoeing around me doesn't work. Say what you want. I don't do subtle. Going forward, especially if we have a child, I need you to promise you will be straight with me. Tell me what you need. Ask me for what you want."

Leah gives me an incredulous look. I smile.

"Social cues are not my strong point." I sigh. "I need you to promise me."

"I promise," she whispers.

"As for my *man cave*, come on, I'll show you." I stand up and hold out my hand.

"I hope you're not leading me to your *red room*," she says, laughing.

I turn and scowl at her. "Red room?"

Leah laughs and rolls her eyes. "Fifty Shades of Grey," she says, as if that explains everything. I then remember seeing the movie advertised.

"BDSM? Is that something you're into?" I ask, captivated. *Is my little Leah into kink?*

"Er, not the whips and chains," she says before shocking me by adding, "But the idea of a little restraint play... well..."

Her cheeks blaze under her words as if she's just remembered who she's talking to.

"Duly noted," I say, laughing. Especially as that does happen to be one kink, I can very much get behind.

I open the door to my room and step inside, drawing Leah in behind me.

"On." The monitors in front of us come alive at my word.

"Wow," Leah says, moving around me, staring at the setup in front of her. She spins to face me. "You're a gamer?"

"I am, but few people know. Not even my family. It's a part of me I keep quiet. Gaming allows me..." I struggle to find the right words.

"Gaming allows you to be you, not Gabriel Frazer. That I get."

I'm surprised at her excitement.

She steps further into the room. "What do you play?" she asks.

I list off a group of games.

"But I prefer *Call to Freedom.*"

"You're kidding me?" she says, spinning around to face me. "What's your gaming name?"

I stare at her. "Why?"

She throws back her head and laughs. "Because I want to know if I've ever whipped your ass," she says.

I raise an eyebrow in her direction. "Unlikely," I say with a dry tone, enjoying how the look of sadness has been replaced by mischief.

"I don't know, I'm pretty good," she says, grinning. This is the Leah I want to see. One who laughs and jokes, pulls my leg. I step towards her and stop.

What am I doing?

The urge to kiss her is overwhelming.

"No one is that good," I say. Knowing *I* am that good.

"Really?" she says, her eyes twinkling. "Come on, *big boy,* put your gamer name where your mouth is."

"Look," I say, pointing to my top-of-the-range gaming chair and console.

"Really?" she squeaks, jumping in the air, clearly not needing a second invite.

My friend Pen is the only other person I've met who is *this* excited about gaming, but looking at Leah right now, she is a close second. But then, I've not discussed my hobby with many people, especially not those I date. This is my private space.

Leah jumps into my chair, and brings up the server where I speak to others on the platform.

Her head spins towards mine.

"No way, you're ExchangeAce69?" she asks. The incredulity in her voice makes me smile.

"That would be me," I say.

I step up next to her, take the controller, and show her my setup.

"Gabriel, this is amazing." Her eyes widen as the main sixty-five-inch screen comes alive with the game while the smaller monitors display the various chatrooms I'm a member of.

"I built it with a friend."

"Really?"

"Yes, I've known them for years. An old friend of my elder brother, Elijah. She introduced me to gaming. Helped me build my first computer when I was thirteen."

My body warms under the scrutiny of Leah's gaze.

"You dark horse." Leah chuckles. "Who would have thought the successful Gabriel Frazer is a secret gamer capable of building his own computer?"

"Pen was at uni with Elijah. She helped him set up Frazer Cyber Security. She is still a shareholder, but life took her in a different direction."

Leah stares at me. "Pen?"

"Penelope Dawson."

Leah's eyes widen. "As in *the* Penelope Dawson. The software developer, whose company branched out into all the fancy hardware. I think I was reading about the new accessibility hardware and software they're developing. The woman is a genius in all things tech. She's made millions. A woman from very humble beginnings who's made it huge in a man's world."

I turn away, amused at Leah's fangirling over one of my closest friends.

"I can't believe you know *Penelope Dawson,*" Leah says, grinning and shaking her head.

"I have done for many years, but enough talk about Pen. So, you game?"

"I do." She grins at me. "Well, I used to. I got tired of watching movies when Vince went out."

My spine stiffens at the mention of her ex.

"So, I bought a Dawson gaming console. It was incredibly addictive. I started with simple games like *Spiderman,* and then moved onto the online platforms when I realised I didn't have to play alone. I enjoy the competitive nature and teamwork."

I got hooked for the same reasons. Something about talking to people online is entirely different from speaking to them face-to-face. Less small talk and a common goal. No one knows my net worth, and gets hung up on it.

"Are you going to tell me who you are?" I ask, wondering who she is. Have I played her?

"I'm AuburnShadow2006," she says, giving me a smug look.

I'm surprised. Pen and I have discussed her. She's a great problem solver, not that I can tell her that.

"I'm impressed," I say. "We will have to set your console up."

Her face drops. "It got fried in the flood," she says.

"Why didn't you mention it? I'd have replaced it along with everything else."

She shrugs, not quite able to meet my gaze. "Gaming was an escape. When I moved into your apartment, I decided it was time to grow up and stop hiding in the gaming world."

"And you can't do both?"

Her eyes lock with mine, and a smile spreads over her face. Her eyes move to the monitors in front of her. "Maybe I can."

I hold out my hand and help her detangle herself from my gaming chair. She laughs as she falls into me. "So comfortable, but grace…"

She laughs again, righting herself as she steps back. Her eyes sparkle up at mine. I don't think I've ever seen Leah look as stunning.

I stop myself from pulling her against me. "Come on," I say. "Let's watch a movie. It's been a long day."

She grins and heads for the door.

"It has," her voice wistful.

"Off," I say as we leave the room, the equipment going into automatic sleep mode.

CHAPTER 24

LEAH

*M*y app bleeps, letting me know it's *that time of the month again.* The past few weeks with Gabriel have been different. The day after my period, he replaced my old console with the latest model and connected it to the television in the main living area. Not quite his set up, but it's more than adequate. There have been several occasions when a yell comes from his man cave, when I've whooped his ass.

I head over to Gabriel's door and knock.

"Come in," he says, his head down as I enter. I wait for him to complete his task.

"Leah," he says when his head comes up, his eyes focus solely on me.

"Er, this is not really the time or place, but you said you wanted to know." Dawning crosses his features. He looks at the clock. "Can I have ten minutes?"

My heart stops. What?

"Er, I was just letting you know for later," I say.

His face drops. "Oh, I assumed."

"A few hours won't make any difference," I say, smiling at him.

"Do you have any plans for lunch?" His question shocks me into silence, so I shake my head.

"Good." He picks up the phone on his desk. "Amanda, Leah and I have an urgent client appointment this afternoon. We'll take lunch and be back mid-afternoon."

"No problem," Amanda answers as Gabriel puts the phone down.

I stare at him, open-mouthed. Breaking up the workday to inject my vagina with his sperm is not exactly what I had in mind.

As promised, Gabriel takes ten minutes. He collects me from my office, and we take the elevator down to his car. Before I know it, he's pulling into the El Castillo, and we're riding the elevator up to his apartment.

"Where is the container?" Gabriel asks.

My lower body contracts sharply at the thought of what he's about to do. His eyes lock with mine, and I swear his pupils dilate. No, that's my horny body playing tricks on my mind. As before, I make my way to my bedroom, change out of my suit and prepare the rest of the equipment.

A knock sounds at the door and Gabriel enters, the sample pot held in his hand.

"Here you are," he says. "There's no rush. Amanda is not expecting us back until later."

"Thank you," I say, taking the pot of his cum.

"Do you want a sandwich?" he asks.

Okay, this is getting more and more bizarre. Even more so when I tell him, "Yes, please, that would be lovely."

Gabriel leaves, and I set about drawing his sample back into the syringe.

CHAPTER 25

GABRIEL

I turn around and walk away from Leah. Not wanting to scrutinise what she's about to do with my cum. My hands ached with the need to touch her as I handed it over. This isn't my first choice in conceiving a child, but then again, I'm her boss and colleague. She's already taking up too much brain matter. I can only imagine what it would do to my brain and body if it knew how it felt to have her in my arms, to deposit my cum deep within her warm, tight pussy. I bite back a groan and move further along the corridor. At this rate, I'll be relieving myself again before we head back to the office, or taking an ice-cold shower.

A scream has me turn on my heels and slam into Leah's bedroom. Leah is sat on the end of the bed, staring in shock at the mess dripping down her hands and face.

The syringe is in two parts, the end unmistakably having exited the casing as she drew my sperm into it. The resultant lack of suction has shot the sperm everywhere.

Her wide eyes meet mine. "I don't know what—"

I don't wait to hear the rest of her sentence. Instead, I

make my way into her bathroom and grab a facecloth from the side, wet it and return to her.

I kneel on the ground, disengaging her fingers from the broken plunger before throwing it into the empty box. I bite down hard on the inside of my cheek, resisting the urge to laugh, as I notice my cum running in thick strands down her face. Instead, I take her hands in mine, wiping them down, removing the sticky residue before drying them off with the towel. Only when I look up, do I find Leah staring at me.

"Drat," she says, giving me a weak smile. "That wasn't supposed to happen."

"The pamphlet stated this was a reasonably clean procedure. Minimal mess. I think those were the words they used."

I watch as her lips twitch. She rubs her eyes with the back of her hand.

"Ouch," she says, obviously rubbing some liquid into her eye. Her tongue darts out. My stomach cramps as I realise she's just licked my cum from her full lips. When she doesn't grimace, a hit of arousal shoots south.

I shuffle backwards as Leah gets up. She's changed out of her suit and into a long t-shirt, her bare legs exposed. I divert my gaze as she walks past, ignoring the possibility she has no underwear beneath it.

"Well, that's today a no-go," she says. "At least it's supposed to be great for one's complexion."

Taking the facecloth from my hands, she wipes her face on the towel and moves to the bathroom.

The videos I've watched suggest multiple attempts at insemination during ovulation. When we decided this, I took it upon myself to find out what it entailed.

"Looks that way," I say, dragging my eyes away from her body.

Leah sighs as she returns, plopping herself down on the bed and staring at the kit lying in pieces.

"I'm not sure what happened. It was really stiff, and then the plunger pinged out of the end and, well, you saw the result."

My eyes follow hers. "Is it worth calling them?" I ask, needing to do something to distract myself.

Leah nods before getting up and heading out of the room, leaving me alone on the floor.

I grab the box and take it with me. I find her in the main living area, her phone already to her ear.

"That's right," she says. "Uh huh, yes..." There's a long pause while she listens to the person on the other end of the phone. Her expression drops, and she pinches the bridge of her nose, closing her eyes. Whatever they are telling her is not what she wants to hear. "What's next?" she asks, sighing. "It is a problem, as I'm ovulating now." Her tone hardens.

I freeze.

She sinks down onto the sofa, her shoulders sagging. I move to sit near her, and she looks up in shock. Did she not expect me to take an interest?

It's a few more minutes before Leah ends the call. She drops back onto the sofa, her hands covering her face, before letting out a frustrated yell.

"They sent me a faulty batch," she mumbles through her fingers. "They'll send me out another set of kits and a spare, but it won't be with us until Wednesday."

I sit forward and rest my forearms on my thighs, staring at the floor. I know what this means, and to Leah, it must be devastating news. It's one more delay towards her dream.

We sit in silence until Leah pushes herself forward and off the sofa. She pulls her t-shirt down over her thighs.

"I'll get dressed and make us both that sandwich," she says, the frustration of the morning clear in her voice.

Her phone rings, and she looks down, scowling at it.

"What does he want?" she says, silencing it and throwing it onto the coffee table.

I look over and see Vince's name pop up on the screen. Not someone I want appearing when I'm trying to conceive a child with his ex. *Am I taking advantage of her?*

If he hadn't left, it would be him trying to make a child with Leah. Is this what fate is trying to tell us? That this is wrong.

Leah runs upstairs to get changed, returning in record time. Her suit is back in place, and her hair is in its severe updo. She heads to the kitchen area and pulls out a selection of food, busying herself.

I get up and make my way to the window, staring out over the city. From the short time we've lived together, I know this is what Leah needs. She needs to do something menial but with a positive outcome. So, I stay out of the way.

I gaze down at the waterways and streets below. The hustle of the week is the same yet different to that of the weekend. A tourist boat floats up The Thames, and mothers and fathers with their children point out the sights. Will that be Leah and me? Probably not. We aren't a couple, and we're creating a child to fill a gap in both our lives. Is that wrong? Loving our child will be our priority as parents even if we don't love each other, surely that is the most important thing.

"They're ready," Leah says.

I turn to see her hold out a plate containing the largest sandwich I've ever seen. Leah averts her gaze, so I take the sandwich, and move to my office.

This is one problem I can't fix. I can't magic an insemination kit. It means we'll have to wait another month. Why does that bother me so much?

CHAPTER 26

LEAH

*G*abriel and I return to the office in silence. I know I wanted to do this the less stressful way, but this isn't stress free, and now I must wait another month before we try again.

We pull into the car park, and I go to release the door.

"Leah, wait." My finger pauses on the button. "Are you okay?"

The concern in Gabriel's voice almost takes my breath away.

"Frustrated more than anything." I sigh. "Who would have thought a syringe..."

Luckily, none of Gabriel's sperm had landed on my suit. I had the foresight to change. A clothing change over a lunch meeting might have been hard to explain, and if we do get pregnant, I don't want our colleagues to think we were sneaking off to have sex at lunchtime. It's going to be strange enough letting them know I have Gabriel's child growing inside me.

"Maybe I should have let you organise for a professional to assist," I say.

"I still can. I can make some calls."

I swivel to face Gabriel. "But what about the press? About people finding out?"

Gabriel shrugs, and it's my turn to glare at him.

"You can't be serious. We've barely begun our fake relationship. Don't you think your family and our colleagues would find it strange we're already at a fertility clinic?" I shudder. "Talk about gossip. Then there's the pressure. We'd be better off having sex than risk other people sticking their noses in."

It's only when I notice Gabriel's wide eyes that it registers what I said.

I drop my gaze. "Sorry," I say, my cheeks heating.

Gabriel's finger lifts my chin, forcing me to look at him.

"It's an option," he says.

"So is a turkey baster, but it doesn't mean it's the right one."

"I wasn't talking about the fertility clinic. I was talking about sex," he says.

I turn to face him, my mouth drops open. "Gabriel, it's not... how could we maintain a professional relationship if ... well, if you...we."

I cover my face with my hands.

"Very articulate."

It's then I realise Gabriel is teasing me.

"Are you laughing at me?" I ask, my eyes clash with his twinkling ones.

"Maybe just a little," he adds, holding up his thumb and forefinger, which I slap playfully. "Look, all I'm saying is, if you don't want to wait another month. There are other options. We can go to a clinic, or you and I could be very clinical about it. No kissing, minimal touching. Just my cock, depositing my sp—"

"I get the picture," I say, my hands flying to my cheeks

once more. "You seem to be enjoying this way too much for someone who is usually a grouch and serious."

"Maybe seeing you coated in my sperm has made me lighten up a little," he adds. I groan. "Anyway. Think about it. It's an option."

Gabriel flicks the button, and the doors open, letting me know this conversation is over and it's time to get back to work. Only Gabriel could drop that kind of bombshell and return to work like he just asked if I wanted a cup of coffee.

* * *

THE AFTERNOON IS A WRITE-OFF. My conversation with Gabriel was not something I can get out of my head. Is he mad? We can't have sex. How will that be professional? It's been hard enough looking him in the eye, knowing his sperm has been swimming around inside me. How much harder will it be if I feel his body stretching over mine. Feel his body shudder as he coats my insides with his cum? Just the thought is getting me hot and heavy. My breasts ache, and my pussy contracts. Damn my hormones.

I close down my laptop. I'm glad my door is closed. My concentration is gone, and I totally blame Gabriel for the problem.

It's five o'clock, so I grab my things and make my way to Gabriel's office.

"I'm calling it a night," I say as he looks up.

His brows furrow as his eyes flick to the clock. "Okay," he says.

I walk in and close the door behind me. "Okay... okay!" I say. "This is all your fault! You've distracted me."

Gabriel sits back in his chair, his arms folding over his chest. "Distracted?"

I growl, and his lips twitch. The nerve of the man.

"How distracted?" he asks.

"I have a million *what-ifs* running around my head. Tell me this, how can you and I go back to being professional if we... you know... do the deed?"

"Do the deed?"

With those words, Gabriel loses his composure. His face crumples as he tries and fails to contain his laughter.

"Don't laugh at me."

I huff, and cross my arms over my chest. What's happening? I'm turning into the grumpy one while he's laughing.

"Leah, *professional* is a construct. It's what we decide. We could decide to be unprofessional by having dinner together, or we can keep it professional as we have done. It's how we view what we do, not the act itself. In this case, we can choose to be clinical."

I stare at him open-mouthed before snapping it shut. Typical Gabriel, an answer for everything. His argument has bones... or does it? I can't think straight anymore. All I know is that I appear to have very unprofessional thoughts about Gabriel Frazer.

"Fine. Can you keep it *clinical?*" I ask, my hands move to my hips, my gaze never wavering from his.

"Yes," he says. "Can you?"

"Of course," I say, ignoring the heat radiating from my face. "Fine," I add.

"Fine," he says before adding, "Fine, what?"

"We'll have professional sex, I mean *clinical sex*... in order to make a baby," I say.

I turn and leave his office. I hit the down button on the elevator, but it seems to be that time of day. By the time it finally arrives, Gabriel is by my side.

We step into the crowded elevator. My body has never been more aware of someone than it is right now. Gabriel and I stand shoulder to shoulder as we head down to the basement and climb into his car in silence.

What have I agreed to?

* * *

I STAND UNDER THE SHOWER. Fluttery sensations flood my chest and stomach. I let my hands slide over my body, my nipples harden and my body grows wet at the thought of what's about to happen. My hands clench into fists, and I lean my forehead against the tiled wall. I sigh as I give in and let my fingers wander to the centre of my body. My lips and clit are swollen, and there's an ache deep in my core that begs to be soothed. It's been months since I last had sex, and a woman has needs, or that's what I'm telling myself. House-warming present or not, it's not the same.

I towel off, careful to leave any natural lubricant in place.

I slip on my bra and a long, oversized t-shirt and make my way into my bedroom. The bed covers have already been pulled back, remaining in the same state as the earlier disaster. A knock sounds at the door, and I clear my throat.

"Come in," I say.

Gabriel steps into the room, wearing a t-shirt and gym shorts. His eyes trail over my bare legs, and I swear he draws in a breath.

He makes his way around to the opposite side of the bed before sitting down on the edge.

I sit down and slide my legs under the covers. Turning my gaze away as he removes his lower clothing. This is a *clinical* procedure and, therefore, does not include me ogling his package. However, I am intrigued by what is coming.

Come on, girl.

I need to get my head out of the gutter.

The bed dips as Gabriel swings his body under the covers.

A rush of warmth floods south. My body prepares itself for the onslaught. It hasn't got the message this is not sex. It's... God only knows what this is. Of course, it's sex, just not that kind of sex. I begin counting down from ten to steady my breathing. All Gabriel is going to do is deposit his sperm directly into my vagina rather than use a container and a syringe.

I lean over and open my bedside drawer, handing him the bottle of lube the girls gave me.

A furrow appears between his brows before he appears to get the idea and squirts some onto his hand. I busy myself straightening the sheet above me, not wanting to appear like a pervert, gazing at my boss as he excites—no, prepares himself. Instead, I shimmy out of my panties and throw them out of the side of the bed. I lie back and stare at the ceiling. It's flawless. Perfect. No cracks to divert my attention. I feel Gabriel moving next to me. His hand slides up and down, up and down. I bite my tongue to suppress the moan that threatens to escape.

Green lentils, large bag, two tins of tomatoes—

"Leah." Gabriel's voice breaks into my distraction, and I look sideways to see him staring at me. "You'll need this," he says, handing me the bottle of lube.

No, I really don't, I almost say, but I hold my tongue. How can I tell him I'm melting in a puddle of goo at the thought of what we're about to do? How my body is in natural sexual overdrive? I can feel the wetness coating the inside of my thighs.

I take it and, squirt some onto my fingers, letting my hand slide between my thighs. The sensation of the cool lubricant on my already overheated flesh is almost more than I can take. I bite my bottom lip to stifle the moan that threatens, hoping it looks like I'm concentrating on the task at hand.

"Are you ready?" Gabriel asks quietly, his eyes burning into me.

"Yes," I say.

I lie back against my pillow and open my legs under the covers.

Gabriel moves, climbing over my leg and situating himself between my thighs. His body looms over mine, so close and yet so far, his t-shirt is stretched over his broad chest, his arms firmly on either side of me, as he takes his weight on his forearms. His aftershave... I stop myself from inhaling deeply.

Green lentils, extra large bag, two tins of tomatoes.

I fix my gaze on a point on the ceiling over Gabriel's shoulder until his voice pulls me once again into the present.

"How do you want to do this?" he asks, his voice so close to my face I can feel his breath on my cheek. I allow my eyes to meet his, almost drowning in their dark depths.

Get a grip, Leah!

Something hard and hot hits my thigh. I jump. My forehead clashes with Gabriel's cheek. He snaps his head back.

"Sorry," we both say together, a flush forming on his cheeks.

"It's fine," I say.

Can this get any more awkward?

"Are you directing, or shall I?" Gabriel asks, moving back over me.

What?

Gabriel must sense my confusion. He cocks an eyebrow. "I could simply stab around in the dark down here, or one of us could guide the other," he says.

I bite the inside of my cheek to prevent the hysterical laughter that's threatening to bubble up.

Come on Leah, you're a mature woman.

"Ah," I say, trying to sound sensible. "Stabbing around is probably not the best idea," I add.

"It may be easier if you direct," he says. He takes my hand and encircles his very hard, very swollen cock with my hand.

Oh, boy! His breath falters, and my heart stalls as my fingers grip him.

Wow, who knew?

His cock jerks. It's hot, smooth skin, not to mention his size. My mouth waters. Gabriel is huge! I tamp down on my desire to explore. Oh boy, whose idea was clinical? Is that even possible! Another rush of heat floods my lower body, my muscles tighten in anticipation of what's to come.

I look up and lock eyes with Gabriel's. His eyes have darkened at my touch, his pupils dilating. I could drown in those pools. I'm just glad he's not a mind reader.

"Okay," I say, "Let's do this." I wiggle my bottom forward, lining him up with my entrance. He continues to hold himself on his forearms, his muscles tense.

My entrance aches. I know my body is more than prepared to accept him. I can feel the moisture running between my ass cheeks. Is he going to know? Too late now.

I stretch my legs wider as Gabriel settles in and presses forward. I bite my lip as the tip of him breaches my entrance.

Green lentils, an enormous bag. Two large tins of tomatoes. A ginormous bottle of wine.

My internal walls clench involuntarily at the invasion, and Gabriel lets out a moan.

"Sorry," I whisper.

"Don't be," he says, pressing forward. My body stretches around his as he sinks further in. His arm muscles quiver. I hold my breath, not daring to move.

"Relax," he says through gritted teeth. "You're really tight."

I concentrate on releasing my muscles and spread my legs further. Gabriel thrusts forward until he's fully seated, his balls against my ass. He resettles his position, the muscles in his arms cord. Our bodies are now joined. Mine is fuller than it has ever been before.

We both freeze, our breathing ragged.

"Are you okay?" he asks, his eyes locking on mine.

I vigorously bob my head. I want to say better than okay. The stretch of my body, the feel of him pressed against incredibly sensitive places, but that's not why we're here. This is clinical sex.

Focus, Leah. Be professional.

Can he see how amazing this feels? Another rush of moisture as my walls contract around him. They say the eyes are the window to the soul. Mine are having a party.

"It's good. Sorry, I'm good," I say before moving my hips, wanting more of the pressure of his cock pressed against that tender spot on my inside walls. I suck in a breath as it finds its mark.

"Is it okay to move?" Gabriel's voice comes out strained.

I stare up at him. "Most definitely," I say, sucking in a breath as he does exactly that.

"Green lentils, large bag—"

"What?"

It's then I realise Gabriel has stopped and is staring down at me.

"You said green lentils. Leah. Are you sure everything's okay?" Concern crosses his face. "I can stop."

Oh no, did I actually say that out loud?

"Everything is fine. I was trying to distract myself." I say.

"Distract yourself?" Gabriel doesn't wait for my reply. Instead, he pulls out of me and rolls onto his back. His arm covers his eyes.

I miss his body already. What the hell just happened?

"What? Why?" I roll onto my side to face him.

Gabriel sits up, and swings his legs over the side of the

bed. "Look, Leah, we can wait. I don't want you doing something you're uncomfortable with. You should have just said." I watch in horror as he reaches down and grabs his shorts from the floor.

"What? No? Oh, shit," I say.

Gabriel turns to face me. "Did you just say shit?" he asks.

"I did," I say sheepishly.

His expression softens. "Look, we don't need to do this. I shouldn't have suggested it."

"You've got it all wrong," I say, realising I've hurt him.

"I don't think I have. Leah. You were reciting a shopping list with my cock buried balls deep in your pussy."

I reach up, placing a finger over his lips. "Nothing was wrong. I promise." Could this get any more embarrassing? "I was reciting a recipe—"

"And that's supposed to make me feel better?" he raises a brow, and I smile.

"No, but it's the reason why," I say. I drop my gaze. "This is embarrassing."

"Leah, either spit it out, or I'm going to leave. We can wait until next month. Go to a clinic."

"Fine," I say, knowing I sound a little huffy. "It felt good. Not just good—amazing. In fact. I was distracting myself, so I didn't."

"Didn't what?"

"Are we really going there?" I ask.

"If we're doing this, then yes. We are going to be completely honest with one another. I'm not going to force myself on you. I'm your boss, for goodness sake."

"And there lies the problem," I say, my temper rising. "How can you say you forced yourself onto me? I was directing proceedings."

"What do you mean?"

I throw myself back onto the pillow and cover my eyes. I

sense Gabriel move and know he's spun himself around to face me.

"Ahhh," I yell. "Fine. If you want to know, it felt good, very good. I was trying to trick my brain into not enjoying it." I open my eyes and face him. "Happy now? I was *trying* to remain professional, damn it, clinical."

He looks confused. "What's wrong with you enjoying it?"

I sigh. "Nothing. Except you're my boss, and tomorrow morning, I'll be in a meeting with you, thinking about how it felt to have you slide in and out of me. How my body—" I stop when I notice his eyes darken. "That's not what this is supposed to be. This is not what we agreed."

"So, it's wrong if we enjoy the sex?" he asks. "Just so I understand? Because I hate to point it out, but in order to give you what you want, I have to enjoy this. Have to orgasm. Is it wrong if you do too?"

Damn Gabriel and his logic. "It complicates things," I know my argument is weak.

"Let me get this straight, it's okay for me to enjoy making our child, but you, who will house it for the next nine months. You're not allowed to enjoy their conception?"

I smack my head back against the pillow. "When you put it like that, it sounds ridiculous," I admit. "But it's not what we discussed."

"Can I say something?"

I turn my head to look at him. "Knowing it felt good makes me feel better. We both want this. You need to stop worrying and overthinking."

"But."

"There are no buts, Leah." Gabriel runs a hand through his hair. "Do you think I won't be thinking about my sperm in your body when you're walking around the office tomorrow? How it's going to drip out of you. How do you think I felt earlier when I handed you the container? I was thinking about how you were going to push it into you, and fill yourself up with my cum."

I moan at his words.

Gabriel reaches over and runs a hand down my cheek. I cover it with one of my own and squeeze. Inhaling deeply, I lock my eyes with his. "Let's do this, properly this time."

"No more green lentils?" he asks.

"No more green lentils," I promise.

"Are you going to allow yourself to enjoy this?"

I bite my lip, and nod.

"Good," he says, moving back onto the bed.

He goes to kiss me, but I block him, covering his mouth with my hand. He places a kiss on my palm and nods in understanding, as he buries his head in my neck, sucking on the sensitive skin beneath my ear. My body presses up and into his, wanting no, needing the connection.

His fingers trail down my body and between my legs, finding my swollen and dripping centre.

He drags his finger through my need and encircles my clit. "This is what I want," he says. I throw back my head and gasp.

"Relax, Leah. There's no guilt. It's only this moment. Only pleasure."

I listen to him, his voice hypnotising. I spread my legs wider, my opening throbs and contracts.

"Ahhh, I want—"

Gabriel moves a finger to my entrance, he circles it, tormenting me until I'm writhing under him. He presses in, my muscles clench hard around him, my back arching off the bed.

"More," I say, my hand snakes lower, searching out the part of him I want to fill me.

My fingers lock around him, and I'm not disappointed. His cock is hard and straining.

He moves back between my legs. I align him with my core, and he presses forward, his swollen head breaching my entrance. We both moan, and I bite down on his shoulder, as my hands move to his back. Gabriel slides a hand under my ass, scooping me towards him as he thrusts forward. My body stretches to accommodate his size and we both groan.

Planting his palm into the mattress he holds his upper body away from mine, before looking down into my face. His cheeks are flushed his eyes scanning.

"How does that feel?" he asks

"Oh, so good." I moan as he grins and twists his hips, rubbing against sensitive places I never dreamed existed.

"No more green lentils?" he asks, resting his forehead against mine.

"No more gree—" he moves, and I lose all rational thought, his pubic bone rubbing against my swollen clit, while his cock torments my G-spot from the inside.

I wrap my legs around his hips, drawing him closer. My fingers dig into the hard muscles of his back. I pull him down and my lips lock onto his neck, nibbling and sucking. His grip on my ass intensifies as his movements increase. Our moans and ragged breathing, the slap of our bodies together, echo around the room.

A familiar pressure grows inside me. "Oh, I'm close," I cry out, unable to stop myself. I'm past caring if this is right or wrong. Clinical be damned. He's right, why shouldn't I enjoy this?

Gabriel moves one of his hands between us, his finger flicks against my clit.

Stars explode behind my eyes and my body shatters. I scream at the intensity.

"That's it." His voice is strained, his breath coming in short sharp bursts as his cock continues its onslaught.

I raise my hand and grip his shoulder as my orgasm

continues to ripple through me, my body convulsing around his, loving the fullness his body offers.

He lets out a grunt and freezes. His body pulses deep within mine. I grip his ass and hold him close as my muscles contract around him, milking him of his cum.

We lie panting, Gabriel's head buried in my neck. He drops a kiss on my skin before gingerly pulling out and reaching above him. He grabs the spare pillow and taps my hip, motioning for me to raise my ass.

"Gravity," he says. "Not sure if it's an old wives' tale or whether it works, but no harm in trying."

I settle my hips onto the pillow, feeling the combination of our bodily fluids on my thighs. I don't think I've ever felt this satisfied. Gabriel pulls the sheet up and over me before dropping onto his back, his arm covering his eyes as he gets his breathing under control. I lie still, staring once again at the perfect ceiling, unable to believe this man just gave me one of the strongest orgasms of my life.

Gabriel moves next to me, standing up before pulling on his shorts, his back towards me. He makes his way to the door.

A chill hits me. I bite my lip against the rush of emotions that almost overwhelm me, blinking away the tears that threaten me. Damn, this is why this wasn't a good idea. One mind-shattering orgasm and I'm turning into a mindless wreck over my boss.

Gabriel pauses, his hand on the doorknob, and I think he's going to say something, but instead, he opens the door and leaves.

I stare up at the ceiling and blink rapidly. What the hell just happened? We seem to have gone from zero to one hundred to minus ten in the space of thirty minutes. Did my having an orgasm freak him out? If it did, there's nothing I can do, and I will not apologise for enjoying myself. Not when he told me to. I've missed sex more than I realised.

A knock sounds at the door, and I rub my eyes in a frenzy. Damn!

"Come in." I pull the sheet a little higher up my body.

Gabriel appears carrying two mugs of steaming tea.

"I thought you might like a drink," he says, placing one of the mugs down next to me.

"Thanks." My throat tightens at his thoughtfulness.

"I can leave you alone," he says, moving back towards the door.

"Or you can stay and keep me company," I say, propping myself up on my elbows but ensuring my hips stay elevated.

Gabriel nods and makes his way back around to the place he just vacated, sitting back on the bed, his back against the headboard.

The next words out of his mouth surprise me.

"What happens next?"

My body shivers with pleasure. Well, I know what I'd like to happen next.

CHAPTER 27

GABRIEL

I rest my elbows on the arms of the chair, my fingers steepled against my chin. I stare out the door onto the office floor and watch those I work alongside, on their screens, telephones or having conversations with one another.

Since uncovering Leah's secret, I've been trying to build a rapport with my employees.

A knock sounds.

"Gabriel, are you coming to pizza night?" Tony, one of my managers, pops his head in.

"I am."

"Great." He disappears.

Leah has organised team lunches and evenings out as I try to engage more with the teams. Not that I didn't before, but this is different somehow.

"Morning, Gabriel. Can I get you a coffee?"

Leah laughed the first time it happened.

"You're creating a community. The staff room no longer goes silent when you enter. Have you noticed?"

I have, and now I'm being asked how my weekend was,

not just my thoughts on the latest market trends. Apparently, my engagement is good for staff morale.

I started Frazer Investment as a boutique hedge fund. We've grown from twenty-two to over one hundred and fifty employees in eight years. But as Leah pointed out, one evening, over dinner. I've left her and Amanda to deal with the staff while I've been caught up in growing the business. I'm not blind to the fact that the professional environment and our success have attracted men like Callahan and his millions to my firm.

Leah has and continues to have an immense impact on this company and on me.

A bunch of flowers walks past my eye line, making its way across the office floor. I jump up. What the hell is he doing here?

I watch the sneaky rat enter Leah's office.

Before I can stop myself, I'm across the room. Fortunately, those around me are paying little or no attention. To them, my presence is normal.

Leah's door is closed when I arrive, so I knock and enter, not waiting to be invited in.

Leah is standing by her desk, her hip resting against it, holding the largest bunch of flowers I've ever seen.

"Gabriel," my brother's voice chips in, breaking my stare.

"Caleb," I say shortly. "Why are you here disturbing my staff?"

I know I sound petty and childish, but I can't help it. Not after the other night. I know Leah said there is nothing between her and Caleb.

"Caleb brought me some flowers," Leah says, placing them down on her desk. She tilts her head.

I turn to my brother, who is sprawled in a chair opposite. "Why are you buying my girl—Leah flowers?"

Leah's eyes flit to the door at my near slip-up. I promised

we would keep our personal life out of the office. Only my family need to think we're in a relationship.

"Because I'm a sap," he says, winking at Leah. He laughs when I let out a growl. "Seriously? Okay." He holds up his hands in surrender. "A group of children were selling them for charity outside. I couldn't simply walk past. What woman doesn't like flowers?" Mr Smooth says. "I was on my way here, so I bought two bunches. One for Amanda and one for Leah."

I turn around to see Amanda returning to her desk, sporting an enormous grin. An identical bunch of flowers are in her hands. Only hers are now in a vase. My hands unfurl, and I refrain from grabbing my twin by the collar and yanking him out of the office. That's not who I am, and since when have his actions bothered me? It's not the first time he's bought Leah or Amanda flowers. That's part of his persona.

I turn on my heels and head to the door. "Stop distracting my staff members."

I know I sound petty. Leah's rigid posture and pinched expression reveal her true feelings. I pause at the door, unable to help myself. "You wanted me to remind you to pick up a large bag of green lentils," I say, enjoying the flush that spreads up her neck.

"Thank you," she splutters.

"Lentils?" Caleb asks, sounding baffled.

"Yes. I make a killer lentil bolognese," Leah says, recovering quickly, her attention returning to my brother, but there is a slight tilt to her lips.

I must admit, I'm impressed, if not a little annoyed. But with no further reason to stay, I leave my brother and my communications officer alone.

I enter my office and drop myself onto my chair, running a hand down my face. What the hell? I'm not the person who storms into someone else's office and interferes in their meetings. Regardless of the meeting's lack of authenticity.

"Hey, what was that about?" Caleb says, coming uninvited into my office and dropping into the chair opposite my desk.

"Nothing," I say, leaning forward and pretending to study something on my screen.

"Horse shit, brother. What's going on?" Caleb says, leaning forward. He's always been good at reading me. Whether it's the fact we shared a womb for nine months, who knows?

"Nothing," I say, looking up. "I just don't want you harassing Leah. She's been through a lot lately," I add, knowing my excuse sounds weak even to myself.

"Are you jealous? Because you know, I'd never go there. I know you and Leah are together." He sighs and runs a hand through his hair. "Maybe flowers weren't the best option. I'm sorry. The kids wouldn't simply take a donation. They wanted me to take the flowers. I should have thought." He's genuine in his statement, and I feel like a heel for making a big deal out of the flowers. He's correct. It's a kind gesture and is very much in Caleb's nature. At least with the women, he's not in a romantic relationship with. My brother's a player. However, he's also one of the most thoughtful people I know when it comes to thinking of others. He's a mixed-up contradiction. This is why, even with his playboy image, he has women falling over themselves to be with him.

"Sorry, it's been a long week," I say, dropping back against the chair. "What are you doing in this part of town?"

Caleb runs a hand down his face. "Can't I pop in and see my brother?"

I raise an eyebrow, and he grins.

"I had a meeting. It finished early, and I wondered if you fancied grabbing lunch?"

I look up at the clocks adorning my wall. Where has the

morning gone? My preoccupation with Leah making me completely oblivious to the fact that it's already lunchtime.

"Sure," I say, getting up. Lunch is easier than evening drinks and busy bars.

"Really?" Caleb grins at me and stands. "Wow, I can't believe you've agreed to have lunch with me without me resorting to blackmail. Who are you? What have you done with my brother? Leah is clearly having an effect on you."

"Ha Ha," I say, glad the office door is closed. "Don't push it. I can still sit down and order takeout."

Caleb pulls a face. "You work too hard."

"I would say you don't work hard enough, but I know that's a lie," I say, grabbing my jacket and following him to the door.

"I know how to work and play," he says, grinning at me.

"As long as you keep your playing out of my office," I warn, my gaze shooting to Leah's office door.

"You *really* like her," Caleb says, catching my attention.

I ignore him. I refuse to discuss Leah and me with him.

"Ignoring me. That has to be a *good* sign." He chuckles.

"Shhh," I hiss. "I promised no one in the office would know until she's ready."

"So, when do I get to meet this new woman of yours?" He exclaims loudly, just as the lift door closes, before gripping my shoulder and squeezing.

I glare at him, making him smirk.

Caleb lets out a belly laugh. "You know you two aren't going to be able to keep your relationship a secret for long. Mother's party is coming up."

I groan and shake my head.

"At least this year, you'll have someone to keep all those social climbing piranhas at bay."

My brother is finding this far too amusing.

"Why me? Why not you? I understand Harper is too

young, Elijah is married, and Kat, well, she's female and in a long-term relationship."

"That probably wouldn't deter some of them." Caleb laughs. "However, I'm the bad boy. My reputation proceeds me. While you're the moody, quiet, incredibly successful, dashingly good-looking, identical twin of said *bad boy*." The elevator opens into reception, and we step out. "I take it you've seen Harper's latest endeavours," he mutters as we step out onto the busy street.

"Mother's about to burst a blood vessel."

I nod. I've seen the newspapers. She calls herself an *influencer*, but our youngest sister also enjoys getting her name splashed across the headlines with her antics. She's in pain, and I get it, but the current self-destruct button she's hitting is not helping her, only fuelling the fire.

We sigh in unison.

"Have you heard from Kat?" Caleb asks suddenly as we arrive at the restaurant.

"No," I say, realising it's been a while since Kat and I last spoke.

* * *

LUNCH IS NOT AS arduous as I feared. We find a quiet table and discuss both his work and mine. He fills me in on the latest project he's looking to undertake, a redevelopment of one of the city's poorer areas, filled predominately with old warehouses and empty shops. Caleb, for all my ribbing, is a shrewd business mind and one of the few people I trust with my money other than myself.

"So, how's it going with Leah?" he asks

"Why all this sudden interest in Leah and me?" I ask, taking another mouthful of food to stop myself saying something I shouldn't.

He quirks a brow in my direction. "I don't know. The fact you haven't dated in, let's say, forever, and now you're in a relationship with someone from the office, something you swore you'd never do. Why the hell is she wearing an elastic band around her wrist instead of the silver bracelet she always wore? I asked if that bastard of an ex took that back too. I can't believe what a jackass that guy turned out to be."

I smart at the level of annoyance my brother has on Leah's behalf. I've observed her missing bracelet but didn't think it was appropriate to inquire. People often use elastic bands to lessen their anxiety levels. Caleb doesn't have the same level of boundaries. He doesn't answer the question, and I jump in before I can help myself.

"What happened to her bracelet?"

Caleb looks up and frowns. "Oh, apparently, it's in her drawer. It was a present from him. She doesn't want any reminders. Not surprising. She said she just needs to get around to buying herself a replacement but hasn't with everything that's gone on."

I remind myself to make sure a replacement is arranged.

We finish lunch, and I head back to the office. Lighter in step and in mind. I drop into my chair and pull up the St Clare website.

CHAPTER 28

LEAH

I stare at the package in front of me. The concierge gave it to me when I arrived home. Apparently, someone has delivered it with my name on it. The vibrant green of the bag lets me know where it has come from. St Clare's is one of the most exclusive brands, alongside Gucci and Chanel. The question is, who and why?

Caleb better not be the culprit, as that would create problems, especially given Gabriel's intrusive entrance into my office when he visited earlier. My stomach knots. What was Gabriel playing at? It's not like Caleb doesn't know about us. Then again, what was Caleb thinking?

To prevent any misunderstandings, I left Caleb's flowers at work in a vase, not feeling it appropriate to bring them home. My office smelled lovely. The gesture showed kindness and thoughtfulness. I stare at the bag and bite my lip.

I busy myself making dinner, my eyes drifting to the little green bag. It's addressed to me. The gift card is very clear. Well, I'll not get any answers staring at the bag. If it is Caleb, I'll put it in my drawer and wait until he visits the office next. I'll thank him, but tell him I can't accept it.

It's been somewhat awkward between Gabriel and me since our sexual encounter a few days ago. We've both walked around on eggshells, not sure how we're supposed to act, or at least I have. He's been Gabriel and disappeared into his man cave.

The whole thing is a little embarrassing, and I'm not sure how to broach it with him. It was as far removed from the disconnected, clinical act we discussed. Who knew the man I worked with all these years has such impressive moves and a physique reminiscent of a Greek god. Mythology tells us that Greek gods possessed irresistible charm and were rumoured to have numerous offspring. I can only hope and pray.

I finish dinner, a vegetable bake, placing it in the oven. Gabriel will be home soon. Otherwise, he can have it when he gets in. He told me he had work to finish up, and then he'd be going for a swim.

Avoidance? Probably.

I drop onto one of the island stools and pull the parcel towards me. I've missed my jewellery, but it seems wrong to wear something Vince bought me, especially after everything. The memory of them has forever been tarnished.

I breathe a sigh of relief as I open the gift card.

Leah

Caleb mentioned your bracelet. I took the liberty of buying you a replacement.

Gabriel.

I STARE AT THE NOTE, reading it repeatedly, unable to keep the smile from my lips. Only Gabriel, so matter of fact. Giving Caleb the credit, when I saw his eyes wandering to the elastic bands I've been wearing around my wrist, I half expected him to say something, but he never has. I reach into the bag and pull out the vibrant box, sliding the lid off. I gasp at the beautiful bracelet with its intricate links, I run my finger over it. Who would have thought Gabriel would have such exquisite taste in jewellery, or did Caleb help to choose? I don't care. It comes from Gabriel.

I slip the bracelet onto my wrist, twisting it around.

The oven dings.

I serve myself a plate as Gabriel is still not home. This is the first time we haven't eaten together in over a week, and I find I miss him.

Gabriel wanders in, just as I'm finishing up.

"Hey," I say. "Are you ready for dinner?"

His hair is still wet from the swimming pool, messy where he's run his fingers through it.

"I'll just grab a shower," he says. I know Gabriel prefers to shower when he gets home, even though there are showers by the pool. He'll usually rinse but then come upstairs.

He disappears without looking at me, and my heart sinks. Is he still annoyed about Caleb? I don't have any control over his brother's actions, but then again, he bought me this beautiful bracelet. Does he regret what we did? Is he now finding it awkward? Was his mention of *green lentils* his way of telling me he was finding it strange? I sigh. There's no closing the gate now the horse has bolted. We will just have to find our new norm. He's the one who told me professionalism is a mindset.

Gabriel returns in record time and picks up the plate I've dished out.

"Thanks," he says, making his way to the table.

"You're welcome, and thank you for the bracelet."

Gabriel pauses for a split second before lowering his plate to the table.

"No problem. I hope you like it," he says, still not looking at me.

"It's beautiful," I say, the fingers of my opposite hand touching it. "You have great taste."

Gabriel says nothing. He just continues to eat his food.

"Okay then," I say after a while. "I'll finish clearing up and disappear," I say the last part, almost to myself.

There's a clatter as Gabriel drops his cutlery onto his plate.

"Leah."

I stop and turn to face him.

"I'm sorry. It's just today..."

I see the confusion and angst on his face and make my way towards him, pulling out a chair and sitting in my usual spot.

"Talk to me," I say. "Do you regret it?" The words catch in my throat.

I jump when Gabriel's hand clasps mine, and he squeezes. "Hell no," he says, and my shoulders sag in relief. "Quite the opposite."

"Then what?"

He lets out a dry laugh and pats my hand, adding to my confusion.

"You told me why you were afraid to let yourself go." His eyes lock with mine. "All I can think about is you."

My cheeks flare at his words, my body clenching in anticipation.

"When Caleb turned up. I didn't react very well. I realised it should have been me buying you flowers, not my bloody twin."

I flip my hand, and interlink our fingers, as relief floods

my system. A small moan escapes my lips when his thumb rubs circles on my palm.

I look up to find Gabriel staring at me, his pupils dilated. There's no question about his lack of regret. My body grows hot and feverish under his gaze until I'm squirming in my seat.

Gabriel rises, coaxing me to my feet, kicking my chair out of the way. He manoeuvres me backwards until my ass hits the side of the glass table.

"It says you should have sex several times during your ovulation period." Gabriel's voice is huskier than I've ever heard it, his body looming over mine.

"I know." My voice is breathless. I stare at his shoulder as a rush of warmth floods my core. Oh yes, please, my mind screams, but I bite my lip.

Gabriel uses his thumb to pull it from between my teeth.

"What do you think?" Gabriel asks.

Unable to find the correct words, I nod, which appears to be all the encouragement he needs. Gabriel scoops me up and deposits me on the table. The chill of the glass is like dynamite against my heated pussy.

He lifts my skirt and pulls down my panties, exposing me to the air and his gaze. A flush spreads over his cheeks as he looks at me with dark eyes.

"Beautiful," he says.

I'm at a loss whether he's talking about me or my neatly presented pussy.

His thumb sinks into my body, before drawing my desire up to my clit. He teases and torments me before moving it around and circling the lips of my sex. I shudder at the sensation, biting down once again on my bottom lip to stop myself from crying out. I let my head rest against the table, the soles of my feet perch on the edge, my knees wide as Gabriel sets to work preparing my body.

My back arches off the table when he inserts first one, then a second finger, twisting and curling, stretching my opening. When he adds a third, I almost rocket off the table, the sensation of fullness almost too much.

I let loose a moan. "Gabriel, please." I pant.

His eyes gleam. He's enjoying the control he has over my body.

"I must make sure you're completely ready," he says, curling his fingers up against my G-spot. "I don't want to hurt you."

"I'm ready... I'm ready. I promise," I hear myself pant.

"I'll be the judge of that," he says, continuing his torment.

An orgasm wracks through me, my body shudders as it clenches hard around his fingers. Gabriel grunts, a small smirk appearing at the corner of his mouth. I know I've made a mess of the glass beneath me.

"Now," I hear Gabriel's zipper as he steps between my thighs. My body is tight from my orgasm as he eases the tip of his cock in. I clench around him.

"That's it, let me in," he says as I squirm restlessly, his fingers curling into my hips as he holds me in place.

"Ahhh," is all I manage as he breaches my entrance, my greedy body stretching, swallowing him whole.

"Amazing," he mutters before sliding back out. I whimper as he withdraws his cock, rubbing it over my swollen mound, teasing and moistening my clit with my juices and his pre-cum.

Who would have thought?

All rational thought disappears as he slams back into me. My legs wrap around his waist, and I give myself over to the pleasure of him filling my body. I don't think I've ever been this turned on. I clutch his forearms, the forbidden is more than a little enticing.

Gabriel's dark eyes hold mine as he continues to move in

and out, his body going deeper and deeper with every thrust. His cock hardens, filling me more. He pulls out slowly before pushing back in hard and fast. I scream, coming hard, my muscles convulsing, bearing down on him. He thrusts home one more time, letting out a roar. His cock jerks, and his body shudders. A flood of warmth, fills my pussy, letting me know he's once again filled me with his sperm. He drops his head onto my chest, breathing hard. I sink my fingers into his hair, massaging his scalp as we lie still joined.

As he softens, he pulls out and steps back.

"Oh dear," he says, running a finger over my still throbbing slit. I moan as he pushes his finger and the escaping liquid back into my body. "We don't want to waste any," he says.

"Oh, my." Is all I manage. My body is almost too sensitive after riding two consecutive orgasms.

"Relax," Gabriel says, slowing his pace, and resting a warm hand over my lower stomach. "One more. Draw all those little swimmers up into your womb."

His words act as an aphrodisiac, and I know he's about to do what no man has ever done before.

"Gabriel," my words are breathless. "I can't." I all but whimper.

"You can. That's it, relax and enjoy. Give your body what it wants," he whispers.

His gaze locks on my pussy as his fingers slide slowly in and out, his thumb working my clit.

I gasp in surprise as the pressure builds once more. This man is going to ruin me for all others at this rate. Professional, clinical. Clinical be damned. I give myself over to him, as my pussy clamps once more around his fingers.

"Perfect," he says, grunting in satisfaction. "Lie still." He pulls my skirt down over my exposed body, moving the chair to rest my feet on the arms before leaving the room. I lie staring at the ceiling, my brain incapable of rational thought, only the fact my boss of eight years has just had me screaming his apartment down, spread out on his dining room table. This time, I don't think green lentils and tins of tomato are going to cut it.

Gabriel returns with another clean facecloth. I reach out to take it from him, but he taps my hand before stepping up to the table and flipping my skirt up. The air of the apartment is cool against my hot, damp core.

"Let me clean up the mess I made," Gabriel says, his attention set on wiping me down gently. My swollen flesh is over-stimulated and sensitive. When he's finished, he throws the cloth to one side before picking up my panties and sliding them back up my legs, making me lift my bottom so he can slide them into place. Before I can sit up, he scoops me up in his arms, carrying me over to the sofa, where he lies me down.

"Movie?" he asks, when I remain silent, my brain unable to form a sentence.

"Great," I croak out.

"I'll make some popcorn."

I watch Gabriel disappear and hear him moving around in the kitchen. I realise he's clearing up dinner. The microwave pings, the smell of buttered popcorn invades my senses. He returns to the sofa, taking a seat at the other end, switching on a movie before pulling my feet into his lap. I lie back as he expertly massages my feet. I bite down on the moan that wants to escape. This man needs to package his hands. My eyes catch on the bracelet he gave me, realising that my ovulation period ends tomorrow. Why does my heart feel heavy at the prospect?

CHAPTER 29

GABRIEL

*T*his time, when Leah's period arrives, I'm not sure how to feel. I can see the devastation in her face, and my heart clenches at her pain.

"Maybe there's a problem," she says over dinner one evening.

"It's still early days," I say, trying to put her mind at rest. "But if you want, I can arrange for you to see someone. Get checked out." I had my sperm count checked before I offered to be her sperm donor.

"Maybe," she says, her hands clasped in her lap.

I place a hand over hers and squeeze. "I'm sure everything's fine. It's not an exact science what we're doing."

In my opinion, the chances of that working are low. She's only utilised an ovulation kit and a thermometer before exposing herself to four samples of sperm. Or maybe that's just wishful thinking on my part. I still can't get the feeling of Leah coming around my cock out of my head, her vice-like grip milking my dick.

I shift uncomfortably in my seat.

"I know," she sighs. "Shall I order some more kits?" Her question surprises me.

My muscles tense.

"Is that what you want?" I ask. My dick protests at the thought.

Colour drifts up Leah's neck. "No," she says, her eyes on mine.

"Clinical sex it is then," I say, a happy dance being done below my waist.

Leah's colour deepens. She opens and then re-closes her mouth as if wanting to say something but holding back.

"Leah, whatever it is you want to say, just say it. I think we're past polite talk."

Her hand goes to the bracelet I bought her, running it through her fingers. "I was... I was thinking." She bites her lip, drawing my gaze to its fullness.

"Leah," I warn.

"I was wondering if we should have more sex. Whether twice a month isn't enough," she says in a rush of words. "I was reading."

I grasp her hand in mine and softly squeeze, stopping her tirade in its tracks.

"It's fine, I was thinking the same thing. But it needs to be your decision."

Her shoulders relax, and she turns her hand over in mine. Interlinking our fingers. I glance down and a warmth spreads through my chest at the sight.

"That's settled," I say.

Leah nods, her eyes shining.

My fingers ache with the need to touch her. I withdraw my hand and get up, needing to put some space between us. If not, period or not, I'm going to be bending Leah over the sofa and sinking into her silky depths. Not what I think she's expecting.

"I have some work to do in my office," I say more sharply than I intend.

"Okay, I'll see you in the morning."

I move away,

"Gabriel," Leah's voice calls after me. "Can I use your bath?"

I stop in my tracks. Heaven help me. I stay facing away from her. The thought of her naked in my bath is more than my dick can take. It wants her. It doesn't understand it has to wait.

"Of course, help yourself," I say, my voice huskier than I expect.

"Thank you," Leah says.

I make my way to my office and close the door behind me. I drop into my gaming chair and stare at the ceiling, before adjusting my swollen cock to make myself comfortable. I stare at the screens in front of me, unable to concentrate. It's going to be a long night.

I close my eyes and an idea begins to form. Opening them, I pick up the phone, and call the one person I know can help.

"Hey, stranger, it's been a while," A chirpy voice answers almost immediately.

"Pen, I need a favour," I say.

A chuckle comes down the phone. "Always the charmer, Gabriel."

I grunt. "You know me," I say.

"I do. So, what can I do for you? I take it this isn't a social call."

I'm not sure what I'm doing, but I want to do it. "I need another console set up."

"Your current one not good enough?" Comes the sarcastic reply.

"Of course it is. I need another *one* set up."

"Interesting. I only gave you our latest handheld console last month. Wow, has Mr Cool, Calm and Collected finally lost it? Or is there another reason?"

"You've developed a large nose today," I say, only to face laughter at the other end of the phone.

"True, but come on, Gabe, loosen up."

I huff. "Only you get away with talking to me like this," I add.

"But that is because we've known each other for years, and we know each other's secrets. They are a powerful weapon."

I would never expose Pen's secrets any more than she would expose mine. We both like our lives the way they are. The idea of that changing is not one either of us wants.

"Fine," I say. "I want a console bank set up identical to mine. It's for Leah."

"Ah, Leah, your new housemate."

"News travels fast." Unsurprised she knows about Leah. She has her ear to the ground and her fingers in more pies than I can count.

"That would be the one."

"Consider it done. And Gabe, I'm happy for you."

"It's not—"

"Hey, it's me you're talking to remember? It's okay to like her."

"That's not our agreement." I bite my cheek when I realise what I've just said.

There's silence on the other end of the line. "It doesn't have to be all or nothing, my friend."

"Maybe not, but it's how she wants it, and who am I to argue?"

"But you want more?"

"Honestly, I don't know. I'm set in my ways, I prefer solitude, and apparently, I'm terrible at relationships, according to every woman I've ever dated. I'm not prepared to lose her friendship. I refuse to take that risk."

"Have you considered that, until now, you just haven't met the right woman. If you want my advice?"

"Always," I say.

A sad sigh comes down the phone. "Don't overthink it. Go with the flow. Life might surprise you. Remember, *no regrets.*"

"Okay."

"Okay? Are you agreeing with me, Gabriel Frazer? That has to be a first. No, maybe a second. Shit, I've got to go. *His Highness* is on the other line. I'll place the order for what you'll need. Give me a week or two. Things are crazy here, as you'd know if you ever read your damned emails."

"Silent partner," I say.

A laugh comes over the line. "Yeah, until you get a brainwave for a new design or game, then you blow up my machine. Oh the accessibility software you wanted is in beta —so far, so good. Anyway, got to go."

Pen hangs up.

I click on to the gaming server. FosterDiamond18 is on. He's eighteen and colour-blind. We were exchanging chat when he told me how much he struggled with some games. I spoke to Pen, and now... Beta testing... wow... Penelope doesn't hang around.

I pick up my controller and send out greetings.

Time to play and take my mind off Leah stretched out and naked in my bath.

CHAPTER 30

LEAH

The apartment downstairs is complete. The furniture has arrived, and the interior designer has been staging the place, but there's been no talk of me moving out. We've fallen into a comfortable routine. We work, eat, game, exercise. We have kept our private relationship out of the office, and it appears no one suspects, likely because Gabriel and I have always been in close contact daily.

"Pack a bag," Gabriel says the minute I walk through the door.

"What? Gabriel, it's Friday night." I kick off my shoes and place them on the rack in the cupboard near the door.

"It is, and it's coming up to *that* time. I heard your alarm go off. I thought we'd go away for the weekend."

I freeze on the spot. What is Gabriel doing? I must admit, he's been amazing over the past two weeks since my period. He's encouraged me to go to the gym, has kept me company. I admit, I haven't had this much fun with anyone other than the girls in a long time. Looking back, mine and Vince's relationship had gone stale long ago. I'd thrown myself into my work and spent more and more time with the girls. He'd done the same. We'd been stuck in a rut. It's unsurprising that one of us left.

"I don't understand?"

Gabriel looks at me with his usual patient glare. "I've been doing my research. Being in a relaxed environment is more conducive to successful insemination." He starts off with facts and figures, and I suppress the laugh that bubbles up in my chest. This man is a walking fact machine. He does nothing by half. My lower stomach flips, the muscles clenching as I think about what's coming.

"The private jet is waiting. We're spending the weekend in Monaco."

My jaw drops as I stare at the man in front of me. What!? He's taking us to Monaco?

"Leah, stop staring, get your things together. You'll want some shorts and t-shirts, a bikini or a swimming costume. We can eat out, although there is a chef on the yacht."

"Yacht?" My voice comes out slightly higher pitched than I expect, making me cough.

"You know I own a yacht. I prefer to stay there than in a hotel. There's more privacy."

My head bobs up and down as I listen to him, my heart racing. Euphoria fills my body. The girls will never believe this. I'm going to experience life on a yacht for the weekend.

"Go!" Gabriel says, and I turn tail and sprint up the stairs, his laughter following me. It's a sound I'm getting used to.

I enter my bedroom and stop.

"Oh, boy," I say out aloud before clamping my hand over my mouth.

Realisation hits. We're not just going to the yacht. We're going to be doing a lot more than just sightseeing and sunbathing. I close my eyes for a moment, my hand coming up and rubbing the place over my heart as my nerves all start firing at once. Clinical sex. Although I think we've gone way past that after the dining table incident. Making me come three times, no hiding under the covers. Yes, we were clothed, but I was out on display, dripping all over the tabletop.

I give myself a mental shake and look at the clock. Damn, I've been daydreaming for too long. I grab my small case and throw it onto the bed, taking out clothes from my drawers and wardrobe, including the dress and top I ordered from Chloe. I rush into the bathroom and grab my makeup bag and products. Throwing them in alongside the rest of my things.

Gabriel appears at the door.

"You ready?" he says, making me jump.

"All set." I zip up the case before lowering it to the floor.

"Here, let me," he says, taking the handle and wheeling it behind him.

Oh boy, I'm in trouble.

Gabriel calls Caleb's driver to take us to the airport, swearing the man to secrecy. I laugh at the seriousness of the driver's face.

"Of course, Mr Frazer. Mr Caleb is also away for the weekend. Not a word," he says as we get out of the car.

"Thank you, Mason," Gabriel says, surprising me by shaking his hand.

The other man grins at him. "Have a lovely weekend. I'll pick you up on Sunday evening."

Gabriel takes my hand and leads me across the tarmac. A beautiful woman in a uniform greets us at the plane's entrance.

"Welcome aboard, Mr Frazer, Ms Walker," she says, offering us a warm and generous smile. We follow her into the body of the plane. The seats are enormous, more like armchairs. The leather upholstery gleams under the cabin lights.

"Where would you like to sit?" Gabriel says, snapping me out of my daze.

"I don't mind," I say. "Where do you prefer?"

He motions to the twin seats on the left of the plane. A large, shiny black table in front of them. "This way, we can eat supper while we're in the air," he says.

I nod, stepping into the seat and moving across to the window seat. I know I shouldn't feel disappointed when Gabriel sits in the seat opposite me rather than next to me.

"Is there anything I can get you?"

"A glass of whiskey for me... Leah?"

My head snaps up. "Er, sorry"

Gabriel chuckles, and the woman standing next to him jumps at the sound.

"What would you like to drink?" he asks, his eyes twinkling. "Champagne?"

"That would be lovely," I say to our stewardess.

"I'll be right back."

"Thank you, Claudia," Gabriel says, his eyes never leaving mine. "Are you warm enough?"

"I'm fine. A little overwhelmed being taken away for the weekend. All this." I move my hand to take in the entire plane. "Not my usual hangout for a Friday night."

"I suppose not. But the plane... we've always had a private plane in the family. Dad, travelled a lot with business. My sister Kat does too. It makes more efficient use of our time. We arrive and take-off as we need to."

I can see the logic in what he's saying. It's just a world away from the life I've lived. Vince and I used to travel business class. Our dual income and no kids meant we could choose how we spent our money, and we had some amazing trips.

"Well, I'm going to sit back and enjoy every moment," I say.

Claudia takes that moment to return with our drinks. Placing them down in front of us.

"Thank you," I say.

"You're very welcome. I'll serve dinner once we're in the air. Until then, if you need anything, please press the buzzer, and I'll return."

With that, she turns and leaves.

"Wow, how the other half live," I mutter.

"You may as well get used to it. When we have a child, this will be your mode of transport if you wish."

"Your mode of transport," I say.

Do I need to remind him that this isn't my life and never will be? When he meets someone else, they won't want to share the family plane with his baby-mummy.

"Yours too, Leah. I meant what I said. I will support you and our child, children, when we have them."

I cross my arms over my chest and stare at him. "Gabriel, I didn't accept your proposition in order for you to keep me. I'm happy earning my salary."

He humphs and I want to smile, but I know it's not the right time. "I get that. All I'm saying is, what good is my money if I can't make life easier for you?"

I'm not and never have been a gold digger. When I got together with Vince, we were not long out of university. He earned less than I did. The fact that he became a front office trader and a successful one, the money was a bonus, but that was not why I was with him.

"I don't want people thinking I'm only with you for your money,"

The words are out of my mouth before I can stop them.

"No, if memory serves me right, you're after me for my sperm." It's then I realise he's teasing me.

"Ha Ha!" I say. "Okay, we'll park this conversation for now. Let's see what this weekend brings."

My cheeks warm, and I raise my hands to cover them. Aware of Gabriel's intense gaze. Oh boy.

At that moment, the captain's voice comes over the sound system. "Final checks are complete. We will be ready for take-off in five minutes."

Gabriel moves to fasten his seat belt, and I mirror his actions as the plane begins to move. I stare out of the window, glad for the distraction. I pick up my champagne and take a sip. The crisp taste and bubbles tickling my nose.

We sit in silence until the plane levels out, and Claudia returns with our starters.

"I hope you don't mind, I ordered ahead," Gabriel says.

"Of course not," I reply, smiling at Claudia as she places the roasted baby tomato and olive ricotta tarts on the table before us. "Thank you."

The starter is light and delicious. The sweet taste of the baby tomatoes and olives against the ricotta, with the peppery taste of the rocket and balsamic vinegar, is perfection.

Next, comes hot smoked salmon with an orange glaze, served on a bed of mango tapenade. The side dish includes new potatoes and baby vegetables. It's like being in a five-star restaurant.

I almost turn down dessert until Claudia announces it's Eton mess. Not the dessert I would have expected, but one look at Gabriel let me know it was his choice after the conversation we had whilst playing a game of Scrabble.

As the plates are cleared away, I show my appreciation. "Thank you."

"I hope you enjoyed it."

I grin over at Gabriel. "Every minute. It's quite the experience."

The captain announces we'll be landing at Nice International Airport in an hour.

"I have some emails to check. I want to take the weekend off," his voice is apologetic.

"Gabriel, stop. It's okay. Remember, I work for you. I know what your job entails. You do what you need to. I'm happy to sit here and read my book."

He nods and pulls out his laptop, placing it on the table in front of him. I reach into my bag and grab my e-reader. I'm pleased that the book I'm reading is electronic, and Gabriel won't be staring at a semi-naked man on the cover. Vince always complained about the *trashy* romance novels I read. Well, now I'm free to read what I want and where I want.

I jerk awake as I feel a finger run down my cheek. Gabriel has sat himself in the chair next to me. "Wake up, sleepy head, we've landed."

Oh god, my hand flies to my mouth. Have I been snoring, or even worse, drooling?

"It's okay. You only let out a few snorts," Gabriel says, his lips twitching. "It was quite a cute sound."

I slap his arm gently. "Oh, don't," I say. "How embarrassing."

I notice my e-reader is back in my bag. Gabriel must have followed the direction of my eyes.

"It was going to slide under the table, so I rescued it. Interesting literature you're reading, Ms Walker."

Ground swallow me up.

I think back to the part I was reading, my hands flying to my cheeks. "Er, well."

Gabriel tilts his head. "Is that what a woman really wants in the office? To be ravished over a desk?"

I gawp at Gabriel, knowing another rush of colour is flooding my cheeks. It's bad enough he now knows my little secret of loving romance novels, but to have fallen asleep while reading a sex scene and then have him pick it up.

Ground double swallow me up.

Luckily, I'm saved from answering by Claudia's reappearance.

"We're ready to disembark," she says.

Gabriel gets up and holds out his hand. I grab my bag, glaring at my e-reader.

"Have a wonderful weekend," Claudia says.

"Thank you, you too," I say as I pass her.

She grins at me.

CHAPTER 31

GABRIEL

The warm, dry air hits me as we exit the plane, and I pause, letting it wash over me. Even though it's nighttime, summer has unmistakably arrived according to the temperature. She turns to face me, her eyes twinkling with excitement, her face softening as the tension and stress of the working week melt away. I hold out my hand, surprised when she takes it, interlocking our fingers. I enclose her smaller hand in mine, and lead her down the steps towards our waiting car.

The driver steps forward.

"Evening Mr Frazer, Ms Walker. I'm here to transport you to your helicopter," he says, opening the rear door to the car.

Leah pauses, her mouth falling open as she shoots me an incredulous look.

I squeeze her hand before helping her into the car. She looks at me with raised eyebrows as I climb in next to her. I lean in, our heads close together, the jasmine scent of her perfume teasing my senses. I stifle a moan at the memories it invokes, instead whispering in her ear.

"It's getting late. This negates the thirteen mile drive. We should be at the yacht about ten minutes after take-off. You'll get to see Monaco and the French Riviera at night from the air. It's quite something."

A slight flush tints the skin on her face and neck, and I watch her tongue as it darts out, moistening her lower lip. Leah turns her head, our faces centimetres apart. My gaze drops to her mouth.

The driver's door slams, pulling us back into the present. We leap apart, my heart racing.

What the hell just happened?

I lock my jaw. This is not the time or place. This weekend is about Leah, about taking time out and giving her the break I feel she desperately needs. She's asked we remain professional. The past few months has seen our relationship change. We've gone from work colleagues to friends and, more recently, lovers. I'm spending more and more time with her in the apartment. This weekend is a change. No external distractions. It's about creating the child. I turn my head and look out of the window as we travel past the hangers. A child, I find myself wanting more and more.

The car transports us to terminal one, where our helicopter awaits. We're seen onboard, and I hand Leah a headset, motioning for her to put them on over the chopping sound of the blades. She smiles once the sound is muffled, giving me a thumbs up. Her excitement is palpable, although she's trying to hide it.

Her hand slides across the seat, gripping mine, and the action is doing strange things in my chest. The helicopter lifts off, and her grip tightens in mine. My stomach drops as the helicopter tilts and sways.

"Whew," Leah squeals.

I smile when she turns to me, her eyes wide.

"It settles once we're in the air," I say, her eyes widening when she realises we can hear each other through the headsets.

"This is amazing," she says, her eyes going past me to look out of the window at the disappearing ground below.

Once we've cleared the airport, the pilot points out some of the sights of the French Riviera on the way to Monaco. The lights twinkle along the beautiful coastline. I never get tired of this sight, but for some reason, tonight seems special. It's like experiencing it for the first time all over again.

"Gabriel, this is..." Her eyes are wide.

"We're almost there," I say, pointing to the landing site in the distance.

"No rush. This is spectacular." Her voice is breathless.

When we finally land and disembark, Leah is bursting with excitement.

She grabs both my hands in hers. "Thank you," she says before going up onto her tip toes and dropping a kiss on my cheek. "Thank you."

I tilt my head, and she smiles. "For the memories. Nothing will ever take these memories away. It's amazing."

Her pleasure is humbling. What I take for granted. Leah is so different from the other women I've had in my life. My fiancée, Rachel, expected this, while the other women took what they wanted. Our relationships were little more than friends with mutual benefits. A give and take. With Leah, however, I'm finding that I want to give her the world. Show her the world. I know she and Vince travelled, but she's open to new adventures.

I shake myself.

"Come on, let's get to the yacht."

A transfer car is waiting for us.

When the driver closes the door, she turns to face me. My hand touches her cheek. "I'm glad you're enjoying yourself. This weekend is all about rest and relaxation."

A flash of colour floods her cheeks, and her pupils dilate. My thumb grazes her bottom lip before I can stop it. "Among other things," I say before dropping my hand.

We both know the reason I brought her here.

The warmth that spreads through my chest is unexpected, so I push it to one side as the driver pulls out.

* * *

THE LIGHTS of the marina dance over the water, welcoming us. The driver opens the door. The captain and one of the crew are waiting, ready to take our bags.

"Evening Mr Frazer, Ms Walker."

"Leah, this is Edward, the Captain of *Francesca's Escape* and Tim," I say, introducing them.

"Pleased to meet you, Ma'am," Edward says. "If you'd care to follow us. Your brother has already arrived, although he and his friends have gone to the casino."

I stop dead in my tracks. "My brother?"

"Mr Caleb arrived this afternoon. I assumed you were expecting him."

"It's fine," I say through gritted teeth.

What the hell is Caleb doing here?

So much for a relaxing weekend with the playboy prince onboard.

The gentle touch of Leah's hand on my arm pulls me back. Her telling smile at my *I'm fine* comment.

"Let's see what he wants."

I huff, only to find myself graced with another one of her stomach-quivering smiles.

CHAPTER 32

LEAH

*T*he view is breathtaking. I've walked past marinas before. Vince and I travelled to some beautiful places, but this is different. I know it shouldn't be, Gabriel is my boss, not my boyfriend, but I can't help it. Deep inside my stomach, anticipation bubbles.

Glancing over at Gabriel, his lips are tight, and have been since the captain announced Caleb is also onboard. I know the yacht belongs to Gabriel, but his family are free to use it. At least I know Caleb. Any of his other family members and it may have been an awkward introduction.

We follow Edward down a concrete sidewalk that runs alongside the waterway. Tim has taken our bags and gone ahead. I stop and take in the sights.

"This is something else," I say, my voice breathless.

Gabriel squeezes my hand in response.

Boats of all shapes and sizes line up along the piers and wooden docks that stretch out onto the water. Tethered by ropes to the pier cleats, the slapping of the water against the hulls, a soothing sound in the maze of boats. Lights, music, and laughter fill the air, drowning out the underlying clinking and wind whistles through the aluminium masts.

We reach our destination. When Gabriel said *yacht*, he meant it. It's at least fifty metres.

"Welcome to Francesca's Escape," Gabriel says. "My escape."

I turn to face him, "Gabriel, this is..."

His lips twitch, and his eyes sparkle. "Do you think you can have a relaxing weekend here?" he asks.

I tilt my head and tap a finger on my lips as if contemplating his question. "I'll try," I say before letting Gabriel lead me up the gang plank onto the yacht.

Tim and our bags are nowhere in sight.

Gabriel leads us past a pool and seating, into the main body of the yacht, and then into the upstairs central stateroom. This is luxury at its finest. Sofas adorn the sides. Windows offer spectacular views, high above most of the smaller boats.

"Would you care for a drink, sir?" a man appears out of nowhere.

Gabriel looks to me and I smile.

"Champagne?" he asks, drawing me down onto one of the sofas.

I smile and nod. What woman is going to turn down Champagne on a yacht in the heart of Monaco. Not this one.

"Two glasses of champagne, Jim," Gabriel says, as the man disappears. He returns two minutes later, with a cooler, two glasses and a bottle of champagne way outside my pay grade and price range.

"To us, and a relaxing weekend," Gabriel says, clinking his glass against mine. "Even if my brother has decided to gate crash."

"To a wonderful weekend. Thank you for thinking of it." I

say, taking a sip from my glass, as I find myself overcome with emotion.

We drink in silence, taking in the surroundings and the gentle swell of the water against the side.

When we have finished, Gabriel stands up, holding out his hand for me to take.

I follow him.

"This is the master cabin," Gabriel says.

My head spins at the sight I'm being presented with. The room is breathtaking. I'm not sure what I expected when Gabriel said we would be spending the weekend on his yacht, but this... well. I look at the king-sized bed, and my stomach somersaults. The room is enormous. Bigger than my bedroom in Gabriel's apartment. Although the blinds have been dropped for privacy, glass windows adorn either side. Stairs lead from the upper deck into an open hallway housing two chairs overlooking the water. The floor is wood, although the bed sits on an enormous velvety rug. I can imagine it's like satin underfoot. The room also houses a large sofa in a separate seating area. This is a suite on a yacht.

"Gabriel, this room. It's gorgeous," I say, walking around.

Gabriel clumsily runs a hand through his hair.

"This room is for you," he says. "I'll sleep in one of the other rooms."

I turn and stare at him. "Um, with Caleb here, don't we need to share a room? He thinks we're in a relationship. If I announce I'm pregnant and he knows we aren't sleeping together—" I don't finish my sentence. Instead, I watch Gabriel clenching and unclenching his jaw.

"I'll take the day bed."

I want to laugh at his words when my eyes dart back to the sofa. I can just imagine him trying to fold his six-foot-two frame onto the sofa. It looks comfortable, but not that comfortable.

"No, you won't," I say. "I'm happy to share the bed if you are. It's enormous. I doubt you would even realise another person is in bed with you." Although my womb clenches in denial. Ignoring his presence is not something I can do.

"I don't want you to feel pressured," Gabriel says.

"Gabriel, it's fine. I promise."

Gabriel continues to surprise me. His tall, dark Mediterranean looks. His bank balance. He could have any woman he chose. Yet here he is, spending time with me. Helping me fulfil my dreams, worried about how I feel about sharing a bed with him for the weekend. No one has ever put my feelings above their own, apart from my parents. But they're pretty special people.

Instead of saying anything else, he moves to a door in the wall. "The bathroom." He opens the door and steps back, allowing me to pass.

The room is marble. A large walk-in shower adorns the far wall. Opposite that is a standalone bath. A large mirror hangs from the ceiling in the middle of a twin sink unit positioned in front of another window.

"The toilet is through there," Gabriel points to another doorway. "And you'll find the wardrobe through that door."

I step forward, peering around the first door before walking into the wardrobe. The walls are lined with hanging and shelving space. A vanity unit sits in the middle, my makeup bag placed in front of the mirror, ready.

I turn around and stare at the rest of the space. It's then I notice mine and Gabriel's clothes hanging up together. The sight warms my chest.

Gabriel follows my gaze.

"Don't worry about it. We're both adults. It's not like we won't be—" I'm not sure how to describe the sex we'll be having this weekend. Baby making? Sperm depositing? "You know." I finish the sentence, and watch his lips twitch.

He turns to face me and rests his hands on my waist. "True. But you were supposed to have the choice of where you sleep. Our relationship is complicated enough. I don't want you to think that with Caleb here."

I touch his cheek. "He'll see through us. Put us on to your mum?" I finish for him. "Stop worrying. We're in a relationship. That isn't technically a lie. It's just not a conventional one."

I watch his muscles relax as I smile at him.

Gabriel nods and rests his forehead against mine.

"What we do or don't do is no one else's business. We're sharing our bodies. Why not share a bed?" I add.

Gabriel laughs, and I realise I'm getting used to the sound. "That's one way of looking at it." He steps back and I miss the closeness. "Do you want to go for a walk, or do you want to have a drink? I'm not sure what time the *miscreant* and his friends will be back."

"Let's have a drink. I like the idea of sipping champagne on a yacht. Something to tell the grandkids."

It's only then I realise what I've said.

"Hopefully, it will be something they're accustomed to," Gabriel says. However, I'm not sure I like the idea that they're *so accustomed to* luxuries they expect them on a plate. Then again, I look at Gabriel and all his siblings. Every single one is successful. Apart from his younger sister, but then Harper is still only that, young. I was only just figuring out life at her age.

Gabriel leads me back through the main deck and onto the upper deck, which holds a seating area and bar. One of the crew is waiting to serve us drinks.

"Follow me," Gabriel says, taking his drink and walking out of the side door.

I follow as we walk to the front of the boat. A hot tub bubbles away on the deck, and a large seating area stretches out behind it.

"They've thought of everything," I say, following Gabriel.

The area is dark. We are above the other boats around us, so the area is private. The light from the pool and the moon the only thing lighting our way. The gentle beat of music and laughter from a nearby yacht is the only other sound.

We take a seat. I drop my head back and close my eyes, allowing the warmth and scent of the salty sea air to invade my senses, disperse the stress of the past few months.

When I finally open my eyes, Gabriel's eyes are fixed on me. His expression is contemplative.

I smile. "This is amazing. Thank you."

"You need to stop thanking me," he says.

"Easier said than done when you keep doing lovely things for me. My mum and dad raised me to be grateful."

The light from the pool lights up his smile. "My parents were the same. We were never allowed to take anything for granted. Things had to be worked for. I won't want it any other way for any child we have."

"I'm glad," I tell him honestly.

"It will happen," Gabriel says, as if reading my mind. "And if it doesn't happen naturally, we can look at other methods."

My gaze clashes with his. "Why?"

He gives me his lip-twitching smile. That tells me he thinks I'm being naïve.

"Because I can't imagine having a child with anyone else."

His honesty shocks me.

"But?"

"There are no buts. You get me. You ask no more of me than I can give. You're honest. All this," Gabriel's hand waves at our surroundings. "You're eager and impressed, but you'll still cook me dinner when we get home, even though you know I can hire a chef to do it for you."

"But where's the fun in that?" I ask. "I grew up cooking in the kitchen with my mum. It's how I learned."

"Exactly, and that's what I want for any child I bring into this world. Normality. Love, despite my wealth."

I'm finally beginning to understand Gabriel. For all his wealth, he strives for a normal life. He still wears the same watch his mother and father gave him for his twenty-first birthday.

"I want that too," I tell Gabriel, my heartbeat picks up as I stare at him. If we have a son, will he pass it to our child when he reaches twenty-one?

When did I start to see him as a man and father? Not just my boss and sperm donor?

We spend the rest of the evening chatting on the deck. Caleb and his friends are still out partying, but I'm struggling to keep my eyes open.

"Are you ready to call it a night?" Gabriel asks.

"Most definitely," I reply, taking the hand he holds out.

He leads me back to the gorgeous room that is ours for the weekend.

"You can use the bathroom first," he says, moving over to the sofa and picking up his phone. "Take your time."

"Thanks," I say.

I make my way through the doors and close them. The opulence of the bathroom once again steals my breath. This really is a total luxury.

I grab my lounge pants and t-shirt from the wardrobe and remove my makeup. I turn on the shower jets and strip off my clothes before stepping into the spray. The water is powerful, massaging my skin. I groan into the spray as the grime of the day washes away.

I grab the scented shower gel and pour some into my hand. I recognise the scent Gabriel uses. I hold my hand under my nose, absorbing the smell. My body tingles as I think of the purpose of the weekend. Tomorrow is my ovulation date. My core clenches at the thought of what's to come.

I wash my now sensitive body, my nipples pebble. I'm not surprised to find my clit swollen and needy when my hand finally drops lower. I rinse off. No time for that. Gabriel is waiting to use the bathroom.

I switch off the jets and climb out. After, drying myself off, I pull on my night clothes. My toothbrush is next to one sink, so I brush my teeth and apply moisturiser before heading into the bedroom.

"All yours," I say, making my way towards the bed. "Which side?"

"How was the shower?" Gabriel asks, looking up from his phone.

"Amazing. Just what I needed."

"Great," he says, disappearing into the bathroom.

"Okay then," I say, staring at the bed. In my bedroom, he'd gone to the left of the bed. Therefore, I'll take the right.

I pull back the covers and sink into the mattress.

What is it about this man and comfortable beds? Does he get them custom-designed for him?

It feels like my body is being hugged.

I hear the shower start and try hard not to think of Gabriel in the shower, his hand travelling over those hard muscles I've seen when we've gone swimming together, or his hand snaking down and touching his—I bite my lip. Hormones! Ovulation and Gabriel are turning me into a raging horn dog. I've never in my life felt so turned on, so desperate for sex.

I roll onto my side, feeling the dampness between my legs, and squeeze my thighs together, only releasing them when I hear Gabriel re-enter the room.

He clicks on the bedside light before switching off the main lights.

The bed dips as he gets in next to me. "Goodnight," he says.

"Goodnight," I whisper.

It's going to be a long night.

CHAPTER 33

GABRIEL

I swear I'm going to fucking kill him.

Groans and moans. Was that a scream? The sounds of my brother and his guest. Shit, that sounds like guests, echo through the darkness.

"Oh, yes... yes... just like that." A female voice moans.

"Harder... oh yes... deeper... oh yes... yes," a second voice pipes up.

I throw an arm over my face and groan, only to hear a chuckle next to me.

"Caleb's guest. Or should I say guests seem to be enjoying themselves," Leah's voice whispers in the darkness, her amusement clear.

"I'm going to kill him," I say aloud this time. Another giggle escapes from Leah. "It's like listening to a bloody porn movie."

Another scream of pleasure echoes through the walls. Does my brother have no shame? We're moored in a marina, for God's sake. The other yachts around us don't need to know what a super stud he is.

"I think they're up for enjoying themselves this weekend," Leah says.

I roll onto my side and stare at the outline of the woman in my bed. "I'm sorry, Leah, this really isn't the vibe I was going for this weekend. It is about helping you relax and enjoy yourself."

"So, orgasms and sweaty sex aren't on this weekend's itinerary?" Leah says, rolling herself onto her side to face me.

I take a deep breath, wondering if I heard her correctly.

"You think I'm not enjoying myself? Relaxing? You couldn't be more wrong. I had a great time tonight, or was it last night? This is more than any woman could dream of. Your yacht is beautiful. Monaco, from the little I've seen, looks amazing, and I can't wait to explore. As for—"

Another loud groan, this time a masculine one, echoes through the darkness. I close my eyes. I don't need to hear my twin getting his rocks off. Not when I'm lying here next to a beautiful woman who I'm aching to take into my arms. My cock hardens at the thought.

Down, boy, it's not time yet. Soon.

A silence descends between us as we listen to my brother come. I'm going to wring his bloody neck in the morning.

I drop onto my back and put my arm over my eyes.

It's only when I feel the bed dip next to me, that I drop my arm above my head.

"Gabriel?" Leah whispers, her voice questioning.

The mattress dips as she moves closer, and I turn my head towards the sound of her voice.

"Leah?" My voice sounds strained even to my ears.

Her hand moves to my chest, just above my heart. Her fingers draw circles on top of the material there. Can she feel the erratic kick of my heartbeat?

"I read that sperm lives for up to five days. What do you say to starting early?"

My breath catches as Leah's lips touch mine, gentle, tentative.

I remain still, allowing Leah to set the ground rules. She's stated that there is no kissing, but her lips are on mine. When she doesn't pull back, and the tip of her tongue touches my lips, I sink my hand into her hair, my mouth crashing against hers. Her tongue dances against mine as I use my free hand to pull her body flush against me.

"Leah," I say as we both come up for air.

She places a finger against my lips, her eyes finding mine in the darkness. I draw it into my mouth, teasing it with my tongue and teeth. Leah moans, and I pull her head back down to meet my mouth, running my tongue along the seam of her lips, demanding entry once more. Our tongues battle and my body tightens with need.

Leah's back arches, pressing her breasts into my chest. With one hand in her hair, I let the other find the base of her t-shirt, sliding my fingers under it and up the smooth skin of her back. She shivers at my touch. Her fingers flex into my chest.

I flip us, trapping Leah beneath my body, her legs opening, cradling me between her thighs. Her head drops back, and she lets out a moan as my swollen cock nestles against her core.

"Has hearing my brother and his friends having sex turned you on?" I ask.

"Yes," she says, panting, tilting her hips, and rubbing herself against me.

I drop my head to her neck, my lips trailing up to the sensitive spot beneath her ear, before nipping at her lobe. "Do you wish you'd been there with him? Riding his dick?" I ask, torturing myself but needing to know the answer.

Leah's hand locks into my hair as she holds me against her. "No. I want you."

"Do you want me to take care of you, little bird?" I ask, my cock hardening at the memories her words are invoking. "You need to tell me what you want," I press. I know it's unfair, but I want to hear her tell me she wants me.

"You, Gabriel Frazer. I want to make a baby with you. I want to ride your cock and enjoy every minute."

I moan at her words, my hand snakes between us, finding her drenched centre hidden beneath her night clothes. I drop my forehead to hers as my fingers glide over and through her damp folds.

"You want me to fill your pussy with my cock?" I ask, circling her entrance with the tip of my finger before withdrawing and returning it to her clit. "You want to ride me? Come with me buried deep inside you." Leah moans. "Look at me, Leah," I demand. Her lust-filled eyes lock with mine. "Do you want me to fill you with my cum?"

"Yes. I want *you* buried deep inside me, filling me with your cum." She pants, her lower body squirming at my touch.

"Leah," I say, dropping a kiss to her open mouth before deepening it once more.

My hands slide under her top. I break our kiss only long enough to draw it over her head. I'm tempted to wrap it around her wrists, but that can wait for another time. Instead, I throw it to one side before drawing one of her pebbled nipples into my mouth. A sharp gasp fills the air as I nip and suck. Her hands grasp my hair tightly as I lavish attention first on one and then on the other.

"Yes," she gasps breathlessly as I pinch one of her nipples between my thumb and forefinger.

She moans as her hips rock forward. I bite the inside of my mouth and count to ten. I can feel her need soaking both our bottoms.

"Please, Gabriel," she says.

"You never need to beg," I say. "Just tell me what you need."

"I want you deep inside me. I want to ride you."

She whimpers as I tweak and tease her nipples.

"At your command," I say, flipping us over I sit up, drawing one of her nipples back into my mouth and sucking hard, her lower body cradling my cock. I press upwards our clothes the only barrier.

"Ahhh."

Leah grips my head hard, holding me to her. Her legs locking around my waist.

One of her hands pulls at the back of my top. I grip it in one hand and slide it over my head.

Leah's head falls back one hand in my hair, the other digging into my now bare shoulder.

"Oh yes," she moans quietly as I flick her nipple with my tongue, my hands slide down her body, her muscles quivering.

I reach the top of her lounge bottoms.

"These need to come off." I move us to standing, and slide them down her legs. When they've gone so far, Leah kicks them off.

"Yours too," Her hands leave mine and travel to my sleep shorts, freeing me to her gaze. She licks her lips and my cock jerks. I kick them off to the side of the bed. We're both now naked in the semi-dark.

Leah pulls my head back to hers, kissing me hard.

My chest presses against her soft breasts, and we both moan.

"I want, I need..." Leah moans.

"What? What do you want? What do you need?" I want to make this good for her.

"I don't know," she says, almost sounding confused. "I want you."

I kiss her hard before trailing my lips down her jaw and towards her throat. Leah throws her head back as I continue my journey. I spend time on each breast before dipping lower.

My hand moves, spreading her thighs.

"Are you ready for me, Leah?" I ask as my fingers reach her pussy. Her skin is wet, a trail of her need waiting for me. My fingers slide effortlessly over her swollen, wet lips. I circle her clit, her hips jerk towards me. I drop to one knee and place a kiss on her stomach before moving my mouth lower.

The scent of her desire driving me wild. I use the tip of my tongue to tease her clit.

Leah pulls my head away.

"Leah?" I ask.

"You don't have to," she says awkwardly.

"Oh, believe me, I want to. Lie down," I say, pressing Leah back until her ass hits the edge of the mattress. I spread her thighs, my eyes never leaving hers as I kneel before her. I let the flat of my tongue swipe from her opening to her clit. "I've wanted to since I had you spread out on my dining room table."

"Ohhh," she says, her fingers gripping my hair as I let my tongue work its magic.

I lift her legs onto my shoulders. My tongue torments her clit while my fingers tease her opening.

"Oh, Gabriel," Leah pants.

I slide two fingers into her hungry pussy, scissoring them before curling them against her inside wall. I find her G-spot, and continue my torment as she rides my hand and mouth.

The sensation of her orgasm almost propels me into my own. I grip myself hard to stop myself from coming over the floor.

Leah's orgasm stretches on, her body milking my fingers hard as I continue to use my tongue to taste her release.

I look up to see her biting down on her arm, my shy girl not wanting to be as vocal as Caleb's guests. A satisfied smile forms on my lips. I move back onto the bed, wiping my mouth on the back of my hand, not sure how she'll take to the taste of herself on my lips.

Lying next to her, I rest on my forearm and place my hand on her stomach, my thumb drawing lazy circles.

I study her features, looking for clues. My eyes have adjusted to the dark.

"You okay?" I ask.

Her hand comes up and holds mine against her stomach.

"Better than okay," she smiles shyly, her eyes still slightly unfocused. "That was—"

"Only just the beginning," I say, rolling over her and settling myself between her thighs, my cock pulsing with the need to sink into her silky warmth.

Leah grunts, her hands reaching up, pulling my mouth to hers, her tongue snaking out, this time deepening the kiss. She moans at the taste of herself on my lips, spreading her thighs wider, her hips undulating against mine. I take my cock, rubbing its head up and down, teasing her clit and using it to spread her juices. Her legs quiver before spreading wider, opening herself for me, her body begging to be filled. I line myself up, pressing in just enough to breech her entrance before pulling back and repeating the move. Stretching the sensitive opening until Leah's fingers dig into my ass as she tries to hold me in place, her hips thrusting up as she tries to draw me into her body.

"Oh, Oh God, please." She pants against my mouth.

I thrust my tongue and my cock into her, swallowing her gasp as her body flexes and stretches around me. Her desire makes it easy to sink into her tight little hole. I pull back before pressing forward, gliding backwards and forwards. The feel of her, of us, skin on skin, her want slick against me. I savour each stroke, every thrust. I twist my hips as I push back in, drawing out another moan.

Ah, she likes that.

I do it again and again until she is whimpering beneath me.

I sink my hands under her hips and tilt her pelvis upwards, driving myself deeper. Finding that place on her front wall, the one I know drives her wild. Leah's breathing becomes more ragged and from the twitching of her leg muscles which are now wrapped around my thighs, I know she's close.

I withdraw abruptly, not wanting this to end. I flip her over, my hands grasping her hips and pulling them up into the air. Leah spreads her knees, her head down on the mattress.

"Please," she whimpers.

I take my cock in my hand, lining myself up once more before pressing forward. The sight of my cock disappearing into Leah's body, her swollen lips glistening with her need. I bite the inside of my cheek.

"Oh, my... deeper... harder."

Leah whimpers into the sheets beneath her as my body sinks further and deeper than before.

I tilt my hips again, and she lets out a silent scream, her hand moving to her clit.

I lean around her and remove her fingers.

"That's my job," I say as she sighs.

My fingers find her swollen bud of nerves.

"Please, oh please," Leah says.

Her body presses back against mine, taking me deeper.

I press forward, my chest against her back, an arm locked around her waist. My hand slides lower, drawing the moisture from her arousal down and over her clit, tweaking it between my thumb and forefinger, making sure it coats the nerves, sensitising it.

I drive home a couple more times, Leah's movements become more and more frantic.

She spreads her thighs, her muscles locking. Her body trembles as she clenches around my cock, milking me. A flood of warmth rushes from her. I pull out and flip her onto her back. She grips my shoulders as I spread her legs before surging back into her welcoming warmth. Her body still contracting around me. I thrust in and out until my balls tighten. I slam home once more, my muscles tense as I follow her over the edge, emptying myself deep within her.

We lie panting, my head buried against her neck. Leah's fingers draw lazy circles on my back.

"Do you need me to move?" I ask, concerned I'm crushing her.

"Don't you dare." Her fingers play with the short hair at the nape of my neck. Her internal muscles clench and twitch around me, making me moan.

She rocks her hips, and my cock hardens.

"You're insatiable, Ms Walker."

"Only with you, Mr Frazer." She widens her thighs and tilts her hips, moving against me.

"Hum. Is that so? I aim to please." I nibble my way up her jawline before making my way to the sensitive lobe of her ear. I blow softly, and her moan deepens.

I drop a hand between us, finding her swollen and ready.

"Let's see what I can do," I say, my lips catching hers once more.

CHAPTER 34

LEAH

I roll over and stretch like a cat, my hand arching out across the sheets, only to find the bed next to me cold and empty.

I sit up, memories of the night before crashing into me. The sheet drops, exposing my naked breasts. Wanton me, begging Gabriel to make me come.

A telltale stickiness coats my inner thighs, a sign of both his and my desire mixed. Not that I can regret it. I've never felt so thoroughly used. My body warms as I remember all that is Gabriel. His dominance as he took charge, as he played my body like a finely tuned instrument. He rang orgasm after orgasm until I was crying with the emotional overload. Then he kissed me and soothed me. Boy, who would have thought Gabriel could kiss like that?

I drop back onto the bed, my chest exposed to the room, my arm flung over my eyes. Flashbacks of how he held me, wrapped in his arms as I fell asleep, my head resting on his chest, his heartbeat soothing me. I haven't felt this close to anyone in years.

Sex with Vince was functional towards the end. I'd come

or not, then we'd roll over and sleep on our separate sides of the bed. I can't remember the last time we spooned. Until last night, I forgot what it was like to connect with another human being. I should be shocked or horrified that it was with Gabriel. We are supposed to be clinical. Last night was anything but clinical.

I will blame the scorching heat and undeniable allure of Monaco.

An incoming notification causes my phone to beep on the bedside table. I stare at it in horror.

What? I never sleep this late.

I jump out of bed and shower. The warm water soothes my tender body as I wash away the evidence of the previous night. I glance in the mirror, telling marks adorn my skin, reigniting the memory of Gabriel's mouth against my skin.

I dress in shorts and a t-shirt and make my way up to the main cabin.

Someone has laid out an enormous breakfast. Gabriel is standing by the railing, his phone planted against his ear. I stop at the top of the steps, taking in the view and enjoying the warm breeze coming off the sea. As if sensing my arrival, Gabriel turns, ending his call.

"Morning," I say, walking up to him, my eyes focused on the table, unable to meet his gaze.

"Morning, Leah," he says, putting down his phone and stepping towards me. His hand comes up, tilting my chin until I'm forced to meet his gaze. My body heats under his scrutiny. "I was going to grab some breakfast for us both. Serve you breakfast in bed."

I check his face, for any signs of regret. Nothing.

"I didn't realise what the time was," I stutter. "I'm not usually so—"

Gabriel stops me, dropping a kiss on my open mouth. My body relaxes against his.

"The purpose of this weekend is rest and relaxation. You had a late night," he says, pulling me into his arms.

Is that a smirk I see gracing his lips? Did he just wink at me?

If I didn't know better, I'd think this mischievous person in front of me was Caleb.

As if summoned, Caleb bounds up the stairs, looking as fresh as a daisy. No sign of his marathon sex session the night before.

"Morning, Gabriel, Leah," he says, snagging a fresh croissant from the table and taking an enormous bite.

"Morning, brother dearest. I take it you had a good night? At least, from the sound of it, you did," Gabriel says drily, still holding me against him.

Caleb shoots me an awkward side glance. "Sorry if we were loud."

I bite the inside of my cheek to prevent myself from laughing.

"Where are your lady friends?" Gabriel asks.

"Er, they headed back to their hotel. I'm going to leave you two alone and join them there. Give you love birds some privacy."

A contrite Caleb is cute and makes him look much younger than he is.

"Have fun," I say, grinning.

Caleb groans. "Were we really that loud?"

Gabriel growls. "You probably kept the entire marina awake."

As twins, they couldn't be more different, or so I thought. Then I think back to Gabriel in bed. When Caleb covers his face, it's not the action I expect from the playboy, but then I doubt he expected family members and friends to overhear his sexploits.

Caleb steps forward and kisses me on the cheek. "You look good on him," he says, winking at me, making my eyes widen. "Don't do anything I wouldn't do," he adds, slapping Gabriel on the back.

"Get out of here," Gabriel growls.

Caleb leans past us and steals another croissant before leaving down the stairs and off the yacht.

Gabriel picks up two plates and moves to the table. The sun is shining, and the Marina is a hive of activity. Gabriel's yacht is enormous, and from the upper deck, we have a perfect view of our surroundings.

"Juice?" I ask Gabriel as he sets the plates down.

"Please," he replies.

His eyes sear into me as I turn and pour us both cold, freshly squeezed juice from the chilled jug.

Wandering over to the table, I take a seat.

"How are you feeling this morning?" Gabriel asks, sitting back in his chair, his fingers steepled.

His eyes are dark, his face a mask. This is calculating Gabriel.

"Amazing," I say, watching as a twinkle sparks in the dark depths. I stretch before I can stop myself, the movement pushing my chest towards him.

His eyes darken, and he runs his tongue over his lips. "Good," he says before breaking our gaze. "I intend to rinse and repeat several times this weekend."

His words shoot darts of pleasure to my core, and I squirm in my seat.

"If that's okay with you, Ms Walker," he adds after swallowing a mouthful of breakfast.

I pick up my juice and use it to wet my unexpectedly dry mouth.

"Fine, Mr Frazer," I squeak.

Oh yes, please, my body screams.

I've never shied from sex before, having had a few lovers in college before meeting Vince. But whether it's my age, my dry spell, or Gabriel Frazer, my body is a *hot, dripping* mess for this man, and I can't seem to control it. It's like he's become an addiction, or at least his magical cock has.

"Great, but first, I thought we'd go on a tour around the main area of Monaco. Tonight, I have booked us into the Monte Carlo Casino for dinner and, if we want, some gaming time."

My heart sinks in disappointment.

"In between each of these events, I intend to strip you naked and feast on your body before filling you with my cum," he says, his eyes concentrating on the food he's loading up. Only when I notice him swallow do I realise he's as turned on as I am. Who would have thought my introverted boss liked to talk dirty?

"I think I can be on board with that," I reply breathlessly as a shiver of longing works its way down my spine.

"Patience, Ms Walker. All good things come to those that wait."

I bite my lip. What the hell is this man doing to me? On Monday, we'll be back to normal, and I'll be facing him across the office, reliving all the delightful things he spent the weekend doing to my body.

"Eat up, we have places to be," Gabriel says.

I take a bite of the croissant he put on my plate, the buttery texture melting in my mouth. "Oh," I say, watching a smile form on Gabriel's lips.

"The home of the humble croissant, or at least across the border."

I devour the croissant and the pile of fresh fruit he adds. Everything is perfect.

Once we've finished, a staff member appears and removes our plates.

"Can I get you any tea or coffee?" they ask.

Gabriel looks at me.

"A latte would be amazing, thank you," I say.

"A latte for the lady and an Americano for me," Gabriel adds.

The staff member disappears, reappearing five minutes later with our drinks. We've moved to the main seating area, allowing a clearer view of everything around us.

"I thought tomorrow we could go out on the boat. Swim, sunbathe, if you'd like?"

I sigh. It wouldn't be hard to get used to this kind of life.

"I keep saying it, but that would be wonderful. I think I need to improve my vocabulary." I laugh.

Gabriel returns my smile and sips his coffee. "This weekend is about you. I want you to enjoy it, Leah."

"Believe me when I say I am. It's like a fairy tale. I'm surprised you can leave this and come back to work."

Gabriel gives me a sad smile. "It's not much fun alone," he says. "It's my haven, somewhere I come to escape. The rest of my family use it too. Hence Caleb."

He stands up and holds out his hand. "Come on, I've arranged for our own tour guide. I know some facts, but I thought you'd like to know the real story."

I take his hand in mine and let him pull me up to stand in front of him.

"If you look at me like that, we won't be going anywhere," he says.

Somewhere between last night and this morning, our openness with one another has moved to a different level, and I can't say I regret it. If I only have this weekend to enjoy this man, then I'm going to embrace it. Gabriel's not only gorgeous but also intelligent and knowledgeable, and he has a dry sense of humour hidden under his serious exterior. Maybe he's not as different from his brother as he thinks, simply more reserved.

"Then I shall have to close my eyes and put my trust in you that you won't let me fall overboard," I say.

* * *

We spend what's left of the morning travelling the hop-on-hop-off bus, taking our time to get off and wander several of the beautiful sites. We grabbed lunch in a small cafe before heading back to the marina. We talk and laugh. I don't think I've ever seen Gabriel this relaxed. Gone is my quietly grumpy boss, replaced by a more relaxed version. Small talk still isn't his thing, but when he talks about the things he's passionate about, he's a field of knowledge.

"I've had some dresses delivered for you to try for this evening," he says as we arrive back.

"Excuse me?" I say, wondering if I've heard him correctly.

"They're hanging in the wardrobe in the master cabin. See if there is anything suitable."

He motions to the door.

"Oh. Do you want to see? Having never been to the casino, I'd like some input," I say, turning towards him.

"Of course, but the decision is yours. I want you to be comfortable."

I smile at his thoughtfulness, my jaw dropping open when I see *the selection* of dresses. Each is a designer brand and gorgeous.

"Oh, Gabriel." I touch the material of the dress closest. "These are beautiful."

"We will be eating there, and I'm not sure who is around, so we may end up talking business." He grimaces, and I smile.

"It's who you are," I say, moving down the line of dresses.

"And you are my communications officer," he says, coming up behind me, snatching a royal blue dress off the rack, and holding it up. "What do you think?" he says.

The dress had already caught my eye, the colour striking. "I love it. Let me try it on."

Gabriel hands me the dress and leaves me to try it on. I step into it and shimmy. The hidden zip, once closed, holds the dress in place.

I stare in the mirror. "Wow," I whisper. No wonder designer dresses go for so much. I've only ever had one, and that was when Vince bought it for me as we were attending a colleague's wedding. It was a who's-who and a lot of flexing of wallets by all in attendance. I don't think the bride knew half the guests her new husband had invited.

But this dress. This is in a different league. It hugs all the places you want it to hug and moves freely where it needs to. The saying *I feel like a million dollars* is probably true.

I look down and notice the shoe boxes and clutch bags under each dress. My eyes and ears pop. Matching sets.

I open the shoe box and stare in awe at the shoes. My size.

Stella would be wetting herself in excitement now. Guilt hits me. I still haven't let them know what's going on. Not fully.

When I get back.

I slip on the shoes that hug my feet, even if they should be entered into society as a dangerous weapon. The heels alone could inflict some serious damage.

I take a few unsteady steps. Heels have never been my strong suit, but amazingly enough, after a few steps, I find these are like walking in slippers.

I step into the main bedroom. Gabriel is lying back on the bed, his arms resting behind his head.

"So," I say, giving a twirl. "What do you think?"

"You look beautiful," he says, sitting up on the bed.

Butterflies dance in my stomach at his words.

When did our relationship change so much? My boss is now calling me beautiful? Has falling apart in his arms set us on a different path? This is dangerous. Gabriel has already warned me that he is terrible at relationships. Our co-parenting is only going to work if I can keep some distance. I can't catch feelings for him. That will be a disaster, especially when I fall pregnant, and he moves on.

A wave of nausea hits at the thought of Gabriel with someone else.

Before I can think, Gabriel is at my side. "Hey, is everything okay?" He takes my arm and leads me to the sofa by the window.

I offer him a weak smile. "Fine."

"It's just you looked like you wanted to be sick," he says, resting his hand against my forehead.

"Honestly, I'm fine. It's passed now."

"It's probably the rocking motion. Although it's not obvious, the boat still moves. It can take some getting used to. I'll get you some water."

Gabriel leaves, heading up the stairs. I make my way back into the dressing room, pulling on one of my summer dresses.

By the time I return to the bedroom, Gabriel is there with iced water and fruit juices.

"You may be slightly dehydrated. We did a lot of walking this morning, and the wine with lunch."

"Thank you, that's thoughtful."

I take the juice and sip, the natural sugar settling my stomach and easing the pressure that was building up behind my eyes. I need to get a grip.

I stand and stare out of the window. The glass is tinted, allowing us to see out but preventing anyone from seeing in. Gabriel comes up behind me, his hands snaking around my waist, spreading out over my stomach. He pulls me back against him and kisses my neck, I drop my head away, giving him access. My body ignites at his touch.

I lean down and put my glass on the table before twisting in his arms, my fingers grazing the short hair at the nape of his neck.

Gabriel continues his exploration of my neck, moving up and nibbling my jawline, before making his way to my lips. I give him access to my mouth, allowing his tongue to dance with mine. I pull his head closer as his hands wrap around my hair, holding me in place while he devours me.

We finally break apart, both gasping for air.

"Leah Walker, what are you doing to me?" He rests his forehead against mine. "I wasn't expecting this," he says and I feel the furrows form between his brows. "You're like a drug. One I can't seem to get enough of." He exhales slowly. "I can't get you out of my head or what it feels like to have you under me, surrounding me."

He pulls away, his hand gripping the back of his neck. I move to his side and my eyes lock on his pursed lips. He turns his head to look at me, his gaze almost pained.

I step forward and cup his cheek.

"This." I look around me. "It's a surprise. You are the most unexpected surprise of all." I let my thumb brush over his lips, only to have him draw it into his mouth. Butterflies take off in my stomach.

"You're not what I expected at all," I say, tilting my head and locking my gaze on his. "We are trying to create a child. Is it so wrong if we enjoy the process? We don't need to look too far into the future or over analyse." I smile up at him. "I know that's your nature, but we need to see how this plays out."

He nods, so I raise a second hand and cup his cheeks.

"I'm a woman, you're a man. I will not complain about amazing sex, and I'm also not going to lie to you. I don't want any misunderstandings between us."

Gabriel goes to open his mouth, but I shake my head. Is this a bad idea? Maybe, but then again.

"Let me finish. All I ask is you promise to be honest with me. Whatever that means. When we got into this, it was to create a child. The day we slept together, we changed the rules. Last night, we changed them again." I pause. "But Gabriel, the more I get to know you, and whatever the future holds, I wouldn't want anyone else to father my child."

Gabriel closes his eyes. When he reopens them, the warmth I see takes my breath away.

"I promise to always be honest if you do the same. I also ask you to be patient with me. I'm no good at this. Relationships and people."

I rise on my toes and press my mouth against his. "I think you're doing just fine," I whisper. "How about you strip me naked and fill me with all that sperm you promised me?"

I've never been one for dirty talk before, never been comfortable enough. Gabriel is undeniably influencing me.

Gabriel licks my lips with his tongue. His smile obvious against my mouth. He pulls my lower half against his growing arousal.

"I think that can be arranged," he says, walking me backwards towards the bed.

He pushes me back, my ass hits the edge of the bed before he kneels between my legs. His hands brush up the inside of my thighs, taking my sundress with them, exposing my panties to his gaze.

"Pretty," he says, his finger touching what I know is a damp patch soaking through the material.

This man only needs to look at me, and I'm a puddle.

"I'm hoping," he says as he plays with the elastic at the edge of my panties. His eyes locked on mine. "That when we get home, and you no longer need to keep all my sperm inside you, I can do all the other things I have in mind."

A rush of warmth floods my core as I watch his eyes darken. He knows precisely what his words do to me. "Would you like that, Leah? Would you like me to take you, in different places, different ways?"

I bite my lip to suppress my moans, as I know that's what he wants.

His finger teases at my entrance.

"Are you going to answer me, or do you need to think about it?" he asks again, the tip of his finger dipping in and out before going up and circling my desire around my swollen clit. My hips lift off the bed.

He continues to tease and torment my body, his hands and mouth everywhere, until an orgasm shatters my equilibrium.

He rises next to me, dropping kisses on my lips, his eyes filled with want but also tenderness.

I cup his cheek and give him a dazed smile. "I think I could be onboard with that, Mr Frazer."

"Good," he says before his mouth descends once more.

We despatch our clothes in record time, savouring each other's bodies. His defined abs and broad shoulders formed by years of swimming, move under my hands. A sharp contrast to my soft curves as they press against his hardness. He makes me feel beautiful in a way I never have before.

When he finally enters me, he swallows my gasp, driving my body higher and higher until we both crescendo together. I contract around him, drawing his cum deep into me.

When Gabriel finally withdraws he places his pillow under my bottom, tilting my pelvis, before dropping a kiss on my stomach and lying back down next to me, his arm thrown over my middle.

I tilt my head and drop a kiss on his nose before I succumb to my exhaustion.

CHAPTER 35

GABRIEL

*A*fter a lazy afternoon in bed and then by the small pool on deck, we take our time getting ready for dinner and a night at the casino. No one should visit Monaco without experiencing life at the Monte Carlo Casino, the home of several James Bond films.

Leah looks stunning, and I'm glad I had the foresight to get a few dresses delivered. I got her to try some others on, as I know she will need them going forward, especially once our relationship gets out. My mother's upcoming birthday party being one such event. I have yet to ask Leah to accompany me, even though my mother invited her. She hadn't been too keen on lying, but things have changed this weekend, so she may feel differently. Our relationship may not be conventional, but it *is* very satisfying sexually. This weekend could not have gone any better. I'm just cautious in case I do something to ruin it.

Dinner is spectacular, and Leah enjoys the blackjack table. We bump into a couple of clients who are determined to talk about work. I watch as Leah shifts their conversation effortlessly from business to their weekends, talking to our clients and partners. Her knowledge of each one is unbelievably detailed. So, this is what it's like to work with someone and socialise with them. Usually, my partners are yawning or trying to capture my attention. Leah understands this is not something I can do when my business is built on offering my clients a personal service. That is what they expect, especially when they are paying the bills.

I'm enjoying my time with Leah, something that has never happened before. Usually, I find myself drawn back into work.

By the time we head back to the marina, it's dark. Leah slips off her shoes and holds them in one hand, her other clasped in mine. Holding hands seems to have become a natural occurrence and I enjoy the physical contact.

When we reach the upper deck, I take Leah into my arms, dropping my lips to hers, our tongues dance, as she kisses me back at a leisurely pace.

"Wow," a voice has us jumping apart. "You two are *hot*."

"Caleb," I say, rounding on my brother.

"Well, if I hadn't seen it with my own eyes. I was wondering if you two were playing us all." Caleb's eyes are twinkling with delight. I have positioned myself between him and Leah, knowing the interruption will embarrass her.

"What are you doing here?" I ask.

"I came back to get my stuff. I was downstairs when I saw you come up here and thought I'd say hi. Sorry to have interrupted."

"Somehow, I doubt that." I huff at my twin.

His expression is one of mischief and delight.

"Look, I'm happy for you both," he says, shrugging. "Mum will be even happier when she finds out you've brought Leah here."

I groan, and Leah rests a hand on my shoulder. "It's okay,"

she whispers, close to my ear. "The cat is out of the bag," she says more loudly.

I lean behind me, wrapping my arm around her waist and pulling her into my side, where she belongs.

Now, where were we?

* * *

MONACO SEEMS LIKE A DISTANT MEMORY. Our flight back to the UK was delayed, mainly due to my brother deciding to hitch a ride. My plans for our return flight and joining the mile-high club with Leah were scuppered.

I made the mistake of checking my inbox when we got home and spent the rest of the night answering emails. By the time I emerged from my home office, Leah had gone to bed. Her own. I didn't think I'd miss her curled up next to me after only two nights, but I did.

Sitting at my desk, I can only think about how yesterday we were lounging in the sun on the open sea, swimming, enjoying each other's bodies. Now we're in the office, not touching, watching her walk around in her ultra-professional suits, hair scraped up in a chignon. All I want to do is pull out the clip, wrap her hair around my hand before pushing her down on my desk, and do exactly what was in her romance novel.

"Gabriel, darling." I snap out of my daydream as my mother appears at my office door.

"Mum, what are you doing here?" I ask, jumping up and ushering her in, shutting the door firmly behind her.

"Can't a mother come and visit her son?"

"You've managed not to for the past eight years," I say, only to have her tut at me.

"That was because you told me not to and before you started dating Leah," she says, taking an uninvited seat.

"Speaking of Leah, I heard you two had a lovely weekend in Monaco."

I'm seriously going to kill Caleb when I see him.

I return to my desk, counting slowly to ten. "Mum, Leah and I have not gone public with our relationship. You can't just swan in here. Leah is professional. I'm a professional."

Mum just looks at me and gives me her gentle, under-standing and totally condescending look. "So, like your father," she sighs, making my heart clench. "He protected me in the office too. Don't worry. Your secret is safe with me. I'm not going to say a word. I was popping by to see if Leah wanted to go for lunch."

I sink back into my chair and stare at my mother. "Mum, don't you think Leah leaving with you for a lunch date is going to raise a few questions?"

My mum wrinkles her nose. "You may be right. However, I wanted to see if Leah could assist with the Frazer Founda-tion. She is, after all, a first-class communications officer."

I groan and run a hand down my face. "Leah works for me, mother."

"I know, dear. But she might be interested. She is, after all, practically family."

"Mum, we've only been dating a couple of months," I say, my eyes wide. Mother is taking my *relationship* to a whole new level. I need to get rid of her before she does or says something else. "Why don't you join us for dinner tonight," I say.

"Wonderful," she says, clapping her hands. "What time?"

* * *

I KNOCK on Leah's office door.

"Hey." She looks up and smiles. "Was that your mother I just saw?"

"It was," I say, my tone making her laugh. "She wanted to invite you to lunch."

Her eyes widen and flick to the door. "It's okay. I invited her over for dinner tonight instead."

"Oh, okay," Leah looks surprised.

"I know I told you I hardly saw my family."

I sigh, sinking down into the chair opposite her desk.

I look up to find Leah biting her lip, trying not to laugh.

"Come on," she says. "Your mum is lovely."

"Except when she's sticking her nose in. She's practically got us married off. She wants you to help her with the Frazer Foundation."

When I look up again, Leah has gone sheet white.

"Hey." I lean forward and take her hand. "It's okay. We can say you're too busy in the office."

"It's not that," she says, pulling her hand back and shooting a look out the door, checking. "I hate lying. You know that."

I sit back and run a hand down my face.

"I like your mum, Gabriel. I hate lying to her."

"We're not lying, not entirely. We are in a relationship. I don't think after this weekend, we can really call our relationship *fake*."

"Maybe not, but it's not heading where she wants it to go. You just said it yourself. She practically has us married off."

"Maybe not the best turn of phrase for me to have used," I say, wanting to kick myself. I was hoping Leah would see the funny side of my mother having us married off. "As for the Frazer Foundation. That's up to you. I wanted to warn you." I get up, not sure what else to say. "She'll be with us at seven."

I leave Leah sitting there. Our relationship isn't conventional, but it isn't *fake*. Her screaming my name as she came violently around my cock was not *fake*. Her curled up next to me in bed, and holding my hand as we walked through the streets of Monaco. None of that was *fake*, or at least it hadn't appeared to be.

* * *

BY THE TIME I walk in the front door, my cock is rock solid, and I can't wait to slide into Leah's welcoming depths and show her how un-fake our relationship has become. Instead, I'm greeted by my mother and *fake* girlfriend chatting over wine in the kitchen.

"Darling." My mother grabs me and pulls me in for a floral hug.

"Mother," I say, hugging her back.

She pulls back and grips my forearms, looking up at me, her eyes twinkling with excitement.

"Leah has agreed to help with the Frazer Foundation. She's going to help Kat and me with my birthday weekend event. Isn't that marvellous?"

My eyes lock with Leah's over my mother's shoulder, and I'm surprised to see her smiling. Not what I was expecting. I know how hard my mother is to turn down when she wants something. Never one to take no for an answer.

"Before you say anything," mum adds. "I know where your mind has gone. I haven't browbeaten her into anything."

"I never thought you would," I say drily, as Leah laughs.

I find myself smiling in response, and before long, we eat and laugh together. The stress of earlier forgotten.

"Come with me," I say, holding out my hand after my mother has left. A warmth settles in my stomach as Leah wraps her fingers around mine. I've missed touching her today.

She gazes at me, searching for answers.

"It's a surprise," I say, causing her to smile. I'm getting

used to Leah's smile, especially when it's directed at me, and I find I want to see more of it.

I lead her to my man cave, and we stand outside the door.

"Close your eyes."

"I'm trusting you. Don't you dare let me walk into anything," she chuckles.

"As if, Ms Walker. I'm incredibly trustworthy." I like Leah's teasing. She makes me want to join in—let go. "Now close your eyes."

I place my hand over her eyes, just in case.

"On," I say to the lights, withdrawing my hand.

After I finished my emails, I'd been too wired to sleep. Leah was tired after the weekend and fell straight into bed. So, I spent the rest of the night building. Pen had come through, delivering everything I needed.

Leah blinks in the light, her jaw dropping as she takes in the setup in front of her. "Oh, my," she says, walking up and running a hand over the chair. "This is—"

"You're own gaming centre," I say. "I've created an identical gaming platform to my own. No more saying I have an unfair advantage."

"This is... I don't know what to say." She looks at me, her eyes glistening. "Does this mean I get to kick your butt while we're in the same room?"

"You can try," I reply, pulling her into my arms, and dropping a kiss on her nose. "I've never had someone to share this part of my life with, apart from those online," I say, wanting Leah to understand the affect she is having on me.

"I get it. None of the girls play. Stella and Nat—they don't understand the draw."

"Do you want to give it a go?" I ask, knowing I shouldn't push. "It's okay, it's late, and we have work tomorrow."

"Are you kidding me? You've just shown me a gamer's dream setup, and you expect me to sleep?" Her excitement astounds me. It's as if I bought her her own yacht. I don't think I've ever come across someone like Leah before. Someone who gets so much pleasure from the little things in life. "Then again, maybe we can find something else to help us sleep... later."

She gives me a cheeky wink, and blood rushes south.

"Unfair," I say as she smirks at me.

"I've whooped your butt before. I'll do it again. Only this time you can blame your dick on your poor performance." Leah grins.

"I didn't hear you complaining about my poor performance over the weekend," I say, getting drawn into the teasing.

"That's because you were on your game. Let's see how good you are with a controller in your hand."

"What does the winner get?" I ask, my competitive streak coming out.

"How about the winner can decide, providing the other person is onboard?"

Blood flow increases further. At this rate, I'm going to be at a disadvantage for sure.

"You're on."

We play for the next couple of hours. As I feared, Leah's strategic play is almost as good as mine. We've both reached the same level and are competing to get to the end. This game is Pen's pride and joy. It's also the market leader and she refuses to let me know how to win, telling me I must figure it out myself. Everyone in the chat rooms is going nuts. No one has cracked the ultimate levels.

"Wow, that was amazing. Gabriel, I can't believe you have that done for me," she says, coming up to stand next to my chair.

"We may need to rename the *man* cave," I say, smiling. "I can see you being in there as much as me."

Leah links her arm through mine and rests her head on my arm.

"Thank you. I don't think anyone has given me such a thoughtful gift."

"You're welcome. But I think, Ms Walker, you need to go to bed. It's been a busy weekend, and it's now two in the morning."

"Really? But I feel so—"

A large yawn escapes, and I raise an eyebrow.

"You were saying?"

"Okay, maybe I *am* a little tired. I'll say goodnight. Thank you, Gabriel. For everything."

We stop at the top of the stairs. Leah goes up on her tiptoes and presses a kiss to my lips.

"Night," she says, her voice husky.

"Good night, Leah." I stand and watch her enter her bedroom and my stomach drops.

I get washed up and climb into my bed.

It feels wrong after having Leah curled into my side for the weekend.

A knock sounds on the door.

"Come in," I say, leaning back against the headboard.

"Hi," Leah stands in the doorway, biting her lip.

I throw back the edge of the duvet and pat the bed next to me. She doesn't need a second invitation. Moving across the floor, wearing simple sleep shorts and a cami, she climbs in next to me.

I pull her towards me. "Miss me?"

She smiles and straddles my lap, her hands resting on my shoulders, drawing her bottom lip between her teeth.

My hand curls up into her hair, and I draw her mouth down to mine. We kiss, but it's not the desperation of the weekend. This is soft and slow, an exploration.

Leah rocks on my cock, her movements slow yet needy.

I lift us both, kicking off my bottoms before removing hers. I let my hand slide between us, but Leah bats it away, instead gripping me in her hand. She positions the head of my cock at her dripping entrance, coating me with her desire, before pressing down, her body stretching and enveloping me in its warm, tight sheath as I sink into her depths.

We moan into each other's mouths as I deepen our kiss. Our tongues tangle as Leah rides me, soft and slow.

My hands move to her hips, my fingers sinking into her flesh, holding her as she rocks me deep into her body. Her head drops back as my cock presses against her most sensitive spot.

I move forward, drawing her nipple into my mouth, nipping and sucking. She grabs at my hair, her hands clasping the back of my head, pulling me closer. She grinds her clit onto my pubic bone, and I feel the telltale buildup of pressure at the base of my shaft. Leah groans, her body clasping around mine. I flip us both, settling myself between her thighs, wrapping her legs around my hips as she continues to milk me. I thrust deeper, adding pressure to her clit, to draw out her orgasm before finally letting go and emptying myself into her body. My muscles lock and shake as I explode deep into her core. I shudder as my cock jerks, coating her insides with my cum. I press my head into her neck, breathing in her scent.

Leah lets out a satisfied moan, and I smile before dropping a kiss to where her shoulder and neck meet.

I withdraw smoothly before rolling onto my back and pulling her into my chest. Dropping another kiss onto her temple.

"Sleep," I murmur as I'm drawn into a blissful slumber.

CHAPTER 36

LEAH

I know it's only been a week, but Monaco feels like a lifetime ago. Life has moved on, and Gabriel and I have fallen into a pattern of work, dinner, exercise, gaming, movies or television shows, spending much of our free time together. Today however is a girls' day.

"So when will you find out if this round of insemination has worked?" Stella asks when we meet up for dinner.

"Next week," I say, wanting to change the subject. The thought of my period coming is horrifying, but then again, more sex.

"Are you blushing?" Nat asks.

"No, why would I be blushing? It's just hot in here," I say, wanting my friends to drop the subject.

"No, it's not. It's bloody freezing," Stella states, pulling on her coat and glaring at the waiter, who quickly walks over and turns down the air-con unit, bashing out ice-cold air from above us.

"Sorry, ladies," he says, eyeing up Stella before he leaves.

Stella watches him go, then dramatically fans herself. "The *temperature* definitely has gone up in this place."

Nat and I burst into giggles. I've missed seeing my friends. When I lived with Vince, we had regular girls' nights, as Vince was often out with his work colleagues, but it's not something we can do while I'm living with Gabriel. It wouldn't be fair.

"When's the apartment going to be ready? They seem to be taking their time." Stella says. "We need to get back to our girls' nights."

The apartment is ready, but Gabriel has been in no hurry for me to leave. We've kind of fallen into a pattern.

"Gabriel is still waiting on some of the furniture," I lie, crossing my fingers under the table. Unsure, I want to tell them how I've not only milked my boss for his sperm but how I'm curling up next to him every night in his bed, even though I'm no longer in my fertile period.

"Where's it coming from? Outer Mongolia?" Stella asks.

I give them an awkward laugh. "Probably, knowing Gabriel."

Stella squints her eyes and stares at me, and I pause. "Something is going on," Stella says. "Look at her, Nat. She's hiding something."

Nat turns and stares at me, my cheeks blaze. "Oh. My. God. You're right," Nat says, turning in her chair and facing me. "Spill sister. Since when do we keep secrets from one another?"

I look between them and feel my shoulders sag.

"I knew it!" Stella says. "Our Leah's been holding out on us. Does this have anything to do with your yummy boss man?"

My hands fly to my cheeks.

"It does," they both squeal together, getting some sharp looks from some of the other tables.

"Shhh," I hiss.

"Then you'd better spill the beans," Stella whispers loudly as she and Nat lean forward.

I draw in a deep breath before letting the air whistle through my teeth.

"Maybe we should get out of here," I say, not wanting to have this conversation overheard.

"That's it." Stella looks at the waiter, who has his gaze fixed on her and calls him over.

"Hi," she says, giving him her best smile. "Can we change our order for one to go? Something has come up, and we need to leave."

"Certainly, madam," he says.

"It's Miss," she says, flicking her hair, making me choke on the water I've just swallowed.

Stella shoots me a glare as he walks away. "Some of us have to get it where we can," she says, wagging her eyebrows.

Stella's cute waiter returns in record time with our food and bill. We clear the bill and head out. Stella chuckles when she finds a handwritten note in the bag along with our food.

"Well, it looks like things may be moving out of the dry era," she says, waving the note, making Nat and I groan.

"It's okay for you two. You're clearly getting some. Have some sympathy for Mr Rabbit. He's been working overtime lately."

"Too much info," Nat says, covering her ears.

"Good for you." I laugh, sliding my arm through my friends.

"Where to?" I ask, when we reach the taxi rank.

"Mine. My flatmate is away, so we have the freedom to talk and when I say talk, sister, you are spilling all the salacious details."

I smile. Gabriel asked me whether I'd spoken to Stella or Nat about our relationship. He was surprised when I said no. He knows they are my friends and can be trusted. However, I wasn't ready to share or jinx what we've started. Protecting my heart was the wiser choice.

A taxi drops us off outside Stella's apartment block. I pay him off before heading upstairs.

"Nat, you grab the plates. Leah, you grab the glasses," Stella says, heading towards the cutlery drawer.

We dish up our food in the kitchen and head to the sofa.

"Spill," Stella says, taking a mouthful of her noodles.

"Fine," I huff. "But what I tell you stays between us," I say, only to be met with, *really* expressions from both my friends.

"I have to say it. Then I get to sleep tonight rather than worry," I say, shrugging. It's something we've always had since college. Watertight friendship when told. "You know Gabriel and I are trying for a baby," I state, and they both nod. "Well, things have kind of changed." I bury my head in my hands until I feel them being pried away from my face.

"Changed?" Stella asks although I can hear the excitement in her voice.

I cover my cheeks with my hands and explain how the artificial insemination kits failed and how we had clinical sex, only it wasn't all that clinical. How he took me to Monaco.

Stella's jaw drops. "I knew it. He's just too hot to keep your hands off. I'm surprised you lasted as long as you did. I bet I'm right. He's a tiger in the bedroom. The quiet ones always are."

I know my wide eyes and puce complexion have just given the game away.

"Oh... Oh... I need to live voraciously through you. Spill, girlie, or I might have to torture you."

Nat looks between Stella and me, her brow furrowed until it smooths out as the realisation dawns. "You're in a relationship with Gabriel?" she says, her eyes as wide as saucers.

"Er, no. We're fake dating. His family thinks we're together. It will be easier for them when the baby arrives to think we were in a relationship."

"Leah, hon, if you're having sex. I hate to point it out, but that isn't a fake relationship. That's a sexual relationship."

I huff. This is why I didn't want to say anything. I knew they wouldn't understand.

"Fine," I say. "If you want to name it. We're in a sexual relationship."

A frown mars both my friends' brows.

"Leah?" Stella says.

I sigh. Stella knows me, perhaps better than anyone. We've been friends for sixteen years.

"I know it wasn't supposed to be like this. When the kits failed, it would have meant waiting another month, and we tried the natural method." I don't go into any more details.

"Okay. So clinical. I can go with that," Stella says.

I drop my chin to my chest. "It started out clinical, only—"

"He turned out to be hung like a horse and knew how to play your lady parts like a finely tuned violin," Nat says, making both Stella and I stare at her open-mouthed.

"What?" she says. "The man is sex on legs. I know I'm with Rory, and I love the man. But I'm not blind. There's no way you could have clinical sex with a man like Gabriel Frazer—" Nat smacks her hand over her mouth.

I bite my lip, trying hard not to laugh. I don't think I've ever heard my friend so forward.

Stella nods, her eyes full of mischief "If you think you can get away with keeping this to yourself, no way, bestie. We need deets."

"Stella!" Nat squeals, laughing. "But she's right... spill."

I roll my eyes. "For me to know," I say.

Something about my relationship with Gabriel doesn't

want to have us giggling about it like school kids. Also, this is going to be the father of my child.

"I have no complaints, though," I say, throwing them a bone, knowing I must be glowing like a lightbulb.

Stella looks at me, her eyes surveying me. "If that's all you're going to say about it, and the fact you're glowing, you must like him," Stella states, taking a sip of her wine while pushing me a juice.

"It's complicated," I say, knowing I'm in trouble. However much I try to tell myself we're only friends with a common goal, the more I know I'm lying to myself. Gabriel has become so much more.

"Please be careful," Stella says.

Too late for that, but if we have a child, at least I'll be able to focus on that when we finally walk away.

* * *

THREE HOURS LATER, I jump in a taxi and make my way to Gabriel's apartment. The doorman greets me with a welcoming smile, and I make my way upstairs. The apartment is dark when I enter, and I wonder whether Gabriel has gone to bed.

I make my way to our games room and tap on the door.

"I've got to go, Leah's home."

"Speak soon, have fun," a woman's voice comes across the speaker.

"You too."

I enter the room, and Gabriel jumps up, walking towards me.

"Who was that?" I ask, knowing I sound jealous and hating myself for it. We don't have and never will have that kind of relationship, but if Gabriel has another woman, I want him to be upfront about it.

"Kat. You don't need to worry." Gabriel wraps his arms around my waist and pulls me against him. "My sister," he adds.

"Sorry, it's none of my business," I say, dropping my chin and resting my forehead against his chest.

"It kind of is," he says then adds, "I will always be upfront with you, Leah. It's the only way I know how to be. Whatever this is between us, we have to be honest and open if it's going to work."

I look up and smile. "Speaking of honest, I told the girls about us tonight."

Instead of being cross, he smirks.

I smack his chest. "No, I didn't tell them any details, only what we're doing."

"Well, Stella thinks I'm *hot*," he says, letting me know he heard my best friend's comment the day I moved in downstairs.

"You heard that, huh?"

"I did, but I waited to see what you said, and I was sorely disappointed you didn't make a comment." Gabriel runs his tongue along the seam of my lips.

I pull back and stare up at him, my hands resting on his waist. "Is that so?" My heart rate picks up. *Did Gabriel fancy me then?*

"Totally. I needed to know whether I needed to reprimand a member of staff for thinking inappropriate thoughts about another member of staff," he adds, raising his eyebrow.

"And what would you have done to reprimand me?" My voice getting huskier.

Gabriel drops his lips to my neck and kisses his way up my throat and along my jawline. It's only when my back hits the wall that I realise he's manoeuvred us backwards.

He captures both my hands in one of his and raises them

above my head, his lower body pressing into me. His free hand snakes up and grips my jaw.

"Now that would depend," he says, his voice low, his breath light against my lips.

I moan as his arousal presses into my stomach.

"But then you didn't, so the point is moot."

Gabriel steps away from me, and I squeak at his loss. He smiles, which is something that comes much more readily to him these days.

I step towards him, this time spinning him around so he's against the wall.

I nibble along his jawline, and he drops his head back against the wall. Allowing me to explore his body with my hands. I kiss my way down his neck, and lower. Before long, I'm kneeling, my hands working on his belt and zipper.

"Leah," he moans as I release his cock from his boxers.

I take his silken shaft in my hand and pump it twice before sliding my tongue over the tip. I run my tongue up and down the underside, teasing the area of skin just below the head. Gabriel's hands sink into my hair, guiding me. His moans spurring me on.

I worship him with my tongue and mouth, licking the pre-cum from his throbbing cock until he grips me under the arms and pulls me up, slamming his mouth against mine before scooping me up and walking to the desk in the corner. He turns me away from him, pulling up my skirt and shoving my panties down. We both groan as his fingers find my soaking wet entrance. Without a word, he runs his cock up and down my slit, coating himself in my juices before slamming home. My body stretches to accommodate him, and I press back against him. We've had so much sex that my body is used to his invasion now. I moan, resting my weight on my forearms as Gabriel pushes into me from behind, forcing the air from my lungs, his hands gripping my hips.

"That feels good," I say, looking over my shoulder at the man commanding my body.

"Only good?" He questions before circling his hips and pushing back into me, hitting my G-spot and cervix over and over.

"Better than good." I pant. "Deeper."

Gabriel practically lifts me off the ground as he circles his hips, plunging into me again and again. One hand snakes around us to my clit. Two flicks and I'm falling apart beneath him.

"That's it -take all of me," he says as he continues to thrust hard and fast into me.

"Oh," I grunt as his balls slap against my clit. My body contracts hard around him and my muscles quiver.

Gabriel slows his tempo, slowly pushing in and pulling out. I can feel the pressure building in his rock-hard cock.

"That's it," he says, and I lower my hand between us and grasp his balls, massaging them.

He freezes and shudders. His cum emptying deep inside me.

He withdraws and grabs a tissue, but not before the evidence of him leaks out.

"I love that sight," he says, his fingers running through the mess we've made, cupping me with his hand.

My core contracts at his words and touch.

Whatever I told the girls this evening, I know I'm in trouble. This man is so much more than I ever imagined, and I'm going to need to find a way to protect my heart if I'm to survive this.

CHAPTER 37

GABRIEL

*L*eah hasn't arrived at work. She messaged to say she was going to be a bit late, but then there's been nothing, and I'm getting concerned. Her period was due last week, but that means nothing.

The elevator alert pings across the office and I breathe a sigh of relief as Leah exits, followed by Caleb. What the hell is he doing here and with Leah, of all things?

Leah smiles at him, her hand resting on his arm before she turns away. She inclines her head at me, smiling. Our relationship is still not public knowledge in the office, and I find I'm hating that. Especially at the symphony of "Morning Leah" that go off as she makes her way to her office.

Caleb turns to my office and frowns when he sees me standing in the doorway.

"Gabe," he says.

I step back and let him enter, closing the door behind him.

"What were you doing with Leah?"

"What?" he asks, taking a seat opposite my desk, while I round it and glare at him.

"Take a breath," he says after a moment. "I met Leah downstairs as I was coming up. We shared the lift. What's going on Gabe?"

I sink into my chair and run a hand over my face. "I don't know." I shrug, honestly. "It's just when I saw you together."

Caleb leans forward in his chair. "Look at me." He pauses until I raise my eyes to meet his. "I would never do that to you," he says, his lips pursed. "You know that."

I nod, holding his gaze for a second before I look away. This is stupid. I know he wouldn't. But after Rachel. She made it quite clear she dated the wrong twin. Had even come on to Caleb, although he spurned her advances.

"It's getting serious between you and Leah?" he probes, unable to keep the grin from his face.

I run a hand over my mouth, and Caleb sits back in his chair.

"Well, that was unexpected, but then again, maybe not. I'm pleased for you." Caleb smiles at me. "Mum's thrilled, by the way. She likes Leah."

I groan and bury my head in my hands.

"Why is everyone so invested in my love life?"

"Maybe because since Rachel, there's been no one of any consequence. No one at all, really." He smirks.

"I've had girlfriends," I say, suddenly feeling the need to defend myself.

"No, you haven't," Caleb fires back, chuckling. "You've had fuck-buddies and a few hookups when the need arose. Admit it, you don't go to parties or socialise like a normal person."

"Like you, you mean?"

"Exactly like me. I put myself out there and give myself a chance," he adds, crossing his arms and legs.

"You look defensive there, brother," I reply, smirking at him.

Caleb glares at me. "You can be smug now you've found Leah."

If only he knew.

"Maybe you need to start up a conversation with someone rather than simply have them ride your cock," I add.

"I talk."

"I'm sure you do. *Harder, faster, that's it, baby.*" I repeat all the phrases Caleb and his partners shouted out the night on the yacht.

He lowers his brow before re-crossing his arms over his chest. "That was Monaco."

"Don't tell me *what happens in Monaco, stays in Monaco* because you couldn't wait to run to Mother about Leah and me. I wonder what she'd think if she knew what you got up to that weekend."

"Time for me to go. You're clearly in a strange mood, and I have a meeting to attend."

I laugh. "Not so much fun when the boot is on the other foot."

"Haha. It's not long until Mother's birthday weekend."

"I know. Mum invited Leah to assist with the fundraiser. We'll both be there," I say.

Caleb grins. "She'll have you walking down the aisle in no time."

I flinch.

"Maybe Mum will set you up with one of her friend's daughters," I shoot back, smirking.

Caleb freezes at the door and groans.

"Heaven forbid."

"A good girl for her wayward son," I add as he throws open the door and steps out.

"I'm leaving now," he says, almost bumping into Leah.

"It's okay," he adds, grinning at Leah. "I know he has a meeting."

"He doesn't actually, but if you want to believe that."

Leah chuckles as Caleb dramatically throws his arms into the air. "I'm doomed," he says, heading off to the elevator. The rest of the office watching him.

"Leah, do you have a moment?" I ask, loud enough for everyone to hear.

"Of course." Leah steps into my office.

I close the door before spinning her around and pressing her up against it, my lips locking with hers.

When I finally let her go, Leah licks her lips and smiles.

"Is that all, boss?" She grins.

"No." I take her hand and lead her to my desk. "Is everything okay? You were late in this morning."

Leah looks away and my heart sinks.

"Leah?"

She raises her gaze to mine, her eyes sparkling.

"I was going to leave this until later, but." She twists her bracelet around her wrist.

"Leah," I warn.

She fishes into her pocket and pulls out a stick, handing it to me.

I stare, captivated by the white stick, revealing two blue lines.

"What? When?" I say, my voice cracking.

"This morning. My stomach's been feeling a little queasy, and when I walked into the bakery yesterday and the smell of the fresh bread. Let's just say I had to leave." Her head tilts, and she stares at me.

I step forward and pull her into my arms, my lips crashing down on hers. This might be the office, but...

"We're having a baby," I whisper, my heart pounding in my chest. "We're really doing this."

"We are. Although it's very early days, and—"

I place a finger over her lips. "A day at a time," I say, dropping my forehead to hers, unable to keep the grin from my face.

She grips my hands in hers and squeezes, her gaze locked on mine.

"You're okay with this?" she asks, and I'm shocked by the wobble in her tone.

"More than okay with it. If we were anywhere other than the office. I'd be showing you just how okay I am."

"You're sex mad." She laughs.

"Guilty as charged, but only with you," I say, realising it's true.

I like sex, I like it a lot, but before Leah, it was an act, something to relieve stress. But now, I love watching her come apart in my arms, of the way her body is so in sync with mine. But it's more than that. When I'm around her, the world seems brighter. I'm finding myself, for the first time, actively seeking someone to share the small things in life with.

"Well, it's a good thing. Some women feel horny during their pregnancy," Leah says, pulling me away from the realisation that things between us are changing.

I tilt her chin and drop a kiss on her open lips. "At your service," I say before stepping back as the phone on my desk rings.

"I'd better go," Leah says, moving towards the door.

"Okay. But don't think we won't be continuing this later," I say, picking up the phone.

Leah grins and waves goodbye, as Amanda connects the call.

CHAPTER 38

LEAH

*W*hether it's my pregnancy or I'm just horny, I can't seem to get enough of Gabriel. Not just in the bedroom, either. Over the past three weeks we have spent more and more time together, either gaming, watching TV shows, or chatting.

I straighten my skirt as he zips up his trousers, wrapping his arms around my waist and pulling my back against his chest. We barely made it in the door before he had me bent over the back of the sofa and was sinking into me, my body a hot mess from his dirty talk all the way home in the car.

"Hum," he says, dropping a kiss on my neck. "I've been wanting to do that all day."

I snake my arm up and around his head, holding him in place. "Me too." I don't remember ever feeling as wanton as I do with Gabriel.

But Gabriel and I have an agreement. This is just us letting off steam, enjoying each other for the moment. When the lust fades, we will return to the status quo we agreed on, and raise the child we've created in a stress free and loving environment. Our child will want for nothing.

It would be very easy to fall in love with Gabriel Frazer and that's not a good thing. My job, my happiness, and that of our child will rely heavily on the relationship we build going forward.

He steps back after one final kiss before making his way over to the kitchen. "Are you ready for the weekend?"

"I am," I say, following behind him. "I saw Chloe. My outfits are sorted. The fundraiser has been finalised. We have some amazing items to auction off."

Gabriel turns and drops a kiss on my nose, his arms encircling my waist.

"Mum is singing your praises. You've made quite an impression. Beware, I think she has high hopes in roping you in on future events."

I stare at him, unsure he's thought this through. When the baby arrives, we'll return to our separate lives. I'm not sure Francesca will want me then.

Oblivious, he adds, "Together we can survive what is known as *my family*."

"They can't be that bad," I reply, only to have him roll his eyes. I pat his chest and let my fears dissipate. I need to learn to live for the moment.

"You have no idea," he says. And I begin to wonder what I've let myself in for.

* * *

WE TURN OFF THE ROAD, passing through two ornate brick pillars supporting equally large metal gates.

"Welcome to Frazer Manor," Gabriel says, as I take in our surroundings. There's no house in sight, just a vast green, open space, and trees that line the road we're travelling on.

"This used to be part of the working farmland. Now it's purely decorative," he explains.

"Is it still a working farm?" I ask, taking in the beautiful surroundings, an air of tranquillity washing over me the further in we drive. This is the opposite of the city. I didn't realise how in need of a *green* fix I was.

"It is, although the family doesn't run it. We rent out the land and it's managed by some of the local farmers," he says, as we meet a high stone wall with brick buildings behind it.

He turns right and pauses, waiting for another set of gates to open. This time solid wooden ones.

The gates open, framing another tree-lined driveway, although this one is shorter. At the end of the driveway, I can see a fountain set in front of shallow, wide stone steps that lead up to an enormous house.

He drives forward. A far cry from the council house and estate on which I was raised. Not that I'm embarrassed. Our home was always welcoming and well-maintained. Both of my parents worked hard for what we had. It's where I developed my work ethic.

The stone building is imposing. The steps lead up to a double height and width wooden doorway, surrounded by clematis. Two stone urns sit either side of the door, their contents offering a vibrant splash of multi-colour against the grey. Enormous sash windows, pepper the walls and must offer spectacular views of the grounds.

I try to keep my mouth from dropping open.

Gabriel turns to me and grins. "Welcome to my childhood home," he says.

"Wow, oh wow," I stutter. "Not what I was expecting."

He jumps out, coming around to my side of the car. I take his hand, still having issues unfolding myself from the car seat, and I know it's only going to get worse when my stomach grows. I wonder if Gabriel realises his car will not cut it with a child and baby seat.

"We had a lot of fun here as children," he says. "It's not as stuffy as it looks from the outside."

I watch a weight lift from his shoulders.

"So many places to hide. Your mother must have had a nervous breakdown trying to keep tabs on you all."

He winks, taking me by surprise. "I'll show you some of the best places."

He keeps hold of my hand as we walk to the front door, which opens instantly.

"You've made it," Francesca says, descending the stairs in record time and throwing her arms around us both.

"Welcome Leah, please make yourself at home. This may be a large house, but there's no standing on ceremony. That's not how this house runs, not around the family anyway," she says, linking her arm through mine and pulling me away from Gabriel.

He drops his chin and shakes his head.

"I've put you in your old room," Francesca tells Gabriel, who is now being accosted by a middle-aged man.

"I'll take care of your luggage, Mr Gabriel," the man says.

"Thank you, Henry," Gabriel replies before catching up to his mother and me as we walk through the large double doors and into the house.

The entrance hall is breathtaking. With a gigantic stone fireplace on one wall. Along with an ornate chandelier and a large curving staircase. I feel like I've been transported back in time.

I turn and face Francesca.

"You have a beautiful home," I say, watching a smile form on her lips.

"Thank you. It's a lot quieter now it doesn't have five children running around. But one day, I hope my grandchildren will fill it."

Oh boy, not too much pressure. I clench my hand against

my side, preventing it from touching my stomach and the tiny life that's growing.

"I'm still waiting for the others to arrive. Elijah and Lottie will be down after Lottie finishes school. Kat has a late meeting but has promised she'll be here for dinner. Caleb is en route, and Harper is around somewhere, recovering from last night."

It's three thirty in the afternoon. It must have been a good night if she's still recovering. But then the press is all over Gabriel's little sister. Influencer and IT Girl. There isn't a week that goes by without her doing something that splashes her over the tabloid newspapers.

"Gabriel, take Leah up to your room, and then you can join me in the drawing room for afternoon tea. Betsy's been baking all morning. Her scones were due out of the oven. So they should still be warm."

Taking my hand he leads me up the impressive staircase. In the centre, it diverts, either left or right.

"West wing, east wing, although a mezzanine balcony connects both sides," he explains as we head right

The walls are wood panelled halfway up, the rest covered with artwork or photographs of the family. Gabriel has four brothers and sisters, and there are lots of photographs of them at varying times in their lives; celebrations, achievements, holidays. Alongside those are pictures of his extended family, which is even greater. We stop by what looks to be a family portrait. An older couple sitting centre stage. There must be thirty people of varying ages. I spot the twins. They look to be in their late teens.

"Cousins, uncles, aunts," Gabriel says as if reading my mind. "My grandparents had five children, my dad being the eldest. The Frazer clan is quite extensive."

"Do you still see them all?" I ask.

"Some more than others," he says.

I can't even imagine what it must be like to have that many relatives. On my father's side, I have two cousins, but as an only child, my friends were the ones who provided me with companionship. It likely explains my close friendship with Stella and Nat.

"Quite a few will come on Sunday, but they're spread out all over the world." He stops in front of a large door. "This is us," he says, pushing it open and motioning for me to step inside.

The room is remarkably light and airy. Two sash windows let in the afternoon light. I move towards the windows, heavy curtains framing them. The view looks over the back garden, where a hive of activity is happening on the lawn.

Gabriel comes to stand next to me, his posture more relaxed than I've ever seen him.

"Over there is the sunken garden and a maze of pathways. We used to love exploring as children. It leads to the vegetable garden, which also wraps around the side of the house, next to the kitchen. There's a greenhouse there too. Mum is very into her organic vegetables and herbs. She's also hands-on. My father used to laugh, telling everyone how she spent a fortune on manicures to get the mud out from under her fingernails."

The affection in his voice is clear. His parents mean the world to him. That's something we have in common.

"It kept her sane after Dad died. She spent hours tending her vegetables and fruit plants. That and the time she dedicates to the Frazer Foundation."

I rest my hand on his arm. He turns his head, looking down at me. There's pain in his eyes, but also something else.

"There's a swimming pool on the opposite side, and the land stretches to the tree line." He points to somewhere on the distant horizon.

Oh boy, I'm not in Kansas anymore.

Gabriel and my life are polar opposites in every way. Our child will undeniably be a child of two very different worlds. My family and I can never compete with all that Gabriel and his family can give it. My heart sinks at the thought.

"This was my room growing up."

I plaster on a smile as we turn away from the window. It's then I notice the large, wooden four-poster bed.

"That's some bed for a child," I say.

Far removed from my tiny single bed at my parents' house. Something Vince would always complain about when we went to stay hence, I often went alone.

Gabriel surprises me by laughing. "This is an upgrade," he says. "When I hit six feet, with no sign of slowing down, my parents realised my feet were hanging off my old bed. This, however, is another upgrade. This might be my old bedroom, but it's also a guest room."

"Were you an untidy teenager?" I ask. "There's a lot of space to make a lot of mess."

"My mum would tell you I had a *floordrobe.* I never remember it being *that* bad," he says sheepishly, making me smile.

"I think most teenagers have their own floordrobe. When we have to buy our own clothes, we just learn that throwing them on the floor is not such a good idea."

Once again, my mind returns to Vince, and the fact he never tidied up after himself, despite having come from a similar background to my own. Maybe it's not so much about what or where you come from but about how we behave. I think about Gabriel's bedroom, everything has a place. His clothes are neatly organised. Not that it matters. Gabriel and I are not a couple and never will be. We are enjoying a sexual relationship and having a child together. Whatever the girls want to think, our relationship has no long term future, and it will never have a fairy tale ending. Gabriel made that clear in the beginning. It's not something he believes in and I have to remember that. Instead, I'm going with a happy for now, at least until our child is born, then I'll have something else to concentrate on, something to look forward to.

"Come on, we better get downstairs before my mother sends out a search party, although maybe she won't," Gabriel says, pulling me into his arms, his lips capturing mine in a kiss that turns my legs to jelly as he walks me back towards the bed.

I root my feet into the carpet, my hands pressing against his shoulders. "We're not keeping your mother waiting," I say, knowing the colour in my cheeks is high.

"You're no fun," Gabriel says, stepping back.

"I'll remind you of that later," I say, spinning towards the door, my hips sashaying away from him.

"Tease," he says, happily following.

CHAPTER 39

GABRIEL

*C*aleb arrives in the middle of afternoon tea. He scoops Leah up into a hug, spinning her around.

"You made it," he says.

The sight of her laughing, her hands resting on his shoulders, sets my teeth on edge. Why does my brother think he can touch Leah at every opportunity?

"We did," she says, sending a smile my way, her eyes softening. She moves to sit next to me, and I place a hand on her thigh. I know the gesture screams *mine*, but I can't help it.

It's at that moment Kat walks in. She looks her usual pristine self, not a hair or item of clothing out of place.

She walks up to our mother, dropping a kiss on her cheek. Mum pulls her in for a hug before reluctantly letting her go.

"It's good to see you, darling," my mother says, her hand cupping my sister's cheek. "You're working too hard."

Mum's polite way of telling Kat she looks tired.

"That's what this weekend is for, some R and R," Kat shoots back with a smile that doesn't quite reach her eyes.

"Kat, no Zach?" Caleb asks.

My brother likes Zach, although I can't fathom why for the life of me. In my mind, he's always been too weak for Kat and too agreeable. She's been dating him for years, but he's never understood her, not the way someone who's supposed to love you should. I watch my sister flinch, although she hides it well. But then, I know her tells and her secret.

"No," Kat replies in her usual blunt manner.

"Apparently, he has to work," Mum adds, her disappointment clear in her tone.

Kat's gaze locks on mine, sending me a silent message before drifting lower to where my hand rests on Leah's leg. Her lips twitch and she steps forward, holding out her hand.

"Hi, I'm Kat. These reprobate's older sister. You must be Leah. I've heard lots about you."

Leah jumps up, grasping my sister's hand in hers. "It's lovely to meet you." A shy smile gracing her lips.

It's at that moment I realise Leah and Kat are around the same age. It's what comes from having a relationship with an older woman, but then Kat and I have always been close.

"If you'll excuse me," Kat says. "I'm going to get changed, and I have an urgent call to make. I want to take some time off this weekend. I'll use Dad's old office."

"You go, darling. Do you want me to get Betsy to send you in some tea or coffee? She's made some scones, your favourite."

"That would be great," Kat says, although her tone is flatter than usual, and I know she simply wants to escape and reset.

We all watch as she leaves the room. Leah's eyes follow her, a crease forming between her brows. I squeeze her hand when she looks at me, a silent message passing between us. I sometimes forget how perceptive Leah is.

It's not long before some of the staff take Mum's attention as they prepare for tomorrow's main event.

"Sorry," she says to Leah. "There are a few issues that need to be addressed."

"Is there anything I can do to help?" Leah asks.

"No, no. You rest up. I'll see you at dinner later."

Mum turns and follows Henry out. Leaving Caleb, Leah, and me alone.

Caleb jumps up. "Well, I'm going to have a lie down before dinner," he says, shooting me a grin.

Leah bites her lip to prevent the laughter I know she's trying to contain at my brother's not-so-subtle attempt at leaving us alone.

"Come on," I say. "We can go for a walk in the gardens."

"Make sure you show Leah the water tower," Caleb says, shooting me a wink when Leah isn't looking.

I scowl at him, which seems to make him grin even more.

"Let me guess, the water tower is where Caleb took all his female conquests growing up," she says, when we are finally alone.

I grunt, forgetting how well she knows my brother. Leah laughs. A sound I'm becoming very attached to. With her hand in mine when she steps in front of me, her eyes twinkling.

"Show me." she says.

* * *

I'll never think of the water tower in the same way again.

"Where have you been?" Elijah's voice accosts us as soon as we enter the house.

"Lovely to see you too, big brother," I reply, squeezing Leah's hand and smiling down at her. "Leah, this is my older brother, Elijah."

She steps forward and holds out a hand, offering him her warmest smile. "I'm pleased to finally meet you," she says, only for Elijah to give her the once over before reluctantly taking her hand.

I bristle at my brother's rudeness.

"Don't mind him, Leah." It's Harper's voice that appears to our right. "He's just a grumpy old bastard."

I turn to see my youngest sister appear. Her bright purple hair is luminescent against the thick black eyeliner and white foundation, clearly her latest look.

"I'm Harper, the baby of the family," she says, stepping in front of Elijah and clasping Leah's hand in hers before pulling her into a welcoming hug. "Sorry I missed you earlier," she says. "It was a late one."

Elijah scowls down at the two women. His monster frame means the women only come mid-chest on his body. I'm six-two, but my brother is at least four inches taller.

I glare at my brother but decide to bide my time before speaking to him about his rudeness.

"Aunty Harper, Uncle Gabe," a voice yells from the stairs.

"Hey, Princess," Harper says, turning to face our niece.

Lottie flies down the stairs and into her arms. There are only ten years between them, and while Harper's life is colourful, Elijah cosets Lottie.

"I love your hair," Lottie says, twisting a lock of Harper's hair.

"Don't go getting any ideas," Elijah interjects at his daughter, who pulls a face.

"When will you grow up?" Elijah says, turning to Harper. His lip curls in disgust as he takes in her appearance. "Don't you think this rebellious stage has gone on long enough?"

"It's called personal expression, dear brother," Harper replies sweetly. "Maybe I'll change the day you get a personality transplant."

Leah's eyes are wide as she stares at my siblings. I tried to warn her, but it has to be seen to be believed. Elijah has got worse over the past few years. When I was younger, I remember looking forward to the summers when he would come back from college and then university, with his friends in tow. Then, everything changed. Now, the rest of us have become immune to his surly manner. Only Lottie, his daughter, seems to bring out a softer side in him.

"Don't be mean, Daddy," Lottie says, wrapping her arms around his waist. "Aunty Harper is an influencer. She's cool."

Elijah's expression softens as he looks down at his daughter. "And what do you know about influencers?" he asks her warily.

The colour rises in Lottie's cheeks.

"Look at the time," I say, grabbing everyone's attention. "We better start getting ready for dinner, or we'll be late."

Lottie shoots me a glance, and I wink. Her eyes widen in surprise, before shooting me a shy smile.

I pull Leah away from my siblings and towards the stairs. Leaving them in the hall.

Leah is silent as we return to our room. Walking in, she settles herself down on the side of the bed.

I run a hand through my hair. I know what she's thinking. "Ignore Elijah, he's —"

"A man mountain, I've seen photographs, but I had no idea," she says, laughing. Choosing to ignore the fact my brother was a rude ass. "I thought you were tall, but he dwarfs even you."

I chuckle. "You sound like Penelope."

I know these two will get on. I wonder if Pen will come tomorrow. She always has, but over the past couple of years, it's got more and more awkward.

"You and she are close?" Leah asks, a hint of something I can't quite recognise in her eyes.

"We are." It's then I realise what I'm seeing. Is Leah jealous of Pen? "But not in the way you're thinking," I say, dropping onto the bed next to her. "Pen and Elijah were at Uni together. Pen used to come down at weekends with Elijah and Darra. I'm like a little brother. I was so shy. She used to sit and talk to me. She got me into gaming and showed me the online community. Helped me build my first computer."

I smile at the memory.

"Build?"

"Yes, build. When Dad saw the impact Pen was having on me, he told her to purchase whatever was needed. It's not like we didn't have the money to buy top-of-the-range, but Pen wouldn't hear of it. She said I needed to understand the components and how they worked."

Leah's eyes widen. "How old were you?"

"Thirteen. It was the same computer I used to track the stock market in the early days. I've built every computer since, with Pen, of course. It allows us to spend time together."

The words are out of my mouth before I realise how they sound.

"Pen is my friend, and I swear she's only a friend. She's like a big sister. She's loud and boisterous."

Leah looks at me, her expression guarded, and I don't like it. "Does Pen see it that way?"

I smile. "Pen only has feelings for one Frazer, and he was always too clueless to notice, and even if he did. Fate had its own agenda."

Leah nods, but I know she doesn't understand.

"Thank you for showing me around. Your family home is beautiful," she says.

I tilt her chin up with my finger, dropping a kiss on her open mouth. "Thank you," I say. "You've given me a whole new opinion of the water tower. I can see its appeal," I say before deepening the kiss. Leah moans into my mouth as I slip a hand under her jumper, finding one of her tender and oh-so-responsive nipples.

She shifts on the bed towards me, her hands coming up and grasping my shoulders.

I moan in protest as she pulls back.

"We need to get ready," she says breathlessly.

"We do," I say before sliding my hand down the front of her trousers and into her panties, feeling the evidence of our earlier encounter still sticky and oh-so wet.

Leah's face crinkles as I slip a finger into her.

"I enjoy feeling my cum in your pussy," I whisper against her mouth as she whimpers as my fingers continue their admiration. "Maybe you need some more?"

Before I can think, Leah has flicked the button on her trousers and is shimmying them down her hips before kicking them away, my hand still buried between her thighs. She goes for my zipper, freeing me from the confines of my trousers. I'm already hard, my crown weeping, as it always does when Leah is nearby.

She pushes me down until I am lying on my back. She kneels over me before lowering herself onto my waiting cock. Her eyes lock on our reflection in the mirror next to the bed. I slide in smoothly, biting back a moan. My cum and Leah's desire makes my entrance easy.

"Do you like what you see?" I ask, moving our bodies so she has a better view of my cock disappearing into her.

"I —"

I move my hand, my thumb brushing her swollen clit. She bites her lip above me as she slides up and down, twisting her hips and taking all of me deep into her body.

"That's it, baby. Perfect. Your pussy feels so goddamn perfect. Watch how well we fit together. That's it, ride me, use me. Take what you need." I watch the colour rise in

Leah's cheeks as she takes in my words. Her hands travel up under her jumper, and I know she's playing with her nipples.

"Oh, no. If you're touching yourself, I want to watch," I say, sliding her jumper up and over her head before unclipping her bra. Leah stalls her movements before starting her ride again. I feel myself growing painfully hard. My thumb returns to her clit while I watch her tweak and twist her nipples. I sit up, pulling her hard against me, my cock finding its way even deeper. I take one of her nipples into my mouth, biting down on it. Leah explodes around my cock. Her muscles clamp around me as she continues to move up and down. Her convulsions are too much, driving me over the edge. Leah drops her head onto my shoulder, breathing hard.

"My beautiful girl," I say, wrapping her legs around my waist before I stand up, carrying her into the bathroom. My cock is still embedded in her. "Now we better get ready before they send a search party out after us."

Leah drops a tired kiss on my shoulder as I pull out of her, enjoying the evidence of our activity as it runs down her thighs. I flip on the shower, testing the water before stepping us both inside. I take the bar of soap and lather it up in my hands, begrudgingly washing away the evidence.

Leah repays me by washing me, first with her hands and then with her mouth.

"We really need to get ready," she says reluctantly. "Your family will get the wrong impression of me.

"Or the one we desire for them to possess. Remember, we're supposed to be in a relationship. This is what they would expect. Me having a hard time keeping my hands off you."

Something flashes in Leah's eyes, but she turns away before I can read too much into it.

She grabs her dress carrier, pulling out the dress Chloe helped her choose. She shimmies into it, showing me her back so I can zip her up. I do, running my fingers up her spine, loving the goosebumps that erupt all over her skin.

I watch Leah as she disappears into the bathroom, leaving me standing in the bedroom. A tightness crushing my chest, churning my stomach. Did I say something wrong?

CHAPTER 40

LEAH

*G*abriel looks gorgeous, as always. His shirt sleeves are rolled up, exposing his muscular forearms, his top button open. I've been looking forward to this dinner, but my chest constricts as we move to join the others. With all the time we've been spending together and the amazing sex, I've let things get away from me. Our relationship is, for all intents and purposes, a ruse set out to make it more acceptable for our families when our child arrives. Somewhere along the way, I've lost sight of that. This will not have a happily ever after where Gabriel and I ride off into the sunset.

"There you two are," Francesca comes forward, pulling me into a hug. My stomach sinks. She's been so welcoming. I hate the fact she thinks there's more between Gabriel and me. The only consolation will be her grandchild when it arrives.

"Let's go through, I'm starving. As I'm sure you two are," Caleb says, smirking.

I feel the colour rise in my cheeks.

"Grow up," Elijah growls at him from the corner.

I'm unsure how I missed it, but the scowl he's shooting my way is hard to miss.

Francesca leads us through to the most opulent dining room. A large hardwood table with high-backed chairs takes centre stage in the middle of the floor. The dining room is beautifully laid out and ready for us. Gabriel takes my hand, leading me to our seats. He holds out my chair like the true gentleman he is. I smile at him as he takes his seat, only to have him lean forward and drop a kiss on my cheek. His public display of affection surprises me, but then it shouldn't. This is all for show. My chest constricts a little more.

A server arrives with the drinks.

"Wine?" she asks

"No, thank you," I say. "Can I have some water?"

"Of course." Her smile is warm and friendly.

"Not drinking, Leah?" Caleb chirps up. "Don't worry, you don't need to stand on ceremony, not around this lot."

"Speak for yourself," Kat chirps in. "Leah can do and drink what she likes. She doesn't need to be bullied by you."

Caleb pulls a face at his older sister, making me smile. I turn to Gabriel as his hand squeezes my thigh under the table.

The first course is served. I sit and listen to the family as they catch up, my brain spinning as I realise how successful each of the siblings is. All apart from Harper, who is still finding her way. I find myself drawn to Gabriel's youngest sister. She's a rebel. Yes. Her hair, makeup, and clothes are outward proof, but there's something more, and I'm struggling to put my finger on it.

"So, Leah. How long have you known my brother?" Elijah's voice breaks through my thoughts.

"I've worked for him for over eight years," I say, picking up my glass of water and taking a sip. Suddenly aware, I've become the centre of everyone's attention.

"And you're suddenly madly in love after all this time of knowing one another?"

There's no missing the sarcasm in Elijah's tone.

Gabriel lays a hand on my arm.

"Leah was engaged until recently. When she split with her fiancé, I saw my chance."

I drop my gaze, wishing the words Gabriel was sprouting were true. Life would be so much easier if they were.

"It's true, he's spent years chasing me away from her," Caleb says, his gaze supportive.

Elijah doesn't look convinced, and I squirm under his scrutiny.

"You fell for my brother on the rebound?"

Elijah's words seem to stun everyone into silence.

Our gazes lock. His eyes are cold, with something else swimming in them.

"Elijah!" Gabriel hisses at his brother.

I squeeze his fingers.

"It's okay, Gabriel," I say, turning and smiling at him before returning my attention to his brother. "Not that it's any of your business, but my relationship with my fiancé was emotionally over way before it was physically over. History and naivety kept us together for longer than we should have been." I smile, unable to help myself. "I've always respected your brother from the moment I came to work for him. He's intelligent, kind, considerate."

"You forgot to mention a billionaire," Elijah says, taking a large sip of the whiskey he has in front of him.

"Enough Elijah!" It's Francesca's voice that cuts through the silence this time.

"Sorry, Mother, but don't you think it's convenient? She splits up with her fiancé and then she and Gabriel shack up together within five minutes. Are you so focused on Gabriel finding a woman that you can't recognise a gold digger when you see one? Leah comes from nothing. She grew up on a council estate."

I raise my eyebrows at his words. Maybe I should have expected the security and cyber expert to have run a background check on me, but I'm not ashamed of my upbringing or how hard I worked to get where I am. I will not let some wealthy prick make me feel inferior because I wasn't born with a silver spoon in my mouth.

"Her fiancé left her. His new girlfriend is pregnant. It wasn't Leah's choice to leave. She found herself homeless without her cash cow of a fiancé. Did you know he's a trader, earning a seven-figure bonus? Leah upgraded when she stuck her claws into Gabriel."

I sit back, unaccustomed to this level of venom being spewed in my direction. The background check certainly explains the instant hostility.

Gabriel is on his feet next to me facing off against his brother.

"Who the hell do you think you are?"

"What?" Elijah pushes Gabriel back, and I'm amazed Gabriel holds his ground due to the size of his sibling.

"Eli, you're out of line," Caleb says.

"Apologise, now," Gabriel says.

I can sense the anger radiating off him.

"What, for speaking the truth? For being concerned that you brother dearest, are being taken for a ride?"

"You don't know the truth," Gabriel hisses in his brother's face. His face a mask of anger. "Not every woman is Darra."

"Maybe not, but it's the truth, or are you too blind to see it? Too taken with a hot, wet —"

I'm drawn to the young girl sitting next to her father, her eyes wide as she stares at the two men.

"Enough," I say, shooting a look towards Lottie, whose eyes have now dropped to the table in front of her.

The two men remain chest to chest until Gabriel finally steps back, returning to my side.

Elijah's eyes drop to his daughter, and he places a hand on her head, his eyes softening.

She pushes her chair back and stands.

"Lottie?" Elijah asks.

"I'm...er...just going to the bathroom."

We all watch as the young girl makes a hasty exit.

"Now the peacocking is over. Maybe we can have the main course," Kat says, throwing Elijah a look of pure disgust. "I apologise for my brother's lack of manners, Leah," Kat adds.

Elijah gets up, shoving his chair back. "Don't apologise for me," He spits out at his sister.

"Then don't be an ass," she says coldly.

My stomach hardens, and the back of my throat burns.

"Stop, please," I say.

I turn to Gabriel, my hand resting against his cheek. A silent message passes between us.

"Leah, don't," he says, his voice almost pleading.

"No, Gabriel, this is not what either of us signed up for, and I'm not letting our relationship affect yours with your family."

"Ignore them. It's none of their business," he says, but I shake my head before turning to the table.

"Gabriel and I are having a baby," I say.

Elijah sinks back into his chair and sighs. "There I was, thinking you are the intelligent twin."

A bang follows his words as Gabriel's palm hits the table, making me jump.

"It's not what you think," I say, squaring up to Elijah.

"Gabriel and I have a professional agreement to have a child together. To co-parent." My eyes turn to Francesca, who is staring at us wide-eyed. "I'm sorry we've misled you.

We thought it would be easier for everyone if you thought we were in a real relationship before the baby was born. I promise I'm not after Gabriel's money. That's the last thing I want."

"This is bullshit," Caleb shouts, his gaze flipping between Gabriel and myself. "I've seen you together."

"Wow, there I was thinking I was the only one who ever created drama around here," Harper says. "Way to go bro, you've outdone even me."

"Shut up, Harper," Gabriel hisses.

I look down at Gabriel, his face a mask, although his eyes hold a sadness I don't recognise.

"I apologise for ruining your birthday dinner," I say to Francesca. "If you'll excuse me. I think I'll go for a walk."

With that, I push back my chair and head for the exit.

"Leah." Gabriel appears at my side, but I shake my head.

"Elijah is only trying to protect you. I get it."

"No. Elijah is complicated. His life has warped his judgement. This has nothing to do with you."

His tone is desperate.

"I need some space." I give him what I know is a sad smile before I turn and head for the door.

CHAPTER 41

GABRIEL

I re-enter the dining room, torn between letting Leah walk away and doing what she asked. I know by following her, I'll only prolong the pain and make things worse. I also need to deal with my asshole of a brother.

Caleb sits back at the table, but his mind is elsewhere. Elijah's expression is like thunder.

It's my mother who speaks up. "Is Leah all right?"

"She's fine, Mum. She's gone for a walk in the garden."

I watch the tension leave my mother's shoulders. I was right when I told Leah my mother likes her. Somehow, that eases some of the pressure on my chest.

A palpable silence fills the room as Elijah and I face off against one another. At five years my senior, he is bigger in every way.

Years of swimming built his shoulders. Subsequent years of gym visits to work off whatever frustrations have overtaken his life have turned him into a man mountain.

"You are out of order," I say, facing him.

"Why, for speaking the truth? Have you learned nothing?" he says, shaking his head at me.

"Learned what? Leah and I are nothing like you and Darra," I spit. "You know nothing about us or our relationship."

"Don't you think it's strange she works for you and then suddenly winds up pregnant?"

I shake my head at him.

"Leah and I have worked together for eight years. Ever since I founded Frazer Investments, she's been my trusted right-hand woman. She's far from a stranger. She's one of the most hardworking people I know, and she is dedicated to my firm. I should know."

I direct my gaze towards my brother for confirmation, but he's still lost in thought, his complexion green.

I run a hand through my hair and sigh, "Leah wanted a baby. I offered to be her sperm donor."

There, I said it.

"Wow, Gabe, who says romance is dead," Harper chirps from the end of the table. "That's a new one, even for you, babe."

"Shut up, Harper," I say, shooting her a look that has her holding up her hands and smiling.

"Hey, don't shout at me. I like Leah, just saying."

She shoots her deadliest look at Elijah before picking up her wine glass.

"What do you get out of this?" Elijah asks, returning his attention to me.

I raise an eyebrow as I stare at him. "An heir," I say, telling him the truth.

The *initial* truth.

I know, however, that's not the most recent truth. Things between Leah and I have changed. She invades my thoughts, my dreams. I find myself wanting to spend more and more time in her company. Not something I've ever felt about another human being. But I haven't processed these feelings yet. Not enough to discuss them with my family, or even Leah. All I know is something inside me didn't like Leah's declaration.

Caleb's chair slides back. "I've seen you together. There is no way this is fake. This is bullshit."

He slams out of the room before I can reply.

I drop my head to my chest and inhale deeply. This is why I hate family gatherings. Why I stay away from people.

"Gabriel, I don't understand. I've seen you and Leah together like Caleb has. She lives with you. You seem so happy together. Was that an act?"

It's my mother's voice that breaks through my stupor, and I hate the hurt I can hear.

"No, Mum, it wasn't an act. What you saw is Leah and me. That's how we are together." I realise I'm telling the truth. We've never put on an act for any of my family. "As for her moving in, that was an accident." I sink back into my chair. "When Leah's engagement ended, she needed somewhere to stay."

"You let her stay with you? Above and beyond for an employee, don't you think?" Elijah's voice cuts in.

"Will you shut up?" I shoot at my brother before returning my attention to our mother. "She initially rented the apartment I own beneath mine. That place flooded, so she moved into my spare room."

I run a hand down my face, knowing I should be with Leah—wanting to be with her—but knowing I need to stop any further speculation before she returns.

"And while she was living with you, she just mentioned she wanted a kid?"

I can hear the contempt in Elijah's voice.

"No, actually," I say, staring my brother down. "She was going to use a sperm bank. I was the one who talked *her* into a co-parenting arrangement."

"Co-parenting?" My mother's voice echoes around the silence that has descended.

"Yes, co-parenting. It's where a couple have and raise their child together, but live separately."

"But why?" My mother sounds concerned. "Why do this? Why not meet someone and settle down? This is so... cold... even for you, Gabriel."

I round on my mother.

"But that's the problem, or at least everyone else's problem." I draw in a breath. "I don't want to find someone to settle down with. I like my space, my life. I'm no good at relationships." Sighing, I take hold of my rising temper. "This works out perfectly for the both of us. Leah gets it. She understands me. One thing I know. My child won't be raised where its parents are constantly arguing."

Elijah lets out a low growl.

Harper holds up her hands. "You have to admit, mum, his love life has been a little sparse. It's why you and your cronies are constantly trying to fix him up."

"What? No," Mum's voice cuts in. "Is that what all this is about? Me trying to fix you up with a date? Is that why you've done this?"

My shoulders drop, and I sigh. "No... partly."

My mother gasps.

"You wanting to set me up started me thinking. Then, when I found out that Leah wanted a child, it seemed like the perfect solution. The best of both worlds. I'm happy, Mum. We both are. It's what we want," I say, although I can't seem to shift the hollow feeling in the centre of my chest.

I meet my mum's gaze, her eyes glazed with unshed tears. "I know you are... I've seen you two together, that's why..." She tails off, and I wonder what she was going to say.

I tilt my head, thinking back to the night after we came

back from Monaco. How she and Leah had laughed over dinner. I hadn't seen Mum so happy in a long time.

"You need to find her, Gabriel. If Leah means something to you, then you need to let her know what she's just told us is okay, that we're okay with it. That as the mother of your child, she *will* be part of our family, even if it is unconventional." I stare at my mum open-mouthed. "And Elijah, you *will* apologise to Leah. I raised you better than this, both of you."

"I'm with Mum on this one," Kat says. "And Elijah, you need to find Lottie. Whatever issues you and Darra have are not that young girl's issues or Leah's. You need to get your *own* shit together before you sling any mud."

We all stare open-mouthed at Kat, who usually keeps her own counsel.

Elijah humphs behind me as if denying Kat's claims until she sends him a glare that would freeze water. I want to smile. My big sister truly is an ice queen when she wants to be.

Elijah grunts.

I need no further encouragement. I leave to check on Leah.

CHAPTER 42

LEAH

I hear her before I see her. Gentle sobs coming from an old playhouse in the corner of the garden. I wipe my eyes, making my way towards the sound. I knock on the door of the old structure. The crying stops as if the person inside is holding their breath.

"Lottie?" I ask, knowing I've uncovered where Elijah's daughter has excused herself.

"I'm fine," she says, her voice catching on the last part.

"Says everyone who isn't *fine*," I say. "Can I come in?"

"Sure." she humphs, and I smile. She has been raised to respect her adults, even when she wants to tell them to *get lost.*

I open the door, and it groans fiercely on its hinges.

"It's safe," comes a voice from inside.

"I'll take your word for it," I say dryly as I crouch down and make my way inside.

"Dad built this for me when I was little. We lived here where I was first born, with Granny and Pops."

"It's amazing," I say, taking a seat on an old, plastic child's chair. "I always wanted a house like this."

Lottie gives me a watery smile. "Dad did lots of things for me here. He always has done."

Her eyes well up. "I'm sorry about the things my dad said to you."

"It's not your place to apologise," I say, leaning forward and squeezing her hand.

"No, but it's my fault he is the way he is."

I look up and lock gazes with the young girl in front of me.

"I don't think—" It's clear Elijah loves his daughter.

Where has she got this notion from?

"It is. He wouldn't have married my mum if I'd never been born."

"I don't know what goes on between your mum and dad, but Lottie, it's clear how much your dad loves you," I say.

Lottie nods, biting her bottom lip.

"I love my mum, but I wish he'd divorce her as he's never happy," she suddenly spits out. "They constantly argue." I move in front of her only to have her wrap her arms around my neck, her wracking sobs shaking her body.

"Have you spoken to your dad about it?" I ask, not wanting to get between Elijah, Darra or their daughter.

Having yet to meet Darra, I can't make a judgement.

"I have, but he tells me it's complicated, and I'm too young to understand."

"Adult relationships are complicated," I say.

"Like yours and Uncle Gabriel's?" she asks, pulling back and staring at me.

"Especially mine and your Uncle Gabriel's."

I sigh, giving her a small smile.

"Are you really having a baby?"

I stare at her in surprise. She'd left by the time I mentioned I was pregnant.

"I was outside the door. I heard what you said." Her cheeks ablaze with colour.

I smile and pat her hand. "It's very early days. Too early really to have told anyone... but yes. I'm pregnant."

A smile breaks out on Lottie's face. "I'm going to have a cousin," she says excitedly.

"I suppose you are." I smile at her.

"Can I babysit?" Her sudden excitement is palpable. The tears of a few moments ago are forgotten.

"That would be wonderful," I say. "I know I'll appreciate all the help I can get."

"Lottie?" A voice comes out of nowhere.

"I'm here, Dad," Lottie calls, wiping her face on her sleeve.

"You look fine," I reassure her.

"Thank you," she says, moving to the door. "You can stay here as long as you want."

"Thank you, Lottie. And if you ever want someone to talk to..." I know I'm playing with fire, I'm not exactly on her father's most popular list.

"Lottie?" The voice is getting closer, so she nods and pushes her way out of the door.

"I'm here, Dad," Lottie's voice gets quieter as she moves towards him.

"There you are. I was worried."

I hear the covered panic in Elijah's voice and my heart softens towards him. The mountain of a man is a soft teddy bear where his daughter is concerned.

"Sorry Dad," she says.

Their voices fade as they walk further away. I wait until I can no longer hear them before I venture out. Elijah is the last person I want to come face-to-face with.

I take the long way around before heading back to the house. I'm halfway up the large wooden staircase before I'm spotted.

"Leah?" I pause at the sound of Francesca's voice.

I drop my head, not needing this right now. I want time to build some walls. My hormones are raw, my emotions too close to the surface.

"Francesca," I say, turning to face her.

"Gabriel has been looking for you. Are you not coming to join us?" she asks, concern written all over her face.

I heard Gabriel calling, but I needed time to get my head together. That had probably been unfair of me.

"I thought I'd have an early night," I say, knowing it's a ridiculous statement as it's only seven o'clock.

She raises an eyebrow, her expression so similar to Gabriel's it takes my breath away.

"I want to tell you, my son... well, I probably don't need to tell you, do I?" She sighs. "I've seen you two together. Please Leah, come and celebrate. You've just given me the most amazing birthday present."

Her eyes drop to my flat stomach.

I hold my jaw tight as I watch her eyes fill with tears.

"I really don't care how —" she adds, her voice cracking.

I make my way down the stairs towards her.

"I'm going to apologise for Elijah. His behaviour is unforgivable. He's gone for the evening."

When I reach her side, she takes my hand in hers and squeezes. I purse my lips and smile.

"Okay." I let her lead me by the hand into the Drawing Room where the others are sitting.

Gabriel gets to his feet as soon as his mother and I enter.

"Where were you?" Concern is clear in his tone.

Guilt at ignoring his call weighs heavily on my chest.

"I was walking. I'm sorry if I worried you," I say, making my way towards him, suddenly needing to be close to him. We need to talk, but I think we have already aired enough *dirty laundry* tonight. I notice Caleb open his mouth, but I shoot him a look, giving a slight shake of my head. He acknowledges me with a nod and sits back. Gabriel pulls me down into the seat next to him, our thighs and arms touching.

"Leah, a baby," Harper says. "When are you due?"

I turn towards Gabriel's baby sister. She's sitting in one of the large armchairs, her leg dangling over the arm. Her thick makeup, unable to hide her natural beauty.

"It's still very early. I'm about eight weeks," I say.

"I'm pleased for you," she says, before adding, "I'll look forward to being an aunt again."

I smile at her, thankful she's broken the silence.

Her gaze never wavers, and it's then I realise there's more to Harper Frazer than the girl who likes the spotlight.

"Are you suffering from morning sickness? If you are, I grow fresh ginger. I can give you some."

My eyes flash to Kat's. Apart from our initial introduction earlier, she is almost as quiet, if not quieter, than Gabriel.

"Thank you," I say, turning to face her. "I've been suffering a little nausea, but it's more a feeling than an actual event."

"Lucky you," comes a voice from the doorway. "I was barfing my guts up when I was pregnant with Lottie. Not to mention the stretch marks. I'm Darra, Elijah's wife and resident pariah."

"Darra, you made it," Francesca says, getting up and moving towards the door. "Elijah has already left."

Darra lets out a harsh laugh. "No surprise there," she says. "Don't worry. I won't intrude. I'll find my daughter and *loving* husband."

Kat's breath hisses on the sofa next to me.

"Congratulations," she says, turning towards me and motioning towards Gabriel. "Make sure you tie him down."

She turns tail before anyone can respond. My gaze shoots

to Gabriel's and I see the concern in his eyes. He places his hand over mine and squeezes. Could this get any worse? We've still got a party to survive tomorrow.

I observe Francesca, whose eyes follow the retreating form of her daughter-in-law, her expression reflects her sadness.

She pauses before turning her attention back to the room, plastering a smile on her face that doesn't quite reach her eyes.

"Caleb, set up, we need to get this party started."

Gabriel leans towards me, his voice low. "It's tradition. Every year we play Monopoly as a family."

"We see who can win the most money." Caleb chuckles and I can see the irony. A room full of billionaires, playing to outdo each other with paper money.

"I'm in," I say.

"Good," says Francesca, shooting me a grateful look.

CHAPTER 43

GABRIEL

*I*t's eleven thirty when we finally call it a night. I'm winning, with Leah a close second. My strategic whispers are likely having something to do with it.

Although Leah is laughing and smiling with my siblings, I can sense her distance. She's put up a wall between us, and I don't like it.

We enter my room and get ready for bed. Leah no longer hides herself from me. There's no need as I know every inch of her body, where she's most sensitive and what she likes. The same way she's learned mine.

She grabs her things and walks quietly to the en suite, avoiding my gaze. I sink into the chair in the corner and pull off my shoes and socks. Tossing them down by the door.

I hear the shower turn on, followed by the tap in the sink as Leah runs through her nightly routine. I would normally be next to her. But tonight, I know I'm not welcome and I don't like the pressure building in my chest, where I keep forgetting to breathe. Leah is my air and tonight that's been withdrawn.

Ten minutes later, Leah comes back into the bedroom and makes her way to the bed, her gaze still avoiding mine.

"Leah?" I say.

"Not tonight, Gabriel. I'm tired. I just want to sleep." She sighs, her tone relaying her exhaustion. She pulls back the covers and climbs into the enormous four poster bed, almost disappearing within its size.

She lies down and rolls onto her side, facing outwards.

I get up and make my way into the bathroom before turning back and reentering the bedroom. I stand in the doorway and face the woman who has come to mean more to me than I realised.

"Elijah, he was out of line. He's got-"

"Issues? Yes, I got that part. He's also looking out for you, and you shouldn't discount that. You and me, we lied to them. Information is his thing. Can you blame him for checking me out? For being suspicious?"

I stare at her. If it's not Elijah, then it must be me. I wrack my brains.

"I fucked up, Leah. I'm sorry."

She gives me a sad smile. "No, Gabriel, you didn't. But what this shows me is how different our lives are. We've been living in a little bubble of our own creation, without a thought of what the future holds." Leah sighs and I move towards her. "Elijah is right. I grew up on a council estate, and my parents still live there, although they purchased their house. I didn't go to a fancy school or highbrow university. My family has worked hard for everything they have, but to people like your brother, that will never be enough."

"Elijah was being a dick. The rest of my family adores you, whatever the circumstances," I say, interlinking our fingers. My temper reigniting. It makes me want to thrash my older brother. That he has made Leah feel less, when she is so much more.

Leah's hand comes up and cups my cheek. "Gabriel, you've been raised in a different world to the one I grew up in. All this, your family home, playing hide and seek in the grounds... the water tower."

A shy smile graces her lips and I wonder if her mind has returned to our afternoon at the water tower, her screams echoing around the inside as I made her come first on my tongue before filling her with my cum as she rode me on an old bench.

"I can't change who I am. Where I come from," I say.

I'm unsure where Leah is going with this, but the crushing vice in my chest tells me I will not like it.

She looks at me in horror. "And I wouldn't want you to. That's not what I'm trying to say." She sighs and sits up, pulling the covers with her. I move to sit next to her.

"You need to explain."

I take her hand in mine. Something I have done a lot of recently.

She lowers her eyes to where our fingers are linked.

"Elijah's words hurt me."

I can't prevent the growl that escapes.

Leah squeezes my hand to get my attention.

"But Gabriel, he won't be the first or the last. Tomorrow we'll face your mum's friends, acquaintances. In our little bubble, we've shut out the rest of the world, but that's not how this works."

"It can. I've done it successfully for years," I say, offering her a smile. "You know I hate this life with all its false smiles and social climbers. The mindless small talk and sucking up, people telling you what they think you want to hear. The fawning. Would they do that if I was a chef or a gardener? No. It's because my last name is Frazer!" I cup Leah's cheeks, making her look at me. "It's why our arrangement, our bubble is so perfect." My final statement seems so empty.

Our agreement has changed. I know this, but I don't know how to tell her without frightening her off, especially after Elijah's little outburst.

"I think you might be downplaying your good looks," she says, her lips twitching, her eyes softening.

I groan and she laughs, the sound warming something within me. "In our social standing, my surname means something. It's like a badge of honour, one many want to add to their portfolio. It started at school, where kids tried to befriend us because their parents told them to. It's been the same with women. Before you, I've never known whether someone wanted me for me, my money, or my name. We might have called our romantic relationship fake, but believe me when I tell you, it's been the most real relationship I've ever been in. We work, Leah. Please don't think we don't. The bubble you speak of, it's where I've chosen to live my life. You've simply entered it. Please don't burst it. I like having you in here with me. The rest of the world can be damned."

Horror fills me as I watch Leah's eyes fill with tears.

"That's the longest speech I've heard you say, outside of work hours." She places a hand over mine, her other coming to my cheek. "I'm happy with our bubble too and those we choose to let in. But Gabriel, this time next year, you will bring our child to your mum's birthday party alone."

My heart jumps at the thought.

"No, *we* will be," I say, knowing I mean it.

Leah shakes her head. "That's not what we agreed. When the baby is born, we'll each be moving on."

My jaw clenches at the thought of Leah moving on. She's mine. When did my feelings change? I'm not one for relationships, the tie, the needs, but with Leah, it's different. The more time we've spent together, the more I've enjoyed her company.

I stay silent.

Leah leans forward, placing her lips against mine. I wait, unsure of what she wants until I feel her tongue snake along my lips.

I sink one hand into her hair, pulling her closer, while the other wraps around her back, dragging her against me.

One thing I know is Leah can't get enough of my body. If that's the case, I shall use every trick in my arsenal to make her crave me so much she can't let me go, and with luck, somewhere along the way, she might even fall in love with my mind too.

CHAPTER 44

GABRIEL

*L*eah has been quiet all morning, and I'm at a loss with how to draw her back. Without mother's party, I would have returned her to the car, driven back to our apartment, and reaffirmed our strong bond. I knew this party was going to be a disaster. Family get-togethers are always intermingled with family drama. At this moment I want to murder my older brother for making her feel this way.

My breath catches, as Leah steps out of the bathroom. Her makeup and hair are perfect, while her royal blue dress gently skims every curve.

"You look beautiful," I say before I can stop myself.

Leah's eyes lock with mine, but they are missing their usual sparkle. We made love last night, slowly. She allowed me to worship her body. But this morning, it's as if a barrier has gone up between us and I don't know how to break it down.

"Thank you," she says, moving over to the bed and collecting her clutch bag.

"Leah."

"No, Gabriel, let's just get through today. We can talk later," she says, heading towards the door.

My agitation towards my brother grows by the minute. How dare he do and say what he did to this wonderful woman? Who the hell does he think he is, interfering in my life like I'm some naïve child?

The party is already underway by the time we make it downstairs. Party goers weave their way through the hallway to the back of the house, where the marquee has been erected.

I take Leah's hand in mine as we reach the bottom step.

Turning her to face me, I cup her cheek, capturing her gaze.

"Ignore my brother. His thoughts are not mine, nor Caleb's or the rest of my family's. You are here as a guest of my mother and me. The child growing inside you is mine. You're not inferior. You are a queen, my queen. Don't let that arsehole wield any power."

I exhale slowly when Leah's eyes soften, and she places her hand over mine, leaning into my palm.

"You're right. Sticks and stones and all that," she says. "We made a choice, and it's our choice. Elijah can have his opinion. That's his right. He made me feel vulnerable yesterday. I should have trusted in us and our agreement. I'm proud of my past and my family. I know he's your brother, but I'm not going to let some privileged ass make me feel less. I'm sorry for pulling away. That was unfair."

Her words are like a blow to my stomach, her trust means more than she can know. My anger towards my brother however has skyrocketed, but now is not the time. I'll deal with him later.

"Come on," I say, leading her through the house. "Let's get this over with."

* * *

ELIJAH AND HIS WIFE, Darra, stand on the opposite side of the marquee, holding audience with several old family friends and hangers on. I've kept my distance, not wanting to create a scene, but I watch them as they work the room. You'd never know by looking at them. They can scarcely tolerate being in the same county, let alone breathing the same air.

I was only in my early teens when Elijah went to university. Every holiday he'd return with a swathe of university friends. Darra hanging off his arm, staking her claim. In retrospect, she had Elijah in her sights and was determined to keep him. During their final year, she got her way, falling pregnant with Lottie. Elijah put on a brave face as his Olympic dreams went up in smoke as he struggled to create a business to sustain him and his new family. My father telling him, if he was old enough to bring a child into the world, then he needed to man up and provide for his family. In true Elijah form, he showed the rest of us what was possible. Not wanting to follow in our father's footsteps, Dad bankrolled his startup. Frazer Technologies and Security has become one of the leading Security and Cyber Tech companies in the world. But my brother was no longer the quick-to-laugh, fun-loving man I remember from my youth.

I turn, realising Leah is missing.

"Kat, have you seen Leah?" I ask my sister, who was deep in conversation with her last I saw.

"She went inside to use the bathroom," Kat replies, patting my arm. "Don't worry about her. She's fine."

I kiss my sister on the cheek and leave the rest of the party behind. It's only when I go to walk around the corner, I hear a conversation that makes my blood boil.

"Have you heard?" a voice says from the hallway.

"No, what?" another answers.

"Apparently Gabriel has got himself an older woman...works for him. It's so cliche. Attractive, but clearly beneath him, socially. A gold digger, if ever I saw one."

There's a sniff, followed by giggles.

"I'm surprised," another voice says. "His mother spoke to mine a couple of months ago. She was hoping to set us up on a date, but then the next minute it's all off."

"No, his mother spoke to mine."

I grimace. What the hell was my mother thinking? As if any of these brain-dead socialites would spark my interest. I'd die of boredom within five minutes.

"Apparently, he whisked her off to Monaco. I hope she enjoyed it, because it won't last."

A flood of giggles follows the comment as a third voice enters the conversation, and I groan inwardly. I can see why women feel like men are treating them as commodities when they stand around discussing them.

"Total gold digger. Probably thinks she's won the lottery."

I'm about to step past the door frame when a hand rests on my chest. I look up to find Leah standing next to me, listening to the vipers spew their poison. My heart stops as she shakes her head. This is not what she needs after Elijah's outburst last night.

I frown, until I recognise the set of her jaw, along with the air of calmness she's exuding.

Leah smiles and I return it. It's like she can read my mind.

"Bubble," she whispers. "I've got this. They're mine."

She reaches up and presses a kiss to my cheek.

My chest swells. I know she heard their catty comments. I've explained how I hate this part of my life. I grew up surrounded by these people. I couldn't stand them then, and it's even worse now.

Before I can stop her, Leah steps forward. "Who's a gold digger?" I want to laugh as Leah feigns her innocence.

The three women pause, observing the new arrival. "We're having a private conversation." One of them says, her disdain for Leah clear in her voice.

I step forward into their line of sight, their mouths dropping open as they gawp at me like goldfish. Leah straightens her shoulders and I struggle to hide my smirk. Look out ladies, you're about to get the Leah treatment. I recognise this stance. It's the one she uses when dealing with annoying clients. Crossing my arms, I lean against the wall. This should be fun.

I vaguely recognise the dark-haired woman who recovers first. "Gabriel... or is it, Caleb? I never could tell the difference." Her laugh is as fake as her cleavage, which is hard to miss as it's practically falling out of her dress. "Lovely to see you again." She giggles at her own joke, stepping towards me. I want to laugh as Leah rolls her eyes, stepping in her way.

Oh, I like this side.

"It's Gabriel. It could be considered quite insulting when they have clear and distinct personalities, especially for someone who professes to know the family so well," Leah says.

The women pause, not sure what to do or say next. "I knew it was Gabriel," another says, clearly not helping her friend.

Their eyes dart to mine, but I mask my features. I'm known as the grumpy twin, so why not play to my strengths?

"Gabriel, darling," Leah says, linking her arm through mine. I bite the inside of my cheek to stop myself from laughing. "These ladies are concerned I'm only after your money."

Leah turns to me, her face feigning shock.

I decide to play along. "Is that true? Are you only after me for my money?" I ask her innocently.

Leah looks back at the women, who are now standing their gawping at us, colour running high in their cheeks.

Leah lowers her voice. "It's not Gabriel's money I'm after."

She pauses. "I'll let you into a little secret, ladies." Leah leans forward, and I wrap my arms around her waist. She looks at me over her shoulder before turning back to the bitches in front of us. "This man really knows what to do to make a woman scream. I've never had so many —"

I pull Leah away, leaving the women staring after us, open-mouthed.

The three women look past Leah, and at me in horror, before their eyes drop to my crotch, their cheeks darkening. Leah laughs, following their gaze with her own. My blood heating.

"What are you doing?" I whisper in her ear.

"Igniting the rumour mill," she whispers, her eyes twinkling. "Now you'll have them queuing up, wanting some of your big, orgasm-inducing —"

I slam my mouth down on hers, silencing her.

"Er... um... enjoy the party."

They call after us, before backing away and scattering.

I tighten my grip on Leah's waist. "Are you being a naughty girl, Leah Walker? Am I going to have to punish you?" I ask against her lips. "Just so you know, they are getting nowhere near my orgasm-inducing cock. That's all yours."

I can feel Leah's grin against my lips and love the fact the twinkle has returned to her eyes. Whatever Kat said to her has undone some of the damage Elijah inflicted.

"I hate gold diggers," she says, laughing. "And money does not equal class."

"Here, here," comes a voice behind us. "I don't know about you, Gabe, but I think I'm in love." I spin to face the one person at this party I can stand apart from family. "Are you going to introduce us?"

I step back from Leah and pull the woman before me in for a hug. "Pen," I say, kissing her cheek. At almost my height, there's little to no bending down.

"Hi Gabe, and this beautiful woman must be Leah," she says, stepping around me before enveloping Leah in a hug of her own.

"Hi," Leah squeaks, trying to catch my gaze, taking in the Amazonian-sized woman in front of her.

Pen is quite something. Standing at six foot, her newly dyed black hair matches the ebony of the dress she's wearing. In true Pen style, she's dressed to shock. I wonder if Pen is where Harper gets her inspiration. The dress is floor length, with an open front split almost to her navel. It's covered in ebony sequins that shimmer as she walks. A chunky chain hangs between her breasts. Her slender figure allowing her to execute it flawlessly.

"I'm Penelope—Pen. Welcome to Frazer World, Leah. It's about time someone put those crazy bitches in their place." Her gaze scowling after the fleeing guests.

Leah coughs to hide her laugh. "Thank you. I think." Leah says before adding. "I love your boots."

Pen grins and pulls up the bottom of her dress. It's my turn to roll my eyes. Only Pen would pair a classic designer dress with biker boots.

"Comfort is key, and I'm tall enough," Pen says, linking her arm through Leah's. "And heels are so bloody uncomfortable."

"Aren't they just?" Leah nods, accepting Pen's arm.

Oh, no. These two together could be bad for my health—mental health, that is.

"I can see us becoming firm friends," Pen adds. "I like Leah, Gabe. You'd better not screw this up."

"You've only just met her," I point out, but when she glares, I raise both hands in surrender. "I'll keep that in mind," I say drolly.

Pen wraps an arm around Leah's shoulder.

"Did Gabe tell you I taught him to game, when he was a moody, non-communicative teenager?" She laughs, shooting me a grin. I roll my eyes as she continues.

"I went to university with the grumpy bastard and beauty queen over there," she says, tipping her head in Elijah's direction. He and Darra having now moved inside. "I came home with him during the holidays, and I've been a visitor ever since."

"You were at university with Elijah?" Leah asks, her brow wrinkling.

Before I can think too much into her response, another voice appears. It truly is the day for it.

"And me...don't forget me...and you're like a bad smell, aren't you Penelope? We just can't seem to get rid of you." Darra swans over, a little unsteady on her feet. I reach out to prevent her from ploughing into Leah.

"Don't start, Darra," I hiss quietly, taking her arm and pulling her away.

"Start what, Gabriel? Making a scene?" She pulls her arm out of my grip. "I'm his wife, the mother of his child. She's just —" Darra doesn't finish her sentence. Instead, she staggers back across the room, whispering something in Elijah's ear. Something that has him looking across the room at us. His expression hardens. I hear Pen sigh and my heart goes out to her. She and Elijah were best friends. An odd pairing.

Pen shakes her head, her eyes betraying the sadness I know she keeps locked inside. A look passes between us before she returns her attention to Leah, as if the past few minutes never occurred.

"Yes, for my sins. Elijah wasn't always this way. He used

to be fun and lighthearted, more like Caleb." She pauses before adding with a chuckle, "But less of a tart. Now he's just—"

"Who are you calling a tart?" Caleb says, sweeping Penelope up into a bear hug, swinging her around.

"You, dear boy," she says when her feet finally touch the ground, her hand pressed against the centre of his chest. "How is your love life? Any woman caught your attention for longer than five minutes?"

A look passes over Caleb's face before he plasters on his usual grin.

"Why would I deprive the female species of this?" he says, waving his hand up and down his body.

We all groan.

Pen shoots Leah a calculating look.

"Aunty Pen." I watch as Lottie catapults her way across the room and into Pen's arms.

"Hey, munchkin. Have you grown again?" She asks, sweeping my niece into an enormous bear hug. "If you keep growing at this rate, you'll be as tall as me soon."

"You always say that," Lottie says, rolling her eyes. "We had to go clothes shopping. My trousers were ankle biters." There's pride in Lottie's voice.

"Well, you have to grow sometime," she adds, giving her a squeeze. "How's your programming assignment going?" Pen sits on the arm of the nearest chair to make herself Lottie's height.

Lottie scrunches up her nose.

"That well, huh? Well, you know where to find me if you need me," Pen says, running her hand over Lottie's hair.

"Thanks Aunty Pen. Dad's been busy," Lottie adds, and my heart goes out to my niece. Her mother is too busy *doing* lunch and whatever else she does to fill her time. My brother hides in his office.

"You have my number," Pen says. "Use it, please."

Lottie nods, but there's a sadness in her eyes. I set a mental note to ask her why she hasn't called Pen or me.

Before I can think, Lottie moves towards Leah and wraps her arms around her waist.

"I see you met Leah. Did you hear? She and Uncle Gabe are having a baby."

A hush falls around us as everyone turns to stare. Leah's eyes drop to the ground, and I step forward, wrapping my arm around her and my niece.

"I know, it's wonderful news, isn't it? I'm hoping I get to have lots of cuddles," Pen says extra loudly. Then looks around her. "Nothing to see here, people."

The nosy crowd turns their nose up at her, making her smirk even more.

"Oh, Pen, I'm sorry," Leah says, and I squeeze her gently.

"It's fine. Ignore them," I whisper against her ear.

"Did I say something wrong?" Lottie says, her eyes flicking between us.

Pen pats Lottie's cheek. "No, munchkin. It's fantastic you're so eager."

She turns and smiles at Leah.

"I'm the pariah, but Mrs F loves me," she says.

"That I do. Are you creating carnage, Penelope?" my mother says, coming up and pulling Pen down for a hug.

"As always," she says, hugging my mother back. "Happy Birthday, Franny," she adds, her voice wavering.

"It's lovely to see you, my darling. It is a shame you couldn't make last night," Mum adds, patting her cheek.

Pen smiles at her. "I know, but I had to work."

"You work too hard." The affection in my mum's voice is hard to miss.

"It's only hard if you hate your job," Pen replies.

Everyone knows she loves what she does.

"Are you still doing business with that slave driver of a son of mine? Is he working you too hard?"

Pen laughs and places an arm around my mother's shoulders. "He couldn't if he wanted to."

Mum huffs. "He's still being a grumpy bastard, then?"

Leah begins to choke.

I grab a glass of juice from a passing waiter and hand it to her.

"It's okay, Leah, I'm under no illusions about my children. Speaking of sons, has my eldest apologised to you?"

Leah squirms.

"I raised him better than that. I'm sorry." I watch in amazement as my mother steps up and pats Leah's cheek. "And you can stop looking smug," she says, looking directly at me. "Don't think last night's discussion is over."

I'm amazed how a woman who stands at just five foot two, can be as foreboding as my mother, but she has it in spades.

"Not any of your business, mother," I add, wrapping both arms around Leah's waist once Lottie steps away.

"Then make sure you look after Leah, or there will be consequences. Your bank balance might be greater than mine, but you're still my son," she says before turning and leaving us to socialise with some of her friends.

"I feel like someone dropped me into an episode of the Twilight Zone," Leah says, leaning back against me.

My arms instinctively tighten around her.

"I often feel the same way."

My gaze catches my friend's, and she grins at me. I return her smile, and her eyebrows almost reach her hairline.

"Leah has that effect on me."

CHAPTER 45

LEAH

*S*tella stands up and pulls me in for a hug.

"I've missed you," she says, before holding me away from her. Her eyes roaming over me.

I grin and step back.

"It's only been a month," I laugh. "How was New York?"

She waggles her eyebrows. "Full of sexy American men, an amazing night life and lots of work, that prevented me from enjoying either," she says dropping back into her seat and laughing.

"Well, you look well on it," I say.

"I feel good," she says. "They say, a change is as good as a rest, and it's just what I needed. Enough about me. How are things with you and Mr Sexy?"

I suck in my lips to prevent my grin. "I'm pregnant," I say with a gush. I hadn't wanted to tell her over the phone. I wanted to see her reaction.

"What!" she screams, jumping up and pulling me out of my seat, oblivious to the other patrons of the coffee shop. "Oh. My. God." She squeals. "I promise to be the best adopted aunty, godmother." She grabs me again in another bear hug, before releasing me and placing her palms on my stomach. "This little one could ever ask for. You are going to be so loved and spoiled."

Tears are glistening in her eyes. It's my turn to pull her in for a hug.

"You daft bat," I say, manoeuvring her back into her seat.

We sit smiling at one another until our drinks arrive.

"Does this mean you're going to be moving back down-stairs?" Stella asks, taking a sip of her drink.

I don't say anything.

"Leah?"

"I don't know," I tell her honestly. "Gabriel and I haven't discussed it."

"But you will?" When I don't say anything, she leans forward and grabs my hand. "Have you fallen for him?"

I think back to our weekend. The bitches and their snide comments, to Gabriel's family, all of whom made me welcome despite our bombshell. All apart from Elijah, but it doesn't take a rocket scientist to work out that man has more issues than a tabloid newspaper.

"Oh, Leah, does he feel the same way?" I look over at Stella, her face a mask of sympathy.

"We haven't discussed it," I tell her honestly.

"I knew this was going to happen. You were never one for one-night stands... clinical sex, my ass. I doubt the man knows what clinical sex is. All the dark, silent, brooding testosterone."

"Enough," I say, unable to keep the laughter in. "Yes, to all of the above. But you don't have to worry about me. I prom-ise. I'm happy. Truly happy. Whatever this is. I'm enjoying myself. When it ends." I take a deep breath and force a smile. "And I know it will. I will have had the best time. I'll also be coming away with an amazing gift."

I let my hand wander to my stomach, where our tiny life is blooming.

A furrow appears between her brows. "But...oh hell. You've fallen in love with Gabriel Frazer."

"No," I say, although I realise the words are a lie as soon as they leave my mouth.

"Really? From where I'm sitting, I'd say that's exactly what you've done. Does he love you too?" Stella asks quietly.

"It's not something that's come up. We told his family about our arrangement at the weekend."

"And?"

"They took it remarkably well. Of course, they were shocked," I admit.

"Leah. I'm worried," Stella says, her face echoing her concern, her hand gripping my forearm.

"I know. But it's complicated." I sigh and shake my head. My heart clenches as I try to articulate what's going on inside my head and heart. "I don't know what to do. I need to talk to Gabriel. Reaffirm the terms and conditions we set out at the very start. Everything has changed. But, if I question them, it makes a mockery of everything I asked of him in the beginning. I don't want our relationship to be awkward. Gabriel made it very clear from the outset that he didn't do relationships. Apart from the sex, nothing else has changed."

Although I know in my heart it has. We're spending more and more time together. What started out as dinner, is now gaming, swimming, curled up watching old movies. But he knows there's an end date. Is he merely pretending to keep me happy while I'm carrying our child? I know I'm over-thinking things, but...

Stella flops back in her chair, her arms folded over her chest. "So clinical isn't how it remained?"

I shake my head, not quite able to meet her gaze. Our sex life couldn't be further from clinical if we tried.

"Oh, Leah," she says. "Be careful. After what Vince did to you."

"Gabriel is nothing like Vince. He certainly hasn't promised me one thing and then gone back on it."

"No, he's made you fall in love with him. Now you're going to have a child together. That links you for a minimum of eighteen years. What happens if he meets someone else, or you do?"

I feel my body sag, knowing she is only voicing the same fears I have.

"I don't know," I tell her truthfully, my eyes welling.

"You either need to talk to him or put some space between you," Stella, the voice of reason, states.

I know she's right. The tightness in my chest has grown since the weekend. I feel like I'm walking an emotional tightrope. But then Gabriel takes me in his arms, and it all disappears. We disappear back into the bubble we've created.

As if sensing I've reached the end of my rope, Stella leans forward and grips my hand. "When's your first scan?" she asks, changing the subject.

* * *

I KNOCK on Gabriel's office door. The rest of the team has left for the evening.

"Hi," Gabriel says, looking up. "How was lunch?"

I told him this morning I was meeting Stella.

"Good," I say, not wanting to discuss what we spoke about here. This is our professional space, and we have kept it that way—mostly.

I move to the window and stare down at the offices and streets below.

Gabriel comes up behind me, his arms snaking around

my waist, before dropping kisses on my neck. When I freeze, he stops.

He's always too perceptive. "What's wrong?"

I turn in his arms and drop my forehead to his chest, my arms around his waist.

"What are we doing?" I ask.

His finger tilts my chin until I'm looking up into his face. I flinch, unsure I want to see what's written there.

"What do you mean?"

"Us?" I twist my head out of his grasp and step back. "Sorry, this is not the time or the place."

I go to move around him, but he captures my upper arm, stalling me.

"What's going on? I take it you talked to Stella. What did she say?" His voice is neutral.

"Nothing. She asked when I was moving out." I look up into his face, and my heart stutters. "I told her about the baby."

Gabriel nods, pulling me between his legs as he sits back against his desk.

"Was she unhappy? Is that it?"

"Oh gosh no, she's thrilled. She can't wait to be an aunty, godmother, whatever title she can adopt." I laugh, thinking back to my friend's excitement.

Gabriel smiles, and my breath catches. I drop my head onto his chest and his arms snake around me, making me once again feel safe and warm. What am I going to do when we finally call it a day?

"Her question threw me, that's all," I mumble against his shirt.

Gabriel pulls back, his body twisting so he can look at me. "Why?"

"She asked me questions I couldn't answer," I admit, finally looking up at his beautiful face. "What are we doing,

Gabriel?" I ask. "We're playing with fire. This is not what we agreed in the beginning."

Gabriel takes my hand and interlinks our fingers. "Are you unhappy?"

My eyes fly to his. "No. I'm very happy."

"Then what's the problem? I know what we're doing is unconventional. But is it wrong if we're happy? Should it matter? Is it anyone else's business? Do we have to label it?" he asks.

He pulls me back towards his body, and I yield. He drops a kiss on my forehead.

"I'm happy, Leah," he mumbles against my hair. "I don't think I've ever felt this happy."

I wrap my arms around his waist as he tilts my head, claiming my lips, his kiss one of ownership and possession. I sink into it, my body unable to resist him.

His hand slides down my back and over my hip before lifting my skirt. His fingers trail over the material between my thighs.

"Always so wet for me," he murmurs against my lips, his finger pushing the material to one side before sinking into me. I gasp and then groan against his lips as his finger pumps in and out, my thighs spreading before he draws my arousal up, using it to circle my clit with his thumb. "Always wanting," he says as I purr at his wicked fingers, my body pressing into his.

"Gabriel," I gasp as he spins me around, spreading me across his desk before moving to stand between my thighs.

I part my legs willingly as Gabriel pulls my panties off, stuffing them in his pocket.

He pushes my skirt up. "Lie back," he says, placing a hand on my chest, pushing me back so I'm resting on my elbows, but can still see everything he's doing.

"Hum," he says, before looking up as if remembering the

office door. He walks around and closes it, flipping the lock. "Just in case."

He smirks.

Gabriel moves back between my thighs, his eyes ravenously fixated on my exposed and now dripping pussy.

He sits down in his chair, scooting himself forward. "Now, Ms Walker, from what I understand, you've worked hard today. Maybe I should give you a reward."

I gasp as his hands slide under my ass, pulling me towards his mouth. His eyes lock with mine.

His tongue snakes out, licking me from my centre to my clit, before his mouth suckles on my sensitive bundle of nerves. My head drops back as his fingers find my entrance, circling and stretching me, just as he knows I like.

"Eyes on me," he demands, pulling my gaze back to his dark one as his mouth continues to torment me, the pressure of my building orgasm growing.

"Gabriel." I moan as he spears me with his tongue, his fingers rubbing faster and faster circles. My orgasm has me clutching his head, my hands locked in his hair as he continues to feed my spasms, until I'm lying across his desk, exhausted. So much for professionalism in the workplace!

Before I can catch my breath, Gabriel's hand slides up my front and under my blouse, cupping my breast. Since finding out I was pregnant, my breasts are tender, but they love Gabriel's mouth and hands. I unbutton my blouse, letting it fall open. The look of possession he has is one I want to memorise.

Gabriel stands up, my juices glistening on his lips. He continues to watch me as he bends over, sliding my bra cup to one side before taking my nipple in his mouth. His gaze holds mine as he slides two fingers into my still-quivering pussy before curling them up against my G-spot.

"I can't," I moan.

"We both know that's a lie." He smirks against my nipple as his thumb brushes my clit, drawing my hips up and off the desk.

Gabriel switches his attention to my other nipple as his fingers pump in and out of me, curling and stroking at the most sensitive spot. He's learned all my weaknesses and knows how to play with my body until it's screaming for more.

I feel the pressure building once more. My muscles begin to clench around his fingers, but he pulls back.

He unzips his trousers, pushing them down, exposing himself. I groan at the sight of him, angry and swollen, knowing it's me who has made him that way.

"This time, you're going to come on my cock," he says, grunting as he presses himself into my opening, thrusting all the way in, in one motion.

My head drops back, and I moan. My body stretches to accommodate his size as he pumps in and out, twisting his hips, hitting my G-spot over and over. My nerves are fired up, needing more of this man. I stretch my legs wider, wanting him deeper.

"That's it, good girl," he says, cupping my ass in his hands and pulling me hard against him.

He pulls back.

"Look at how well we fit together. You spread out on my desk," Gabriel says, making me look down at his dick, glistening with my juices.

I bite my lip as he inches back in.

"This is not quite right," he says suddenly, and it's then I realise he's recreating the scene from my e-reader. "If I remember rightly."

He pulls me up and spins me around, pressing my chest down onto his desk. My feet touch the ground, and he nudges them out. Before I can breathe, he is thrusting back inside me. My body welcomes him, drawing him deep. We both moan at the sensation. Gabriel drops himself over me, his mouth finding mine in an awkward kiss.

"I'm never going to look at my desk without thinking of you, and your hungry pussy," he says, sliding in and out, my desire running freely down my thighs.

His hand snakes around, his fingers finding my clit, rubbing circles until I'm squirming beneath him.

"Ahhh, Gabriel," I say.

"Are you happy?" he asks, his lips against my ear.

"Yes...so happy," I say as another orgasm rockets through my body, squeezing him. Gabriel continues to circle my clit, wringing every ounce of my orgasm out of me, his own body twisting and thrusting until he too freezes. I feel him jerk deep inside me, coating my insides once more with his cum. He collapses onto my back, breathing hard.

"Good girl," he says as he withdraws from me.

The exact words the character used in the book I was reading. Unlike the fictional character, however, Gabriel wipes away the evidence, pulling my skirt back into place before turning me around and straightening my bra and blouse.

"Panties?" I ask.

The wicked glint in his eyes is all the answer I need.

The distinct sound of the elevator door opening makes us both freeze.

Chatter appears, followed by the distinct sound of the door being tried. A key rattles in the lock.

"Shit."

I straighten my hair and scoot around Gabriel's desk, dropping into the chair opposite him as he does the same, zipping himself up as he throws the evidence into the bin.

The door opens, and the cleaner steps in, freezing at the sight of us.

"Oh, sorry," he says. "I'll come back later."

"If you don't mind, thank you," Gabriel says, his attention focused on his screen.

I bite down on the inside of my cheek to prevent myself from laughing.

The door closes, and Gabriel looks up, his eyes sparkling.

"I can understand the thrill," he says, as I giggle.

We narrowly escaped getting caught having sex in his office! Who am I, and what have I done with the professional Leah of old?

CHAPTER 46

GABRIEL

"*O*f course, send him up."

I hear Amanda's voice on the telephone and wonder who's about to appear.

The elevator pings, and I wait patiently. My attention today is a little off-par. Leah is wearing the same suit she wore last week when I spread her out over my desk. The memory is playing havoc with my concentration. It's strange because it's not like I'm sex-starved. Since falling pregnant, Leah's been insatiable. Not that I'm complaining. Thinking back to Monaco, she was insatiable then. I smile at the memory. I love how wanton she is, how she feels, coming on my dick, how she's unafraid to tell me what she needs.

An enormous bouquet walks past my door.

"What the?"

Those legs definitely *do not* belong to my brother.

I'm on my feet before I can stop myself.

All eyes on the floor follow the stranger and the flowers, and they stop outside Leah's office. It's only then I see the face of the person responsible.

What the hell is Vince doing here? Why is he bringing Leah flowers?

My stomach drops, and a sour taste fills my mouth.

Leah's door opens, and her face is a picture of shock. Her response settles some of my unease.

"What are you doing here, Vince?" she asks.

"You've blocked my number," he says. "I need to see you."

"My blocking your number should be enough of a hint," Leah says, her hands resting on her hips.

"Don't be like that. We had ten good years together. Don't you owe me the chance to explain?"

I watch Leah's jaw drop open at his words.

"I don't *owe you* anything. You left me, remember?"

"And that was a mistake. I'm here to apologise."

I've heard enough. I step out of my office. Leah's eyes going wide as I move towards them.

"Is there a problem?" I ask, facing Leah, but shooting Vince a look.

He's the same height as me, so his eyes lock with mine.

"I wanted to see Leah," his voice is whiney.

"Leah is working," I say.

I want him gone and as far away from Leah as possible. Perhaps their ten-year history unsettles me.

"Surely she's entitled to a break. I've been waiting downstairs for you to take lunch," he says, returning his attention to Leah.

"I ate at my desk," Leah chirps up.

"Well, then you can have a coffee with me. Half an hour. Surely your boss can't deny you that?"

He sounds smug having thought he's circumnavigated the rules.

Leah looks past Vince and me to the rest of the staff. All of whom have stopped what they're doing and are now watching the events unfold.

Leah looks at me.

"The choice is yours," I say.

It's not like I can stop her. She's a grown woman and our relationship is still a secret amongst our colleagues.

Leah's eyes widen.

"See, your boss is fine with it. Please, Leah. Half an hour."

Leah shoots me a questioning look, but all I can do is shrug. I want to deny his words, but I know I can't. It would cause too many questions, so instead I say, "We have a new client coming in at four."

Not that Leah needs to be there, but it gives her an excuse should she need one.

"I won't forget," she says, her shoulders relaxing.

Vince thrusts the bouquet at Leah, and I'm please when she takes them and drops them onto the sofa with little thought or care. I enjoy seeing the frown that mars his brow.

"Fine. Let's get this over with," Leah says, grabbing her phone and handbag as she storms past Vince and me and heads towards the elevator.

Vince shoots me a smug look, but I ignore him. Calmly making my way back into my office, even though my insides are churning. I'm not Leah's keeper. She needs to be free to make her own choices.

Since her lunch with Stella, and our chat, Leah's been more relaxed. I told her I don't want her to move out, that I like things the way they are. She seems to have accepted that, but as I watch her leave with Vince and the doors close, taking her away from me, my breathing becomes quick and shallow. I press my hand against my chest almost to the point of pain. What have I done?

I go back into my office and sit down, I reopen the document I was struggling with before, but close it. I run a hand through my hair before pulling up the latest market newsfeed.

Concentrate!

CHAPTER 47

LEAH

The elevator door closes, my eyes locked on Gabriel's until the last moment. What was he thinking? He could have stopped this. Given me an out. Coffee with Vince is the last place I want to be right now. But then maybe Gabriel is right. Going for coffee now means I can set Vince straight. He never was good at taking a hint and I know he won't let whatever it is, go, until he says his piece.

Vince steps closer, and I move away.

"What do you want?" I say, turning to face him.

"Don't be like that, babe," he says, his face softening as he stares at me. "I've missed you."

I stifle my laugh with a cough.

"Missed me?" I choke on the words, but I'm given a reprieve as the elevator opens into the reception area, letting us out.

Vince's hand moves to the small of my back, so I sidestep. My skin crawls at the contact. I can remember my mother saying to me years earlier. When you go off someone, you can feel your skin crawl when they touch you. I never believed her until now.

He thankfully takes the hint as we walk in silence to the coffee shop around the corner.

"What can I get you?" he asks. "You get us a seat."

"A decaf latte," I say, which causes him to pull a face.

I leave him to order while I find us a table. There's one in the window, out in the open. At least here he'll have to behave himself.

He eventually returns with two mugs of coffee.

"Decaf," he says, placing the mug in front of me.

"Thank you," I respond, wrapping my hands around it and staring at the steaming liquid.

Vince sits down opposite me, silence descending.

"I'm sorry," he says eventually, his eyes staring into mine.

I used to love his blue eyes, but now all I can think about are dark, almost black eyes, surrounded by ridiculously long lashes. Lashes that would make most women jealous.

I shrug, not sure what he wants me to say.

He runs a hand through his slicked back hair. I want to laugh, as I can only imagine how sticky his palm will now be.

"Don't be like this. Talk to me," he pleads.

I sigh. "What do you want me to say, Vince? It's okay?" I shake my head at him. "Because guess what? It's not okay. There is another woman who is pregnant because of you. You turfed me out of my home and moved her in. You threw ten years of our life together away, without even a thought for my feelings."

I'm surprised when he has the good grace to look sheepish.

"I know. I could have handled it better." He runs a hand over his face this time, pausing at his mouth.

"You think?"

"Look, I'm sorry. It was all a lie. I miss you. I want us to give it another try."

He reaches across the table for my hand. Which I pull away.

I stare at him wide-eyed.

"You're kidding, right?" I say.

"No, I mean it."

His hand comes across the table again. This time when I move, I spill coffee onto the table, just avoiding my skin.

"Don't be like this. You love me," he pleads.

"No, Vince, I don't," I say.

"You do. I hurt you, I get that, but we can overcome that. Just come home, give me another chance. I love you, Leah. I always have."

His whiney tone is grating on my nerves.

I shake my head, unable to believe what I'm hearing. This is a man who was threatening me with solicitors less than six months ago. Now he's here begging for a second chance.

"What about Yasmin?"

I'm amazed as I watch the muscles in his shoulders relax. Oh wow, he thinks he has a chance.

"That's over. She and I are history. Everything got out of hand. Yas, she was supposed to be a bit of fun, something to lighten the load. The boys, they encouraged it," he tries to explain, as if somehow, that makes everything magically better.

"What about the baby? You can't just ignore the child you created."

A flush of red tinges his cheeks.

"It's not mine," he says, his eyes dropping to the table.

My eyebrows raise at his words. Did I just hear correctly that the child isn't his?

"Excuse me? Not yours?" I say, slowly.

My mind goes back to the night at Tristan's Bar, a night

347

that set me on my current path. A night when Yasmin had purposefully told me she and Vince were having a baby.

I can no longer contain my laughter.

I look up to find Vince staring at me.

"No. It's her ex-boyfriend's. He dumped her when he found out she was pregnant, but had second thoughts and has come back," Vince explains, looking at me, as if I've lost my mind.

I dab at the tears that are now freely running down my face.

"So, you thought you'd settle and come back for me?"

"No," he says firmly, but I know he's lying. Vince has never done well on his own. He can't cook. I wonder if he has learned how to use the washing machine.

"I love you, Leah. I always have." His tone is pleading.

"I'm sorry Vince, but it's too late. I've moved on," I say.

"Impossible. You love me," he says again, reaching for my hand.

This time I place it in my lap.

"No, I don't. And it's probably the reason you had an affair. We'd grown apart."

"No, it's not. She tricked me."

I stare at him, giving him a small smile. "Tricked you into bed? I don't think so."

He sinks back into the chair. "You and I, we were having difficulties," he adds, as if that makes everything okay.

"We were planning our wedding. Not much more civil than that," I say, crossing my arms over my chest, wondering how I got myself into this situation.

"I got cold feet. Can you blame a man? Marriage is a big step. But it's one I'm willing to take now. We can get married this weekend. Go to a registry office. Stella and Nat can be our witnesses."

He sits forward, excitement on his face at his suggestion.

Does the numpty not realise it takes at least four weeks to get a marriage licence? This isn't the movies, but he gets a gold star for enthusiasm.

Instead of correcting him, I shake my head. "As I said before, we're over."

He leans forward, "But-"

I cut him off. "I'm pregnant."

Vince sags back in his chair. "What? How? Who?"

"You know how," I say. "As for who, it doesn't matter."

I desperately need to leave this place, go back to the office, and find comfort in Gabriel's arms. Everything with him has been perfect, despite us only being together for a few months. He has never made any false promises. He has always been open and honest. Whatever our future is, it will be better than my past. I bet money on it.

"I don't care," he blurts out. "We can raise your baby together. I love you and I know you love me. The spare room is a nursery. It's all ready and waiting."

I stare at Vince open-mouthed.

"You're willing to accept my child as your own?" I ask, intrigued and horrified in equal measure.

"Yes, if it means you'll come back," he says, his head nodding frantically like a bobbing dog.

"And the nursery is already set up?"

I repeat his words slowly, his head bobbing enthusiastically. How on earth did I stay with this man for ten years?

"It is. I have bought and prepared everything," he says, sounding smug.

I stand up.

"Goodbye Vince. Please don't ever contact me again. I wish you a nice life."

I turn and head for the door, only stopping when a hand clamps around my upper arm.

I stare down at the offending limb.

"Let me go, Vince," I say, shaking my arm.

But his hand remains firm.

"You are not walking away from me," he hisses. "I deserve better than that."

"No Vince, you don't. I deserve better than you. You think I'll accept being second choice? That I want a nursery that was decorated and chosen by the woman you left me for? *I most definitely* deserve better than that and always have. I suggest you look up housekeepers. You'll find one who can fulfil your needs."

My heart rate increases when his hand remains.

"When did you become such a bitch?" Vince spits, his eyes wide.

"When I realised being a doormat wasn't conducive to my wants and needs." My eyes drop to where his hand has tightened further on my bicep. "Sorry Vince, but I really need to leave now. I have a meeting to get back to."

A man from a nearby table gets up and moves towards us.

"I think the lady wants you to let her go, man," he says, coming to stand next to me.

"Stay out of this. My fiancée and I are having a conversation." Vince hisses.

"No Vince, this conversation, and our engagement are over. Please remove your hand and let me go. If not, I will ask this kind gentleman to call the police," I say as my heart races.

I don't think Vince would ever hurt me, but there's a kind of maniacal look in his eyes that I don't recognise.

My rescuer makes a slight move towards us, and Vince drops his hand.

"Fine, but when you regret this, don't think you can come crawling back," he says

"Don't worry, Vince. I promise I won't."

The gentleman looks at me. "Will you be all right?" he asks kindly.

I nod.

"Thank you," I say before making my way to the door without looking back.

I know the guy is waylaying Vince, allowing me time to make my escape. Stepping out and into the sunshine, my heart lightens. If I hurry, I'll be just in time for Gabriel's meeting.

CHAPTER 48

GABRIEL

*M*r Paine shakes my hand.

"I look forward to doing business with you, Gabriel. I'm sorry I missed Leah. Please send her my regards," he says.

I nod, but my mind is elsewhere. It's amazing I've managed to convince him to take us on.

After saying goodbye, I watch as Amanda walks him to the elevator, before I head down to Leah's office. Her door is open, but when I look inside, she's still absent, her bag not in its usual place.

I turn to Rob, who sits outside her room.

"Rob, have you seen Leah?"

He looks up as if shocked to see me at his desk.

"Sorry, Gabriel, not since she left with her fiancé," he says awkwardly as if he's somehow dropped Leah in it.

"No problem. If you see her, can you tell her to pop in and see me?"

He vigorously nods in agreement.

Where the hell is she? She left over two and a half hours ago.

My stomach roils, and a sour taste fills my mouth. This is not like Leah.

I enter my office and drop into my chair, checking my phone for messages or a missed call. But the last message from Leah was yesterday.

The hairs on the back of my neck stand up.

What if Vince has convinced her to go back to him? Will she go? What if he doesn't care she's carrying another man's child? They were together for ten years. They have history. I know Leah says they're over, but is that her way of coping with his desertion? What if they are right now, at their old apartment, Vince sliding in and out of her body? There's no way any man could resist her. The flowers reveal he's finally come to his senses and wants her back.

Bile rises in the back of my throat as I think of Leah and Vince together. Of her moaning his name, the way she screams mine. Of her coming on his cock, squeezing him hard.

Shit!

Things between us were perfect before my mother's birthday weekend. Then Elijah ruined it with his questions. Then her friend Stella, questioning her, making her doubt us. I thought after making love in my office, all this was behind us. But now? Was Leah pretending? Does she still doubt what we have? I told her I was happy. Was that not enough?

I glance at the clock. Damn, it's the middle of the night for Mark. I pick up the phone.

"Gabriel?" Caleb's voice comes over the line. "What's up?"

"How do you know something's up?" I ask.

"You never call me unless something is wrong or you need something," he replies, and I realise it's true.

"I'm sorry," I say.

"Don't be. It's who you are, Gabe. Talk to me," he says, surprising me.

"Leah's gone," I say.

There's a pause. "What do you mean, she's gone?"

"Her ex turned up and made her go for coffee with him."

"Okay." Caleb is clearly wanting more.

"Two and a half hours have passed since then," I say.

"And you're worried?"

I run a hand through my hair, a habit I seem to have picked up since Leah entered my life.

"Have you tried messaging her? Calling her?" he asks.

"She hasn't messaged or called me."

A moment of silence follows. "Gabriel, you and Leah are in a relationship. You are having a child together. I know it's unconventional, but there's more between you than either of you are admitting. A blind man would pick up on the chemistry that sizzles between you two."

"Have you been reading romances again?" I ask Caleb. He's always had a penchant for romance. It's why I'm surprised he's never settled down.

"Nothing wrong with a good romance," he laughs. "You can learn a lot, but Gabe, if you're worried, call her, send her a message."

"What if she thinks I'm interfering? Overstepping?"

An exhale comes down the phone, and I know Caleb has sat down. "Do you love Leah?"

That was not what I was expecting.

"Er..."

"Let me put it another way. When you are with Leah, does she make you smile? Do you want to share your thoughts with her? Your worries and fears? When you touch her, does it feel safe and natural, like you've come home?"

I stop and listen to my brother's words, half shocked and more impressed. When did he become insightful?

"You are not useless at romance, Gabe. It's just you never met the right woman. You and Leah fit together."

"But —"

"But nothing. If she makes you feel that way, then you have to tell her. Don't let Vince sweep in because they have history. Not that I think Leah is that naïve. She has feelings for you. Every time she looks at you, it's written all over her face. You just started wrong." Caleb sighs. "What have you got to lose?"

I think about what he's said.

"I'll call her."

I pick up my phone and dial Leah's number. It rings, and I hold my breath. When it clicks to voicemail, I immediately redial.

When the same thing happens, my muscles tighten. Why wouldn't she be answering? Unless she doesn't want to speak to me, or face me?

"No answer," I whisper.

There's a pause. "There may be an explanation. Maybe her phone has died, or she's dropped it," Caleb says.

"Or she doesn't want to talk to me," I say, laying my thoughts on the line.

"I can't see Leah doing that. She's an upfront woman," Caleb says.

"Is she? No one knew for two months her engagement had ended."

"All I'm saying is, try not to read too much into it."

There's a knock at my door. I look up to find an ashen-looking Amanda in the doorway.

"Sorry to interrupt, Gabriel. There is a Stella Long on the phone. Apparently, Leah has been in an accident. She's at the hospital."

I'm on my feet before I can think. "Where?"

"St Andrew's," she says.

"Gabriel, I'll meet you there," I hear Caleb shout before the telephone goes dead.

I grab my jacket and make my way to the door.

I pick up Amanda's phone. "Talk to me, Stella."

"Oh, thank goodness," a teary voice comes over the line. "Leah's in hospital, she was in an accident... she's unconscious. Since her phone was smashed, I came through reception."

"I'm on my way," I tell her. "Stay with her."

"I'm not going anywhere. See you soon."

I put the phone down and turn to Amanda.

"Go," she says, her own face filled with emotion. "I've got everything covered."

I race to the elevator, smashing the button over and over until it finally pings. I head to the reception. Taking my car would be pointless. I'll never park. I grab a taxi that is dropping off and steal it from another couple.

"Sorry, an emergency. My girlfriend has been taken to hospital," I say.

"Go," they both say. "We hope everything is okay."

I nod, amazed, as I never talk to strangers, but it seemed the right thing to do. Leah has that effect on me.

"Please, Lord, let nothing have happened to her or the baby," I whisper, hoping someone is listening.

* * *

I THROW money at the driver as he pulls up outside the hospital, then race inside. Caleb is waiting for me.

"Breathe," he says, grabbing both my shoulders and giving me a shake. I'm not sure whether the motion is more for him or me. I don't think I've ever seen Caleb look rattled.

"Leah's in A&E. They're running tests."

I step away, moving towards the entrance, but he grabs my arm and pulls me in the direction we need to go.

"Come on," he says. "Let's go and find your girl."

I allow him to lead me. My brain floods with an excess of thoughts, possibilities, and what-ifs. The journey over has taken too long. Rush hour in the city is not the time when you need to get somewhere. Not when someone you care about is in trouble.

We burst through the doors to the A&E department, heading to the reception desk, where an orderly queue is formed. I press forward, but Caleb holds me back.

"That's not how it works. You know that," he says.

"I don't give a fuck," I hiss, only to have the woman in front of me turn and glare.

"Sorry, he's stressed. His pregnant fiancée has just been brought in," Caleb says, holding up a placating hand.

"Oh heavens. Please go ahead of me. I hope everything's all right."

I leave Caleb and his charm, moving towards the desk.

"Leah Walker?" I say. "She was brought in by ambulance."

The lady behind the counter smiles and taps on her keyboard.

"Here we go, yes, Leah Walker. Who are you?"

"He's her fiancé and the father of her unborn child," my brother chirps up, reappearing at my side. The woman he was talking to is now being seen by one of the nurses. A smile a mile wide on her face. Trust Caleb.

Fiancé? I look at my brother but choose not to contradict him. If I have my way, that's precisely what I'll be, if Leah pulls through this and will have me. This past half an hour is not one I want to repeat. If it's shown me anything. I can't lose her, I won't.

"I'll get someone to come and take you through. Please give me your name and take a seat."

"Gabriel Frazer."

The nurse shoots the pair of us another wider smile. "Of course, Mr Frazer."

I turn and look at the overcrowded waiting room and grimace. The room is full of people with varying degrees of illness or injury. One man is sitting pressing a towel to his head, dried blood smeared down his face. Another is clutching his arm to his chest. That's naming only two. The room is packed with people waiting to be seen.

The seal on the inside door whooshes, and a male in scrubs comes through. He walks up to Caleb and me. "Are you Mr Frazer?" he says to Caleb.

"That's me," I say, finally finding my voice.

The guy smiles warmly. "I'm Dr Hanson. If you'd like to follow me, I'll take you through to Ms Walker. Her friend Stella told us you were on your way."

Caleb and I follow him through the doors.

"How is she?" I ask.

"Leah's fine. She received a nasty bang to the head and lost consciousness for a few moments. She is currently having a CT scan to check if there's any damage, but initial tests show this is precautionary. It looks like she might have sprained her ankle in the fall. We're sending her down for an x-ray to be sure. Unfortunately, the cyclist who hit her was travelling at speed."

"What about the baby?"

Dr Hanson turns and smiles. "Baby appears to be unharmed. Tests have shown a strong heartbeat. I would, however, suggest Ms Walker take it easy for the next week. Baby is still very young."

"She won't be moving off the sofa, you have our word." Caleb chirps up, making me smile. The doctor looks between us and smiles back.

We're led into a side room. Stella sits in a chair, her eyes red from crying. She jumps up when she sees us, throwing herself into my arms, her tears restarting.

My arms instinctively wrap around her. She's Leah's best

friend, the dynamo who stood up for the woman I'm very much in love with.

"Sorry," she says when she finally pulls away. "When they called... and then..." She chokes on her words.

I lead her back to her seat and sit her down. Caleb grabs a plastic cup of water and crouches down in front of her.

"Here," he says, wrapping her hands around the cup. "Drink."

Stella nods, taking a sip.

"Leah is down having a scan," she says finally. "She's all bruised, and they want to check her ankle." Stella flinches at the thought.

"Do they know what happened? She went out for coffee with Vince and never returned," I ask.

Stella shakes her head. "Apparently, according to witnesses, the traffic was at a standstill. Leah stepped out, not seeing the courier bike travelling down the inside. She was thrown into a stationary car, hitting her head."

I pace the room, exhaustion taking hold. I pinch the bridge of my nose.

"She's going to be fine," Caleb says, handing me a coffee.

I hadn't even noticed he'd left.

"What's taking so long?"

Caleb raises an eyebrow. "This is a hospital. There are queues."

Dr Hanson takes that moment to pop his head into the room. "Leah will be back up shortly."

"Thank you, doctor," Caleb says, gripping my forearm. His voice is surprisingly shaky.

"Yes, thank you," I mumble, my head in a spin, full of the what-ifs that follow an accident. I could have lost Leah and our child today.

My heart is racing. I feel the cup taken out of my hand, and Caleb grabs both of my arms, shaking me.

"Gabriel, she's fine. She isn't Dad. She's coming back to you."

Only my brother understands.

The door opens wider and an orderly wheels Leah in. She's sat up. My eyes fly to her face. A large bandage has pride of place on her forehead, a graze on her cheek. As soon as her bed is in place, I'm by her side, grabbing her hand in mine, every protective instinct racing to the surface.

"Hey," she says, giving me a weak smile.

"Hey, you," I say, drawing her grazed knuckles to my lips. "You gave me quite a scare."

Caleb moves a chair behind me and urges me to sit.

"Hey, beautiful," he says over my shoulder.

Leah looks up and smiles at him. "Caleb," she says. "What are you doing here?"

I turn to look up at him, and he raises an eyebrow at her. "Where else would I be? You're family. I was also on the phone when Gabriel took the call from Stella. There's no way I was waiting for a phone call to let me know how you were. And with you out of action, someone has to look after him," he says, nodding at me.

Leah smiles, squeezing my hand.

As she goes to move, her face scrunches as pain radiates from somewhere. I'm on my feet before I can stop myself.

"I'm okay. My ankle is twinging, and I have the mother-of-all headaches, but I'm okay. Baby is fine, too."

I sit back in my chair and drop my forehead to her hand.

"What happened?" I ask.

"I left Vince in the coffee shop and was walking back to the office. I wasn't concentrating and stepped out. The poor cyclist," she says, earning a scowl from me.

"He shouldn't have been weaving in and out," I say, unhappy she's sticking up for the person who put her in the hospital.

"That's what they do. He's only doing his job. I'm the numpty who stepped out. Luckily, no actual harm was done," she says, cupping my cheek.

"Vince?" I ask.

"I don't think he saw what happened. It was away from the coffee shop. A guy was waylaying him."

My muscles tense at her words. "What do you mean?" I ask slowly.

"He was a little upset I wasn't tripping over myself to take him back."

She rolls her eyes and chuckles before grimacing.

Stella steps around the other side of the bed. I freeze, wondering if she thinks Leah should take Vince back. We've never discussed what her friends think of our relationship.

"I hope you told him to take a hike," she says.

"I did." Leah smiles. "You'd have been really proud of me."

Her hand goes to the bandage on her head, her face screwing up.

"Can I get you anything?" I ask.

"No, thank you. I just need to rest."

"That's exactly what I was going to order," Dr Hanson says, appearing in the doorway. "We're moving you up to one of the wards." When I go to open my mouth, he holds up a hand. "Purely precautionary. You've had a nasty tumble with the pregnancy and a bump to your head. I want to monitor you."

"Are there private rooms?" I say. "If there are, I'm happy to pay. Make a donation, whatever it takes."

"Your brother has taken care of it... however, donations are always welcome, Mr Frazer," Dr Hanson says.

I wondered where Caleb had gone.

"Leah, we will move you in the next half an hour. Visiting hours start again in the morning." He looks across at me. "You'll be welcome back then."

I go to protest, but Leah squeezes my fingers.

A pressure builds in my chest at the thought of Leah leaving my sight.

As if sensing my unease. "Hey, I'll be fine. I promise. It's only for one night." She looks down at the hospital gown and grimaces. "Can you go home and grab me some fresh clothes?"

I nod, not wanting to add additional pressure to the situation.

Instead, I lean forward, placing my lips against hers.

I'm surprised when her mouth moves under mine, her hand coming up and clutching the back of my head.

I pull back and stare into her eyes.

"I'll be back. Try to behave yourself," I say.

"Yes, Sir," she says, smiling.

I lean forward, close to her ear. "I like the sound of that. Don't make me tie you to the bed."

Leah lets out a low moan.

I drop another kiss on her open mouth and pull back.

"I'll be back as soon as I can. In the meantime, I'll drop you off one of the new office phones. Stella said your old one was smashed."

Stella steps forward, the shattered phone in her hand.

"I'll switch out the SIM," I say. "That way, if your parents ring, you have a phone."

"Oh, heavens. Please tell me you haven't called them."

Her eyes dart between Stella's and mine.

"Calm down," Stella says, gripping Leah's other hand. "No one has called them. We all wanted to see how you were doing."

Leah's shoulders visibly sag.

I rub my thumb over the back of her hand. "You need to tell them. I'm not having your mum yell at me for not letting them know."

Leah grins. "Scared of my mum?"

"Damn right," I say, altering the next words out of my mouth. "She's our child's grandmother, I'd be silly not to be."

Leah throws her head back and laughs, then grimaces.

"I think that's enough. Leah needs to rest," a voice comes from the doorway.

We all turn to see a woman standing with her arms folded. Stella leans forward and kisses Leah on the cheek.

"I'll call you tomorrow," she says before shooting me a look and leaving.

Leah smiles before gripping my hand more tightly as I move away.

"Thank you, Gabriel."

I turn back, dropping a chaste kiss on her lips.

"I'll see you later."

I offer her a smile before turning and walking away. The greater the distance, the heavier my heart.

I make my way towards the exit.

Caleb has disappeared again, no doubt sorting out everything I should have done for Leah. But as twins, we've always had a way of knowing what the other needs.

"Gabriel."

I turn to find Stella chasing after me.

"Stella. Are you okay? Do you need a lift?" I ask, wondering why Leah's best friend is chasing me down.

"No, but thank you. I just—" She stumbles over her words.

"Whatever it is, talk to me," I say, stopping in the middle of the corridor.

"I just wanted to say thank you for being here for Leah. Ever since you came into her life, she's been happier. She'll probably kill me for saying that, but I've noticed the change, and we've been friends for what seems like forever. Please don't hurt her. She survived Vince. I'm not sure she'll survive you."

Her words knock the wind out of me.

"I promise you I have no intention of ever hurting Leah," I admit.

I know I will do everything in my power to make sure that doesn't happen.

Stella smiles at me. "That's what I thought." She pauses before adding, "When I saw you together."

Caleb appears out of nowhere.

"You two ready to go?" he asks.

"Just heading to the Tube," Stella says. "Thank you both for taking such good care of my girl."

Her eyes well.

"Our girl," Caleb says. "Come on. Mason, my driver, is picking me up. He can drop you both home."

"The office, please. I need to collect one of the phones. My car is also there."

"I'm fine, honestly," Stella says.

"Stella, get in the car. You've had a shock. We want to see you home safe," I say, knowing it's what Leah would want.

She doesn't argue as Mason pulls up at the kerb.

CHAPTER 49

LEAH

*a*s promised, an orderly appears and wheels me to one of the wards. We chat openly. I fill him in on my mishap, and he tells me about his grandchildren.

"Thank you," I say when he finally gets me settled in a private room.

"There's an en suite there, but with your ankle I suggest pushing the button here. Any issues, just buzz."

He hands me the buzzer before leaving.

I look around. The room is clean, the large window looking out over nearby houses. I must be at the edge of the hospital.

"Leah Walker?" A woman close to my mum's age appears in the doorway, looking down at a chart.

"Yes," I reply.

"Hi, Leah. I'm Tammy. I'm the nurse on duty tonight. How are you feeling?" she asks, coming to stand by the side of my bed.

"Like I got hit by a cyclist," I tell her, smiling.

"Well, according to your notes, you're in as a precautionary measure. It says here, you're about nine weeks pregnant. You've had a nasty knock to the head, but there are no signs of internal bleeding and you've sprained your ankle."

"That about sums it up." I grimace. How could I have been so stupid?

"Well, I'm here if you need anything."

"Um, my partner is bringing me a phone because mine got totalled in the accident," I say, wishing Gabriel could be here with me.

"No problem. As soon as he shows up, I'll bring it to you."

"Thank you, Tammy."

"You're welcome. Remember, buzz if you need anything. It's what I'm here for."

I nod, sad to see her leave.

I flick on the television and channel hop, but the throbbing in my head makes it hard to concentrate. Damn Vince. Why on earth did I agree to go for coffee with him? I doubt he even knows I've been in an accident, or at least I hope he doesn't. This is the last place I want to have to face him. How could I have been so stupid? But then again, I have no one to blame but myself at the end of the day, it's my fault. If I hadn't been so irritated by him, I wouldn't have stepped out onto the road.

An hour later, Tammy pops her head around the door.

"There's someone here to see you," she says, grinning.

Gabriel steps around her.

"Thank you," he says.

"You're welcome. But you can't stay long," she tells him, stepping back and closing the door.

I know I'm staring when Gabriel comes towards the bed.

"One phone, an e-reader, a change of clothes, nightwear, toiletries," he says, smiling.

"You know I'm only here for one night?" I laugh, staring at the enormous bag he's just brought in. "Gabriel, how?" I ask.

The orderly had told me there was little to no chance of Gabriel getting back in tonight. Strict policies.

Gabriel shoots me one of the grins I'm getting used to. "A large donation," he says.

"What?"

"Worth every penny. The staff have been amazing. I was talking to Dr Hanson."

"Gabriel," I say, grabbing his hand and pulling him towards me. He comes with little resistance.

"I wanted to see you," he says.

"Well, I'm glad you have."

I pat the bed next to me, and he sits down, his fingers interlink with mine. "I'm so sorry for all the stress I've caused."

"No. I'm sorry. I should have kicked Vince out of the office. But I felt I would have been out of line." He drops his chin to his chest.

"I wish you had," I tell him truthfully. "Although there was something quite satisfying about telling him to get lost."

Gabriel's eyes meet mine. "Did you? Did you tell him it's over?"

I frown, tilting my head. Does Gabriel think there's a chance I'd have gone back to Vince, after everything we've been through?

"Of course. Gabriel. I know what we have isn't conventional. But I like our little bubble. There's no way I'm going to go back to Vince. Whatever happens between you and me. I wasn't lying when I told you, he and I are over."

He brings my hand to his mouth, his eyes closing.

"I thought I'd lost you," he admits.

I use my other hand to brush his hair away from his forehead.

"You can't get rid of me that easily."

He drops his head forward until our foreheads touch, careful to avoid my bruise.

"I —"

"Sorry to interrupt, but the doctor is on his way to do final rounds. I need to get you out of here Mr Frazer."

Gabriel pulls back and stands up. His expression torn. He was about to say something when Tammy walked in.

"I'll be back in the morning," Gabriel says, dropping a kiss to my lips.

"I'll see you in the morning," I reply, wanting nothing more than to beg for him to stay. But having him kicked out won't help either of us.

"I'll be back in a moment, Leah, to help you get showered and changed."

I smile at Tammy as she whisks Gabriel away.

* * *

TRUE TO HER WORD, Tammy returns.

"That is one gorgeous man you have there," she tells me. "Hold on to him. Although I don't think he's going anywhere soon. That man is caught -hook, line and sinker."

I laugh at her expression. "He is special. But our relationship is complicated."

"Complicated is what *you* make it. Nothing *has to be* complicated."

"You're right. We have a lot of talking to do."

I'm unsure why I'm telling a stranger this, but it's been a long day, and my head hurts.

She pats my hand and smiles. "If you're talking, then half your problems just disappeared. Everything can be resolved, if you communicate. Take it from someone who knows."

"As a communications officer, I can vouch for that," I tell her as she helps me hobble into the bathroom.

I'm horrified when I catch sight of myself in the mirror. What must Gabriel have thought? I'm surprised he didn't run for the nearest exit. I also realise how lucky I've been. The accident could have been far more serious. My hand drops to my stomach.

"Try not to think about it," Tammy says, patting my hand.

She helps me get washed and dressed.

I'm exhausted by the time I swing my legs back onto the bed.

"You missed dinner," Tammy says. "I'll see what I can organise. You must be starving."

I nod my head, forgetting about the pain but wanting to thank her for her kindness and consideration. My eyes fill with tears of gratitude.

"Hey, none of that. You look after yourself and that little bean you're growing. I'll provide some TLC."

My new phone pings

GABRIEL:

Did I remember everything?

I smile, and Tammy looks over.

"I'll leave you to it. Call me if you need anything."

"Thanks Tammy." When she leaves, I place my hand on my stomach. "That's Daddy checking up on us. I'm sorry little bean. Mummy promises to be more careful in future."

My throat clenches at the thought of what might have been. I know I need to stop, or I will drive myself mad. I pick up my phone and open Gabriel's message.

ME:

Everything is perfect. Tammy has helped me get changed. I'm back in bed.

Three dots appear instantly, and I suppress a smile. I can

just imagine him sitting there on the sofa, staring at the phone, waiting for me to reply.

GABRIEL:

How are you feeling?

ME:

Hungry

GABRIEL:

Do you need me to get some food delivered?

My heart beats a little faster at his thoughtfulness.

ME:

No, Tammy's gone to sort some out.

GABRIEL:

If you change your mind, I'll get Jason to package some up and have it delivered.

I smile. It's seldom, but occasionally when we've been working late. Jason is our go-to restauranteur when we're both too tired to cook.

ME:

Jason is on the opposite side of town.

GABRIEL:

If you want it. I'll make it worth his while.

I smile, knowing he would, even if he had to collect and drive it here himself.

ME:

Honestly. The food Tammy brings will be fine.

GABRIEL:

How's your head? Your ankle?

ME:

I'm in one piece. I can't believe I was that stupid. When I think of what could have happened?

My hand goes to my still flat stomach.

GABRIEL:

Elijah pulled up the footage. The cyclist was weaving in and out.

ME:

Cyclists do that. I've lived here all my life. I know how to cross the road. I was an idiot.

GABRIEL:

I'm just grateful you're okay.

There's a pause.

ME:

What are you doing?

GABRIEL:

Sitting here, missing you. The apartment is very empty.

My heart skips a beat. I miss him too.
My phone pings again.

GABRIEL:

Get some sleep. I'll be with you as soon as they let me in.

ME:

But you have your big client meeting in the morning.

GABRIEL:

I'm not even going to answer that. You and our child are my priority.

GABRIEL:

Amanda's moved it. Now stop worrying and go to sleep.

ME:

Goodnight xx

My throat closes as I re-read his words, knowing I'm done for. One reason I stepped out in to the road was I'd been thinking about how much trouble I was in. How deeply I've fallen in love with Gabriel Frazer.

* * *

BREAKFAST HAS BEEN AND GONE.

Jenny, a young nurse, helped me get washed and dressed, Tammy having gone off duty at seven. I finally fell asleep around midnight, although I awoke several times with my heart racing as flashbacks hit.

Me stepping out, the frantic ringing of a bell, and then the pain.

My hand continues to sit protectively on my lower stomach. I know how lucky I am, how lucky we are. One moment and my dream of motherhood, of our little bean, could have been over.

I remember how pale Gabriel looked when they wheeled me back into the room. Of Caleb, who is becoming the brother I never had. Looking out for me. It's amazing how accepting they've all been.

A knock sounds at the door.

"Hey stranger," Caleb's head appears.

"Caleb." I peer around him. "How have you got in? Visiting hours aren't for another twenty minutes."

I wave him in, telling him to close the door.

He grins.

"I come bearing gifts." He holds up a bag from my favourite coffee shop. "Decaf and a blueberry muffin," he says placing them on the table next to the bed. "I thought you might appreciate something other than hospital food."

"It's actually not been too bad, but coffee and cake, what girl can say no to that. Thank you," I say, opening the bag and letting the smell of the muffin waft out. "How on earth did you get in? Gabriel managed a flying visit last night but had to leave."

Caleb's face falls. "He should have told me. It's who you know," he says. "One of the consultants bought my old apartment. We've been friends since." Caleb pulls up a chair and drops into it. "How are you feeling?"

"I'm good," I say. "My ankle aches, and I've been warned to rest it for a couple of days, but the headache is now only a dull ache. I feel more of a fool than anything. I can't believe I stepped out without looking."

Caleb drops back into his seat, resting an ankle on his knee.

"What happened? Did I hear something about Vince?"

I drop back against the pillows. "I had a row with Vince. He wanted us to get back together. I told him I've moved on and that I was having a baby." I sigh, still shocked at Vince's response. "It didn't put him off. He informed me, it was fine. That he'd already decorated the nursery."

Caleb looks confused, and I laugh.

"His ex, who he thought he was having a baby with. They'd already decorated the spare room."

Caleb's face is a picture as the realisation of Vince's statement sinks in.

"Is the man a complete moron?" Caleb asks.

I giggle. "He didn't see the problem."

"The answer to my question then is yes."

I chuckle, and Caleb's face becomes serious.

"Maybe he's realised his mistake and wants to rectify it. The grass isn't always greener."

I shake my head.

"Too bad. I told him to look into a good housekeeping service." I smile at the memory of Vince's face.

"Ouch, you have claws, lady," Caleb chuckles.

"Only when threatened. Vince and I are history. You don't need to worry. I'm not leaving Gabriel to return to my ex. If that concerns you."

Caleb looks at me from under his brows. "Am I that obvious?"

I smile. "Maybe, but I don't blame you. If I had siblings, I'd be the same."

"What is going on between you and my brother?" Caleb asks.

"None of your business," a voice sounds from the door, making Caleb jump. "What are you doing here?" Gabriel asks.

Caleb spins in his seat. "Bringing my niece or nephew's mummy some proper food."

Gabriel storms into the room.

"That's my job," he says, placing down another bag of goodies from my favourite coffee shop.

I bite my lip to hide my smile. Their identical faces, showing opposite expressions. Caleb's amused, while Gabriel is highlighting his favourite grumpy expression, one I haven't seen for a while.

"Instead of scowling at your brother, maybe I can get a good morning kiss?" I freeze, immediately realising I may have overstepped the mark. Sure, he always kisses me good morning at home, but...

I watch Gabriel's expression relax and he steps towards the bed. He wraps his hand around the back of my neck, his mouth coming down on mine in a show of possession. I sink into his kiss. I missed his arms around me last night. Something I never thought I'd say.

When he finally pulls away, he rests his forehead against mine, careful to avoid the bruise. That is going to be a continual reminder of my stupidity for the next week or two.

"Never scare me like that again," he says, pain and worry reflecting in his eyes.

"I'm sorry," I say, running my thumb over his lip.

We're both distracted by a movement out of the corner of our eyes. We turn in unison, only to watch Caleb fanning himself with one of the magazines, the nurses brought me to flick through.

"What are you doing?" Gabriel's brow furrows against my skin as he takes in his brother.

Caleb laughs. "You two are hot. There I was fearing... fake relationship! My arse!" Caleb stands up, taking one of my hands and raising it to his lips, earning him a growl. "You lovely lady, have completely put my mind at rest. My work here is done."

He glances at his watch. "Now I have a meeting to get to. Some of us work for a living." When Gabriel's scowl deepens, I turn his face back to mine, dropping another kiss on his lips. Caleb gives a dramatic sigh. "I will love you and leave you."

Without another word, he turns and leaves the room.

Gabriel pulls back and unloads the treats he brought with him. I smile at his thoughtfulness. But then he continues to surprise me. He's not the aloof and introverted man I thought he was. Introverted with strangers, yes, but with those he knows, who have access to his inner circle. He's loyal, caring.

We tuck into our muffins and coffee in silence.

Another knock sounds at the door. The doctor enters.

"Morning Ms Walker, Mr Frazer," he says.

"Morning, Dr Hanson," I reply.

"How are you feeling this morning?" he asks, picking up my chart and studying it.

"Like an idiot," I say.

The doctor chuckles. "You've been lucky. Your scans were clear, so apart from a headache, there should be no further complications. Your ankle is likely to remain swollen for a week or so, so you will need to take it easy. I'll bring some crutches, but you're going to need to rest, keep your weight off it."

"Don't worry, doctor. I'll make sure of it," Gabriel says.

"Ah, Mr Frazer. Your fiancée needs to rest."

I watch as colour floods his cheeks. "Don't worry, doctor. I shall personally see to it," he says.

Gabriel turns and looks at me. There's something I don't recognise in his gaze.

"Perfect." The doctor smiles at us. "Before I discharge you, I want to do another ultrasound. Check the foetus is happy." I nod. The nurses told me the doctor would want to and brought me a jug of water to drink. "You've had no discomfort or bleeding?"

"No," I say, breathing deeply. I'd never have forgiven myself if I harmed our little bean. It may still be in my first trimester, but I already love our child, with all my heart.

"Are you ready to see your baby, Mr Frazer?"

Gabriel nods, moving to my side and interlocking our fingers. His hand shakes in mine, and I look up, surprised at the emotion resonating in his eyes.

The doctor wheels in the ultrasound machine, lowering the back of my bed until I'm lying flat.

"If you can pull up your top," he says, placing a paper towel along the top of my trousers and under my jumper to protect the material. "Sorry, this is going to be cold," he says, squirting the gel onto my stomach. My muscles contract, but I smile as he places the probe against my skin.

He moves it around smearing the gel.

He turns to the screen, pointing at a little pulsating blob. "That's your baby's heartbeat."

He flicks a button, and the sound fills the room.

Gabriel's grip tightens on mine, and I look up to see his face filled with wonder.

I bring his hand to my lips, as we both stare in amazement at the life we've created.

The doctor says nothing for a moment, letting us take in the miracle before us.

The doctor hits another couple of buttons, and pictures of our baby print out of the machine.

"A keepsake," he says, handing the photographs to Gabriel, who's staring at them in awe.

"Thank you," he says as if the doctor just doubled his fortune.

"No problem. Everything looks to be fine, but I want you to rest for the next week. Providing there is no bleeding or pain, sex may resume as normal. But if anything changes, come back in, or see your local doctor."

My cheeks burn at his words, especially when Gabriel brings my hand to his lips, holding it there, his eyes lock on mine. That's one thing that isn't complicated or fake. Our sex life is phenomenal, and the thought of Gabriel and I together, by choice. Gabriel's eyes darken as if he's reading my mind.

"I'll arrange for your discharge. Look after yourself, and no more stepping out onto the road."

"Yes, doctor," I say, dragging my gaze away from Gabriel, finding the doctor grinning at us both.

* * *

GABRIEL GATHERS MY THINGS, while a nurse gives me a lesson in crutch walking. It's a lot harder than it seems. Gabriel chuckles in the corner. "You're a liability," he says.

"Why do you think I steer clear of heels?" I say, shooting him a fierce look.

He walks up behind me and grips my waist. Showing me how to move. With his help, I get it in no time.

When the nurse is satisfied, she places me in the chair and goes to find a wheelchair to transport me out of the hospital. I'm not allowed to walk. As promised by Dr Hanson, the paperwork is all signed and letters will be sent to my local doctor's surgery.

"You ready?" The orderly from the day before says, wheeling a chair into the room.

"Yes," I say, looking over at Gabriel, who's been busy fielding emails and answering calls for the past thirty minutes. Guilt overwhelms me. He should be at the office, not here with me.

Gabriel ends his call, before looking up and smiling. "Let's go home."

My chest swells at his words.

"Let's."

CHAPTER 50

GABRIEL

I come out of the home office to find Leah sitting on the balcony, staring out over the water below.

"Hey," I say, coming up behind her and dropping my head to hers, stealing the kiss I've been longing for.

"Hey yourself," she says looking up and smiling. It's been three weeks since the accident. Her ankle is down, but I'm making her stay at home, much to her frustration. "Rob and Leon both called. They've sent you emails but said it's nothing that can't wait until Monday. Amanda also called. She and I have gone through the latest press releases. If I didn't know she loved being your secretary, I'd be worried for my job."

She may not be in the office, but it doesn't mean to say she's stopped working. She and Amanda are working side by side, sharing their two roles to ensure all jobs are done by either one or the other.

I grip her chin and tilt her head, dropping a more passionate kiss on her lips. "You've nothing to fear. You're stuck with me. I don't care whether you are my PA, communications officer, or bed warmer. I'm —"

She slaps my arm, locking her hands behind my head.

"Is that right? Bed warmer?"

I swing around, dropping myself onto the seat beside her, pulling her into my arms.

"What I meant to say," I say nuzzling her neck. "Is I don't care about titles providing I have you in my life."

"Well, you're stuck with me and our little bean," she says, taking my hand and placing it on her stomach.

"I'm not sure he or she is a bean anymore. More *peanut* sized," I say, gently stroking where the life we've created is growing. Her body changing week by week, highlighting the miracle.

"True, and soon he or she will be a bowling ball. Not that we're a secret anymore."

Her accident outed us. My mad, frantic dash and protective response left no one in any doubt something was going on between us. What shocked me the most, was their lack of surprise. The outpouring of love towards Leah and her well-being, showed me I wasn't the only one who saw her true value. I'm the lucky man however she has chosen to be with.

Vince came and saw her, when he heard about the accident, but Leah closed him down. I was privy to their conversation as she met with him here. He didn't seem surprised when he found out, I was the person Leah was now with. When I walked him out, he told me I was a lucky man.

We stare out over the city below us, a comfortable silence stretching between us. The streets below are still busy, although we get to enjoy the silence being this high up. Important in a city that never sleeps.

Leah snuggles in and I wrap my arm more tightly around her. "Today was crazy. I was hoping to finish early so we could go out."

She looks up at me, her chin resting on my chest, understanding reflecting there. "Don't apologise, Gabriel. I know the company and what it demands of you. It's who you are, and I'll never ask you to change. The fact you're even here with me and not at the office is more than I expected."

"I'm the boss." Something my mother pointed out to me, shortly after Leah's accident. I can still hear her words.

"Gabriel Frazer, you have a baby on the way. You need to learn to prioritise!" She proceeded to lecture me on parental duties and that of being a partner. You'd never have thought I ran a billion-pound company and people trusted me with their money. I left her like a little boy with his tail between his legs.

"You are. But there's a company and its clients who rely on you. I don't want to take you away from what's important. Don't get me wrong, I appreciate it, but I can't be selfish."

I run a hand through my hair as I stare down into the face I've come to know so well.

"What is it?" she asks, sitting up and taking my hand in hers. "Talk to me."

A furrow forms between her brows, and I brush it with my thumb. "Gabriel, what's going on?" I can tell from her tone I'm scaring her, but I'm scaring myself more. What I'm about to say has far-reaching connotations.

"The past three weeks." I look at her, my eyes swimming with the emotion I can no longer contain. "When you didn't come back... I thought... Then Amanda came in, and I spoke to Stella... My world stopped." I run a hand over my mouth. "I've never been so scared, not since my father's accident. The thought of losing you." The tightness in my chest grows at the sheer thought.

Leah turns to face me. Her hand comes up and cups my cheek. I turn into it, placing a kiss on her palm. I close my eyes briefly and relax into the feel of her.

"You haven't lost me," She whispers. "I'm not going

anywhere as long as you want me here," she admits. My eyes fly open. I know how vulnerable she's made herself.

I cover her hand in mine.

"I want to change our contract."

Leah sinks back into the sofa, her expression one of confusion. "Our contract?"

I interlock our fingers in a way I've become accustomed to.

"I want you here with me. I don't want you and our child living downstairs, where I only see you for a snapshot of time." I grip my hair, not sure if I'm making sense. I pause, inhaling, before slowly releasing my breath. "I know I told you I don't do relationships. It's true. I haven't, at least not successfully. I'm not saying I'm not going to fuck up. I can almost guarantee I will. But Leah, these past months with you. I've never felt like this. I know I said we would fake it. But this doesn't feel fake. At least not to me, anyway."

I stare into Leah's eyes, watching as they fill with tears.

Oh hell, I've made her cry.

I grab both her hands and drop to my knees by her feet. "Marry me. Be my fiancée for real. Be my wife until we're old and grey," I say before I can stop myself.

Leah's eyes widen, the moisture escaping from the corner of her eyes, making tracks down her cheeks. I let go of her hand and capture the droplets on my thumbs.

"I know this is not what we agreed. Or the proposal you deserve or I wanted to give you, but —"

She lifts her hand to mine and squeezes, before placing a finger against my lips. I fall silent and wait. I watch in amazement as her face alights with the brightest of smiles.

I take her hand in mine and grip it, bending my head and holding it against my forehead. "I want us to be a proper family, not co-parents. I want us to share in the mundane and the special moments. Watch our child, hopefully, children take their first steps, say their first words. When this little one is born, I want to make another one."

I grip her hand, and when I raise my head, Leah is openly crying, but her smile lets me know they're happy tears.

"Yes," she says. Her eyes twinkling. "A billion yesses. I don't need a fancy proposal. Actions speak louder than words. Although your words... who knew?" She chuckles and I smile. "I love you Gabriel Frazer, so much."

"I love you. Maybe I should have started with that. But since you came into my life. I can't think straight. You've changed my life, my world. Made me look at myself, question everything," I say, dropping my head to hers.

Leah's laughter fills the air.

"I love you so much," she says, leaning forward, her hands coming up and wrapping themselves around the back of my head. She pulls my mouth down to hers, my little communications officer, demanding my lips. For eight years this woman was under my nose, and I didn't see what I had. It wasn't our time, but I'll be damned if I'm letting her get away now I've realised she is the other half of me.

Without breaking contact, I lift her up and carry her back into the living area. Placing her gently on the sofa. I slow the pace of our kiss, savouring the feel of her against me.

"Make love to me, Gabriel," Leah whispers against my lips.

"It will be my pleasure," I say. "I'm going to worship you for the rest of our lives. I love you, Leah. I was blind for so long. You've made me open my eyes."

I spread her thighs, moving between them, dragging my mouth from hers trailing my lips down her jaw to her neck, my hands weaving their way up and under her jumper, pushing it over her head. My fingers make quick work of her bra, freeing her breasts to my gaze and mouth. "Beautiful," I say, moving my mouth to one of her nipples, sucking and teasing until Leah bucks beneath me, her fingers, gripping my hair.

I move to the other, teasing and nipping, taking my time until Leah is squirming beneath me. Her skirt is bunched around her waist. My hand snakes up under her skirt before finding the material of her panties. Leah gasps as my finger trails under the elastic. As always, she's wet and ready for me. My cock stiffens to the point of pain with the knowledge.

I return to her lips, pressing myself against her, my fingers tormenting as I know she likes. She gasps as I breach her entrance with two fingers. Our kiss deepens as she rides my hand, our tongues tangling in desperation. The sound of our heavy breathing echoes around the space.

"I want you naked," I say, slipping my hands into the waistband, pulling both her panties and skirt down.

"Beautiful," I say, spreading Leah's legs wider, exposing her to my gaze. I should have realised I was a goner the night I took her on my dining room table. Sinking into her welcoming pussy was like coming home.

I let a hand trail down her stomach, watching in delight as the muscles contract and jump under my touch. Rising, I drop a kiss on her stomach, where it's beginning to swell with the life of our child growing within her.

I look up to find Leah's eyes on me. Love I never thought I'd see radiating brightly. I drop my mouth to her core, my eyes never leaving hers as I lap from entrance to clit, teasing her swollen flesh with my teeth, tongue and lips. Her thighs stretch, the noises she's making telling me all I need to know. I smile against her skin as her fingers dig into my scalp, her hips rising up to meet me.

When I curl my two fingers against her front wall, I watch her explode. Her body clenching and shaking as her orgasm shatters her.

I continue gentler movements until she's purring beneath

me. It's only then I place my lips against hers, sliding my tongue into her mouth, my fingers still buried deep inside her.

"I'll never get tired of watching you come apart in my arms and on my mouth," I whisper as she mewls beneath me.

"I'll never get tired of you making me. Who knew the man in the expensive suit has such a magical tongue and fingers," she says, wrapping her legs around me and rubbing herself against me.

"What about my cock?" I ask, just as she sucks on my tongue, shooting a pulse of pleasure south.

Leah doesn't say anything. Instead, her greedy fingers are untangling my trousers and freeing my painful dick. When she gently squeezes me, I let out a loud moan.

I shove my trousers and boxers down without breaking contact. Leah grips me and presses me against her entrance.

"I'm yours," she says, turning her head, her eyes glazed with passion. "Gabriel, I want you now," she says.

I spin us around, dropping us to the floor onto my thick rug. My body beneath hers, our lips clashing, knowing she can taste herself, but she doesn't blink, instead she deepens the kiss. Moaning into her mouth, my cock finds her entrance and sinks in. I thrust forward until my balls stop me going any further.

"I love you," I say against her lips.

"I love you more," she says.

"I don't think that's possible," I say as I begin to move.

Our foreplay means this is going to be over quicker than I want.

"Make me yours, truly," Leah says. "Coat my insides with your cum. We have forever to take it slow. I need to know I'm alive, and we're together."

"Your wish is my command."

My hands grip her hips as I slide in and out. Her breasts

press down against my chest, my mouth on hers. I feel her orgasm begin, her muscles contracting around me, milking my dick. My body speeds up, and I thrust harder until the pressure takes over, and I follow her over the edge, my cum filling her up, as she wanted. This is where we started, but that's all it was, the start. This time, it's with love. Although I think the love has been hiding under the surface for a long time, both of us too scared to voice our change of heart.

Leah collapses on top of me. I pull the throw over our naked bodies. Her hand draws circles on my chest.

"Thank you for trusting me," I say against her hair.

"Thank you for loving me," she says, and I smile.

"I think I've loved you from the beginning. It just took my conscious brain some time to catch up."

Leah pushes herself up and stares at me.

"What will your family think? We're going to give them whiplash."

I chuckle, her look one of confusion.

"Have you not realised they love you? They already know I'm madly in love with you. They know me better than I know myself, I think. Knew the only way I would have put a baby in your belly was if I had powerful feelings for you. I'm the luckiest man alive that you've fallen for me, too. "

She places a hand against my cheek. "The same goes for me. There were so many reasons I shouldn't fall in love with you."

"We're not having a long engagement. I want to call you mine as soon as possible."

Leah laughs at my words. "Patience," she says dropping a kiss on my lips. "We need to wait for my parents to come back from their trip. I'm not sure they'll forgive us, especially my dad, if he doesn't get to give his only daughter away," she says, her mouth closing over mine.

I wonder how quickly I can charter a plane to Australia.

CHAPTER 51

GABRIEL

Four Months Later

I haul myself out of the pool and grab my towel, drying myself off before pulling on a t-shirt and some joggers. Leah headed back upstairs a little while ago, her growing pregnancy meaning she can't do the number of lengths she did before. After I proposed, we went to St Clair's and purchased the ring Leah wanted. It was a lot less flashy than most of the women I knew would have wanted, but it suited Leah down to the ground. A simple, square-cut, flawless diamond in a platinum setting. Her mum and dad were over the moon. They are due back in a couple of months. The idea of becoming grandparents shortly after nearly had them cut their trip short. It took a lot of convincing to have them see out their trip, and the promise that if Leah was to go into labour early, I would get them home.

Our life is crazy, although Leah has replaced the stock market as my favourite pastime and is helping me get some

perspective in preparation for the baby's arrival. Not everything has stopped. We still game, make love. We annoyed
Pen, having finally figured out that each of the latter levels
required players to pair up to complete them. Teamwork was
the key. One Leah worked out. Ironic, as neither one of us
got to proclaim ourselves as King or Queen of the Games
room on this occasion, but somehow, I don't think the battle
will be disregarded. My communication officer and
completely sex-mad partner has quite a competitive streak.

"Mr Frazer."

I look up as one of the concierge team approaches.

"Billy," I say, making him smile when I use his name.
Another thing that has rubbed off on me from Leah. She got
him moved across from her old building when she knew a
position had opened up. She knows every staff member's
name, and it's paid dividends. The staff will do anything
for her.

"Ms Walker called down. She would like you to return as
soon as possible, please."

My heart pounds as I make my way to the pool entrance.

"Did she sound distressed?" I ask, not that Billy is likely to
know.

"No, but it might have something to do with the young
girl who just turned up. She asked to be let up. She looked
distressed, and when I called Ms Walker, she told me to send
her straight up."

"Thank you, Billy. You did the right thing."

The elevator arrives, and I jump in, tapping my foot
impatiently as the door seems to take forever to close.

There's only one young girl we know, and that's Lottie.
Why would she be here?

I enter the apartment to the sound of heart-wrenching
sobs. Leah is sitting on the sofa, with my niece encased in her
arms.

"Lottie?" I say, sinking down in front of her. "Hey pumpkin, what's happened?" I try to keep my voice neutral, but my stomach's churning. I scan her for any signs of injury but come up blank.

I look at Leah, who's as equally distressed as I am. I send her a questioning look, wondering if Lottie has given any more information on her state.

"Lottie," I say again, her wracking sobs breaking my heart. "Talk to us, sweetheart. We can't help you unless we know what's wrong."

She pulls up, her expression one of pure agony, her eyes red and puffy, her face scrunched. I cup her face in my hands, wiping away some of the tears that continue to stream down her cheeks. Leah's arm is wrapped around her shoulders.

"Talk to us. Let us help you."

She sucks in a shuddering breath as she tries to get her emotions under control.

"You...you can't help. No one can," she says, the devastation in her voice and on her face, telling me she truly believes no one can help her.

"Why can't we help?" Leah asks tenderly, taking one of Lottie's hands in hers.

Lottie looks at her. "He's not my biological father. She's going to take me away from him."

A look of confusion crosses Leah's face, her gaze shooting to mine. I shrug until Lottie's words sink in.

Oh, shit... everything becomes clear like the sun breaking through the clouds on a dull grey day. Leah sees the horror in my expression as realisation dawns. I school my features, not wanting to broadcast them to Lottie.

Is this why Elijah never left? Why he and Darra never divorced? None of us could understand why he stayed, especially when it's so clear they make each other miserable. Lottie's words play over in my mind. Lottie is Elijah's world, and has been since the day she was born. I remember watching my older brother pacing the floor, getting his newborn daughter to sleep. Wiping her tears when she grazed her knee. Building her the playhouse that still sits in the gardens of Mum's home.

Shit. How long? How long has he known? I think back to their relationship. When did everything change? When did my brother change from a carefree, fun-loving man to a work-obsessed tyrant?

Lottie's body continues to heave in Leah's arms.

"What do you mean?" I say, taking her shoulders and holding her so she can look at me.

"Lottie," I say again. "What do you mean?"

She turns her tear-stained face to me, the devastation of what she's heard written all over her face.

"Mum and Dad were arguing. It was so loud. She told him if he didn't do what she wanted, then she would take me away. We'd leave." She sucks in a breath. "He then... he then said. I may not be her biological dad, but I'm not letting you take her away from me." Her eyes are wide when she stares at me. "He's never left her. He's stayed because of me."

There's a hammering at the door. What the hell? Only one person would have been able to get past security and upstairs. Mainly because his company installed the system.

"Lottie? Lottie, are you there? Gabriel, open this damn door." Elijah's voice echoes through the apartment.

Lottie freezes.

"I know you're in there, please, darling." Elijah's voice changes as if every ounce of fight has left him. I don't think I've ever heard my brother sound so desperate, helpless.

"Lottie, I'm going to speak to your dad. Are you okay if I let him in?"

I don't know if there is more to the story, but I am not going to traumatise my niece if she needs five minutes without my brother breathing down her neck. I'm quite happy to step in. I still haven't forgiven him for his treatment of Leah.

Lottie nods before wrapping her arms around Leah, dropping her head to her shoulder. Leah's bump awkwardly sat between the two of them.

Elijah hammers once more. "Gabriel... please."

I'm up and on my feet, making my way to the front door. Leah pulls Lottie into her arms, holding her tightly as she continues to shake.

"Elijah," I say, opening the door to my frantic brother. His face is ashen. He looks like he's aged twenty years.

"Gabriel, is Lottie here?" he asks, looking around me, his movements manic. "I tracked her phone."

"She is." When he goes to push past me, I press my hands into his shoulder, stopping him. He shoots me an impatient look.

"She's distraught, Eli. Whatever she heard."

I watch as he crumbles in front of me. His face screws up as if he can no longer contain the pain. His enormous frame folding in on itself. He lets out a mewl like a wounded animal.

I grip his shoulders and shake him when his breathing becomes erratic.

"Eli. Listen to me. There's a very confused little girl in there. She needs her dad. That man is you. You need to pull yourself together and be that for her."

Elijah looks at me, and I watch his all-too-familiar mask fall into place before he straightens his shoulders.

"I've got you. We can talk later, but first, you need to see Lottie."

He moves to step around me and stops. "No one can know," he says turning towards me.

"I won't say a word."

He nods, before stopping in the doorway. His eyes locked on Leah and his daughter. It doesn't take a rocket scientist to work out that my fiancée is comforting his daughter.

"Dad," Lottie mumbles, her tears reigniting.

She stands up and throws herself into her father's arms. He scoops her up, holding her tight. His eyes close as if she's his lifeline.

"I'm sorry, Lottie. So sorry. You were never supposed to find out."

My heart breaks as I listen to my brother and watch his life unravel before my eyes. Leah moves around them to stand beside me, wrapping her arms around my waist. The look in her eyes lets me know she's grasped the severity of what we've just been told. Her heart is aching for the two people who are now crying in our living room.

"Oh, Lottie," Elijah says, eventually putting his daughter down and wiping his eyes on his sleeve. He sits down on the sofa, pulling her into his side.

"Lottie, look at me," he says, using a tone he's only ever used for Lottie.

"But Dad, I heard what Mum said," she says, her voice breaking.

Elijah recoils at her words.

"I may not be your biological father, but I'll always be your dad, princess. I never want you to doubt that. You were mine from the moment they placed you in my arms. I love you. You're my baby girl. You may not have my blood running through your veins, but you have my love and heart. Nothing can or will ever change that."

Lottie throws herself at Elijah, and my vision blurs at the nightmare unfolding in front of us. I wrap my arms more tightly around Leah, pulling her into me. She comes willingly, encasing me with her love. I'm so happy I have her in my life. That I overcame my fears and allowed myself to feel.

Elijah looks up at us, his eyes connecting with mine over his daughter's head. They radiate his helplessness. Only time and some seriously good lawyers are going to fix it. His gaze moves to Leah, and I freeze. He bows his head, mouthing the word, "Thank you."

Leah acknowledges him before motioning towards my office. Elijah nods as we walk away. They need time to talk but know where we are when they're ready. That's what family is for.

As we walk into the office, our own child kicks against my hand, making themselves known, my heart melts. Elijah's reaction to Leah and I makes more sense now. What had he felt? I can't easily forgive him. Leah is a good person and didn't deserve his attack, but maybe I can try to understand him.

EPILOGUE

CALEB

*M*y hand goes to my eyes, my fingers rubbing over my eyelids to try to open them. Wow, last night. Snippets of the evening come back to me. My cock hardens as I'm flooded with the memories of the previous evening. A hot, tight body. Screams of pleasure echoing around the suite. Soft, demanding lips. *Coming* harder than I ever have before.

My ears tune in to the sounds around me. It's far too quiet. My hand snakes out, only to find cold, empty sheets. I listen for the sound of the shower, nothing.

I sit up. The sheet covering me drops to my waist. Suddenly awake, my eyes struggle to focus on the darkness. The heavy blackout curtains doing their job. I flip on the bedside light and look around. My clothes litter the floor, where they were abandoned in our speed to get to each other's bodies. But it's only mine. My little dancer's clothes are gone.

I drop back and fling my arm over my eyes.

"Fuck."

I throw back the covers and dive out of bed. Breathing a sigh of relief when I find my wallet in my jeans, untouched.

Dragging them on, I walk barefoot into the main area. The family suite is extensive. They are in all the family hotels. Fully catered and set up to allow the family to stay with minimal disruption. My grandfather had started it, my dad and sister have continued the tradition. I can't complain. With the amount of travelling I do, it's nice to have a home from home.

I scan the room, checking for any sign of the woman who joined me last night. When I find nothing, I run a hand through my hair, frustration blooming in the pit of my stomach.

Did she sneak out?

Nothing seems to be missing. She must have simply got up and left when I finally fell asleep. I look at the clock.

Seven-thirty.

We got back to the room at three. There was not much sleeping as we enjoyed each other's bodies.

I pull on a jumper and head downstairs, hammering on security's door.

"Mr Frazer. Um… Can I help you?" A man in uniform opens the door, his face not hiding his shock at finding me there.

"I came back with a woman last night." I'm not really thinking how that sounds until after the words leave my mouth. "Bert," I say, reading his name tag before giving him one of my most dazzling smiles.

He looks at me, his expression blank.

"I want to know who she is and where she went."

He steps back and lets me into the room. A wall of screens monitor different parts of the hotel, from the lobby to the dining room. Even the bar area.

"Was your visitor a guest of the hotel?" he asks, taking a seat at his desk, his fingers poised over his keyboard.

I grimace.

Maybe this wasn't such a good idea. I'm about to admit to a member of my sister's staff that I spent the night with a stranger I brought back to the family hotel and know next to nothing about.

Kat is going to kill me!

"April. Her name is April," I say, praying he doesn't ask me for a surname.

He types into his terminal.

"Not a guest," he says, turning his head to look at me. Nothing but professionalism showing on his face.

"We came back at around three AM," I say, pulling up a chair and dropping into it next to him.

He pulls up the lobby feed, finding the time I gave him and letting the feed run. Sure, enough April and I appear. We're laughing, my arm around her, her hand resting on my chest, as she looks up at me. My stomach clenches at the sight of us.

"That's her," I say. Watching as we disappear off screen.

It was two minutes after this, we were in the lift. Me pressing her against the wall, our hands roaming freely. We barely made it to the suite before we were tearing each other's clothes off.

Shit! I scan the monitors, letting out a sigh of relief—no lift cameras.

Kat really would kill me!

Bert skips the feed until April reappears. He lets the feed run, and I stare at the woman who has left me sleeping upstairs. Her clothes are in place, her hair scraped back, her face clear of any makeup. She walks confidently out of the front door without a backward glance.

I check the time stamp. Five AM.

My heart sinks. April is long gone.

"Is everything alright, sir?" Bert asks. "Did the lady steal anything? If she did, I can call the police."

I give him a weak smile. "No, she didn't steal anything," I tell him.

My eyes move back to the screen, and the picture Bert has frozen. I stare at April's frozen image.

Not anything you can see, that is…

* * *

READ CALEB and April's Story in The Playboy Billionaire.

For more Gabriel and Leah, download their bonus scene and 3 of Leah's favourite vegetarian recipes https://dl.book funnel.com/no30wf7y1m

END #

ABOUT THE AUTHOR

Zoe Dod writes emotionally intense billionaire fiction, with complex characters, swoon-worthy romance and a host of plot twists that will leave you guessing until the end. Her books are written in British English.

Prior to becoming a writer, Zoe began her working life as a software development manager in The City of London. In her mid-thirties she retrained as a primary school teacher, and loved teaching children to write and tell stories. She left teaching to spend more time with her family, and it was then she uncovered her love for writing romance.

Zoe lives in The New Forest, Hampshire, England with her husband, two adult children (when they're back from uni) and her four rescue fur babies.

She loves reading and writing. When she's not doing either of those, she's on long walks in The New Forest or attending Zumba classes

Sign up for her monthly Newsletter www.zoedod.com
    You can follow Zoe on
    Instagram: @zoedod_author
    Facebook: Zoe Dod - Author
    Tik Tok: @zoedod_author

ABOUT THE AUTHOR

ALSO BY ZOE DOD

* * *

* Coming 2024

^Coming 2025

Made in the USA
Middletown, DE
05 March 2025

72249078R00223